Emilian Kavalski is Lecturer in Politics and International Relations at the University of Western Sydney and author of *Extending the European Security Community* (I.B.Tauris, 2008), editor of *The New Central Asia* (2009) and *China and the Global Politics of Regionalization* (2009), and co-editor (with M. Zolkos) of *Defunct Federalisms: Critical Perspectives on Federal Failure* (2008).

LIBRARY OF INTERNATIONAL RELATIONS

Series ISBN: 978 1 84885 240 2

See www.ibtauris.com/LIR for a full list of titles

25. *France and Iraq:*
Oil, Arms and French Policy Making
in the Middle East
David Styan
978 1 84511 045 1

26. *Nuclear Inertia:*
US Nuclear Weapons Policy After the Cold War
Tom Sauer
978 1 85043 765 9

27. *Politics of Confrontation: The Foreign Policy*
of the USA and Revolutionary Iran
Babak Ganji
978 1 84511 084 0

28. *Australia and the Middle East:*
A Front-line Relationship
Fethi Mansouri (ed.)
978 1 84511 209 7

31. *Syria and Saudi Arabia:*
Collaboration and Conflicts in the Oil Era
Sonoko Sunayama
978 1 84511 302 5

33. *Britain and Japan in the Twentieth Century:*
One Hundred Years of Trade and Prejudice
Philip Towle and Nobuko Margaret Kosuge (eds)
978 1 84511 415 2

34. *Islam and Political Violence:*
Muslim Diaspora and Radicalism
in the West
Shahram Akbarzadeh and Fethi Mansouri
978 1 84511 473 2

35. *Climate Change Politics in Europe:*
Germany and the International Relations
of the Environment
Lyn Jaggard
978 1 84511 409 1

36. *The Anglo–American Oil War:*
International Politics and the Struggle for
Foreign Petroleum, 1912–1945
Fiona Venn
978 1 84511 458 9

38. *Cyprus At War:*
Diplomacy and Conflict during the 1974 Crisis
Jan Asmussen
978 1 84511 742 9

39. *India's Fragile Borderlands:*
The Dynamics of Terrorism in North East India
Archana Upadhyay
978 1 84511 586 9

40. *Managing World Order: United Nations*
Peace Operations and the Security Agenda
Richard Kareem Al-Qaq
978 1 84511 580 7

41. *Darfur and the International Community:*
The Challenges of Conflict Resolution in Sudan
Richard Barltrop
978 1 84511 977 5

42. *Greece and the American Embrace:*
Greek Foreign Policy Towards Turkey,
the US and the Western Alliance
Christos Kassimeris
978 1 84511 876 1

43. *Counterterrorism and International Power*
Relations: The EU, ASEAN and Hegemonic
Global Governance
Cornelia Beyer
978 1 84511 892 1

44. *The GCC and the International Relations*
of the Gulf: Diplomacy, Security and Economy
Co-ordination in a Changing Middle East
Matteo Legrenzi
978 1 84511 921 8

45. *India in the New South Asia:*
Strategic, Military and Economic Concerns
in the Age of Nuclear Diplomacy
B. M. Jain
978 1 84885 138 2

46. *Mediterranean Frontiers: Borders, Conflict*
and Memory in a Transnational World
Dimitar Bechev and Kalypso Nicolaidis
978 1 84885 125 2

47. *India and Central Asia: The Mythmaking*
and International Relations of a Rising Power
Emilian Kavalski
978 1 84885 124 5

48. *International Intervention in Local Conflicts:*
Crisis Management and Conflict Resolution Since
the Cold War
Uzi Rabi (ed.)
978 1 84885 318 8

INDIA AND CENTRAL ASIA
THE MYTHMAKING AND INTERNATIONAL RELATIONS OF A RISING POWER

EMILIAN KAVALSKI

TAURIS ACADEMIC STUDIES
an imprint of
I.B.Tauris Publishers
LONDON • NEW YORK

Published in 2010 by by Tauris Academic Studies, an imprint of I.B.Tauris & Co Ltd
6 Salem Road, London W2 4BU
175 Fifth Avenue, New York NY 10010
www.ibtauris.com

Distributed in the United States and Canada exclusively by Palgrave Macmillan
175 Fifth Avenue, New York NY 10010

Copyright © Emilian Kavalski, 2010

The right of Emilian Kavalski to be identified as the author of this work has been asserted by the author in accordance with the Copyright, Designs and Patent Act 1988.

All rights reserved. Except for brief quotations in a review, this book, or any part thereof, may not be reproduced, stored in or introduced into a retrieval system, or transmitted, in any form or by any means, electronic, mechanical, photocopying, recording or otherwise, without the prior written permission of the publisher.

Library of International Relations 47

ISBN: 978 1 84885 124 5

A full CIP record for this book is available from the British Library
A full CIP record is available from the Library of Congress

Library of Congress Catalog Card Number: available

Printed and bound in India by Replika Press Pvt. Ltd
camera-ready copy edited and supplied by the author

*The elephants' bodies bent the earth
and created quakes the world over.
All that monstrous ivory made
the face of the world into a chessboard.*
     Amir Khusrau (1287)

CONTENTS

List of Abbreviations ix

Acknowledgements xi

1. Introduction: Framing India's International Interactions 1

2. Trajectories of India's Post-Cold War Foreign Policy 21

3. The Myth of Assertive Posturing and India's Post-1998 Foreign Policy Making 47

4. The 'Look North' Policy: Uncovering India's Discourses on Central Asia 79

5. The Peacock and the Bear: Shifting New Delhi's Relations with Moscow in Central Asia 111

6. An Elephant in a China Shop: India's Search for Pragmatic Relations with China in Central Asia 133

7. The Porcupine meets Mars and Venus: India's Interactions with the West in Central Asia 167

8. Conclusion: The No Influence of the 'Look North' Policy 195

Notes 213

Bibliography 225

Index 249

LIST OF ABBREVIATIONS

ABM	Anti-Ballistic Missile Treaty
BJP	Bharatiya Janata Party
CAO	Central Asian Organization
CFSP	EU Common Foreign and Security Policy
CAEC	Central Asia Economic Community
CIS	Commonwealth of Independent States
C/OSCE	Conference/Organisation for Security and Cooperation in Europe
CSTO	Collective Security Treaty Organization
C(N)TBT	Comprehensive (Nuclear) Test Ban Treaty
C(N)TBTO	Comprehensive (Nuclear) Test Ban Treaty Organization
EAEC	Eurasian Economic Community
EC	European Commission
EU	European Union
FRY	Federal Republic of Yugoslavia
GoI	Government of India
GUAM	Organization for Democracy and Economic Development of Georgia, Ukraine, Azerbaijan, and Moldova
ICC	International Criminal Court
ICCR	Indian Council for Cultural Relations
INC	Indian National Congress
ISI	Pakistan's Inter-Services Intelligence Agency
JWG	Joint Working Group
MTCR	Missile Technology Control Regime
NATO	North Atlantic Treaty Organisation
NPT	Nuclear Non-Proliferation Treaty
OCAC	Organization of Central Asian Cooperation
PfP	NATO's Partnership for Peace program

PRC	People's Republic of China
SCO	Shanghai Cooperation Organization
SES	Single Economic Space
UN	United Nations
USA	United States of America
USSR	Union of Soviet Socialist Republics
XUAR	Xinjiang Uyghur Autonomous Regions

ACKNOWLEDGEMENTS

There are a number of individuals and institutions whose assistance made this book possible. The Andrew Mellon fellowship generously offered by the American Institute of Indian Studies helped set off this investigative journey. It allowed me to spend several months in New Delhi perusing the libraries at Jawaharlal Nehru University and Delhi University as well as the multitude of bookstores in Daryaganj. My stay in Delhi would have been barren without the support and friendship of Saponti Baroowa, Mridula Chakraborty, Kavita Bhanot, Rashmi Joshi, Neelakshi Surayanarayan, and S.K. Vij. It would have also been unbearable without the home that Ms. Kishori Kaul provided for me among the worlds of her paintings seemingly anchored at her house in Babar Lane. It was there that this manuscript began. The bulk of the writing however occurred in Edmonton (western Canada), far away from the warmth and embrace of Delhi. There, Rob Aitken and Gita Sud were patient recipients of news on the progress of my scripted 'skeletons' and also made possible several much-needed sojourns away from the laptop. Their 'mother-henning' is very important to me. I would also like to thank Jean McBean and John Whorton for sharing their house by the ravine where this volume took shape. The School of Humanities and Languages at the College of Arts, University of Western Sydney (Australia) kindly provided a stimulating collegiate atmosphere and a hospitable institutional environment for finishing this project. I am also grateful to Rasna Dhillon, my commissioning editor at Tauris Academic Studies, for her professionalism, assistance, and understanding. My largest debts, however, go to Raycho Kavalski for his unending love, trust, and conviction and to Magdalena Zolkos for being a true partner and friend; for me, it is her 'faces', support, and sharing that make this world such a worthwhile and colorful place.

1

INTRODUCTION: FRAMING INDIA'S INTERNATIONAL INTERACTIONS

> *Over the years the Indian leadership, and the educated Indian, have deliberately projected and embellished an image about India that they know to be untrue, and have willfully encouraged the well-meaning but credulous foreign observer (and even more the foreign scholar) to accept it. What is worse, they have fallen in love with this image, and can no longer accept that it is untrue… India is much too important today, and its potential far too significant in the coming decades, to be held hostage to this simplistic mythmaking.*
>
> Pavan K. Varma (2004, 4)

Investigative Scope

Grappling with the nascent international agency of regional powers with global intentions has become a dominant topic in the study of world affairs. This rash of attention to the emergent dynamics of international interactions has been facilitated by the break-up of the Cold War order which has allowed a number of actors to extend their international roles and outreach. India features prominently among those actors and its agency in global life is subject to a growing public, policy, and scholarly interest. This book inscribes itself within this literature. In this respect, it is about the patterns of India's post-Cold War international interactions, especially as indicated by its relations with Central Asia. At the same time, it is a book about the language of international relations in India. The focus is on the discursive articulations of India's projected rise to global prominence through the simultaneous adaptation to and realignment of the dynamics of world affairs. Indian commentators reveal that the narrative emplotment of foreign policy needs to take into account 'the domestic audience' on whose behalf it is articulated since publics at home 'must be able to locate the components of [their country's external relations] within their norms/value system or through their unique historical system' (Narayanan 2007, 657).

Central Asia, therefore, is treated here as a prism for teasing out both the underpinnings of New Delhi's external strategies and the discourses through which they are articulated. In other words, the region is perceived as a transformative context for studying the articulations of India's international agency. Such a narrative process-tracing illuminates the process and strategies through which the reformulations of national identity in the wake of India's 1998 nuclear tests have furnished a platform for the discursive mythmaking of New Delhi's extended influence in Asia and beyond. Thus, while many of the commentaries on the modalities of India's engagement in Central Asia are primarily aimed at making empirical contributions, this book offers a theoretically-informed reflection on their debates. The contention is that the emphasis on analytical observation allows for eliciting the logics of India's foreign policy making which tend to remain occluded in the data-driven investigations that focus on energy resources, ethnic conflicts, and regional 'new' and 'old' 'great games'.

While drawing on insights from recent developments in the study of international relations, this examination of India's involvement in Central Asia engages in an extensive analysis of the domestic justification of New Delhi's foreign policy making. As I will discuss shortly, a close reading of Indian accounts of the country's diplomatic relations informs the *narrative imbrication* approach adopted by this book. At the same time, the focus on Central Asia facilitates a confrontation with the discourses of India's rise as a global power. The veteran political commentator and scholar Davendra Kaushik (2003b, 31) has remarked that 'the public mind in India has been in general clear about [the] high Indian stakes in Central Asia on account of our age-old vital cultural and economic interests in the region and concern for our security arising developments in our neighborhood'. This volume engages the perspectives embedded in these Indian representations of Central Asia's impact on New Delhi's anticipated emergence as one of the most important 'movers and shakers' in world politics.

In particular, Chapter 2 and Chapter 3 detail the perceptions that underpin the centrality of India's fledgling international agency. It needs to be mentioned here that objective renditions of the notion of 'emerging powers' in global life identify them as:

> middle powers on the ascendant: states that have the capability and intention to maneuver their way into great power status. India, from this conceptual vantage point, is a quintessential emerging power. It should be pointed out that India's emergence is more likely to be in the realm of international political economy than that of international security. (Sahni 2005, 84–85; emphasis added)

Said otherwise,

> emerging powers are more than 'intermediate states' or 'regional powers'; they have the potential of playing a system-shaping role in the future and are in various ways signaling their intention to do so. [That is], they are sufficiently powerful to defy any great power attempt to force them to behave in a manner against their choosing. For instance, India could not prevent the setting up of the global nuclear non-proliferation architecture, but it could certainly choose to opt out of the regime. (Rajagopalan and Sahni 2008, 6–7)

This understanding underscores the analysis in Chapter 4 of the 'Look North' policy—the external relations narrative of India's relations with Central Asia (Asopa 2006; Bal 2004; Banerjee 2004; Batabyal 2007; Roy 2001). The constructs of its discursive engagement (as its appellation suggests) follow the logic (and intimate a desire for emulation) of India's post-Cold War 'Look East' approach to Southeast Asia (Devare 2006, 28; Jain 2008, 51; Kale 2009, 55; Menon and Nigam 2007, 171; Reddy 2005; Sharma 2005, 62).[1] As Chapter 4 elaborates, the narratives of the 'Look North' policy reflect the broader pattern of *inter-regional* international relations adopted by New Delhi. The proponents of the 'Look North' policy observe that

> The growing international competition for establishing spheres of influence in Central Asia is causing serious con-

cerns to India. New Delhi has come to realize that it can no longer remain an indifferent onlooker and watch the blatant attempts by outside powers to change the geopolitical balance in Central Asia, which is fraught with grave consequences for the strategic balance in South and West Asia. (Asopa 2003, 188)

Consequently, the discursive articulations of the 'Look North' policy assert that India's engagement in Central Asia is guided by 'the ancient tradition of the Great Silk Route' which was known for 'its spirit of religious tolerance and cultural pluralism rather than the competitive spirit of the "great game"' (Singh 2003, 196). Chapter 3 exposes the mythmaking logic underscoring such proclamations. Their articulations, however, illustrate that the 'Look North' policy is construed as an 'Indian approach' which is 'not inclined to favor the projection of the current Central Asian scenario as a new version of the nineteenth-century "great game"' (Kaushik 2003b, 32).

Prior to engaging with the narrative tendencies implicit in the 'Look North' policy and their impact on India's interactions both with Central Asia and the world, this chapter outlines the methodological approaches assisting the investigation of this volume. For the purposes of clarity, the following section clarifies the meanings that the designation 'Central Asia' has acquired in the conversations of Indian commentators. This exposition is important for understanding the discursive strategies employed in the articulations of the 'Look North' policy. Finally, this chapter sketches the arguments developed in this volume about India's external affairs and, in particular, about the narratives of New Delhi's strategic vision in Central Asia. Such a synopsis offers a glimpse into the formulation of India's foreign policy as a reflection and a projection of internal afflictions.

What is Central Asia

Since *Central Asia* is one of those notions whose ramifications are open to contestation, its geographical boundaries in this investigation follow the functional designation of the region in the immediate post-Cold War period—namely, the area occupied by the five post-Soviet 'stans': Kazakhstan, Kyrgyzstan, Tajikistan, Turkmenistan, and Uzbekistan. In the overwhelming majority of cases, Indian commentators identify with this definition and describe Central Asia as 'a new geopolitical creation' (Roy 2001, 2273). Such a designation reflects a belief both in the common historical traits of the people and polities of Central Asia, as well as the shared patterns of post-Soviet transition. This perception of similarity underpins Indian perspectives on the strategic responses required by regional posers:

> The Russian withdrawal from Central Asia after the disintegration of the Soviet Union gave rise to a host of security problems. The region was left without a security manager. Intra-regional rivalries eroded the possibility of region-wide cooperation and consolidation [...] The Central Asian republics had, therefore, to contend with domestic insurgencies, cross-border terrorism, growth of militant Islam, drugs and gun-running, etc. The republics witnessed the emergence of authoritarian regimes, poor governance, and rampant corruption. These problems have made the Central Asian region a fertile ground for outside intervention in the form of big power rivalries. (Sharma 2004a, 268)

This understanding of the Central Asian label notwithstanding, there have been some nuances in its definition. In fact many of them reflect the not-so-distant exigencies of the Cold War period when *only* Afghanistan and Mongolia were perceived as constituents of Central Asia (Rahul 1981). Consequently, there has been some proclivity to (occasionally) include both Mongolia and Afghanistan in the discussion of regional dynamics because of their distinct experience of Soviet modernization, a process that has not been unlike that of the Central Asian republics. In particular, this has been the case with Mongolia, which 'like other Central Asia states was transformed from a backward, medieval, and conservative society to a developing modern state' (Patnaik 2004, 154; Sengupta 2002; Soni 2002). As the following chapters illustrate (especially Chapter 4 and Chapter 7), the case for the inclusion of Afghanistan in the discussion of India's policy towards Central Asia is usually linked to its impact on both the dynamics of intra-regional interactions and the involvement of extra-regional actors. At the same time, it is ascertained that 'geographical contiguity, racial and religious affinity, and long-established transborder communications have provided a strong basis for cross-border fraternization between the people of Central Asia and the adjoining [territories of] Afghanistan, [which are] popularly called Northern Afghanistan and historically known as Afghan Turkestan' (Warikoo 2003, 143).

Likewise, for reasons of shared Soviet experience and the growing strategic significance of their natural resources, the countries of the Caucasus (especially those in the vicinity of the Caspian Sea) tend to (sometimes) make it into Indian calculations for Central Asia (Asopa 2006). Such analyses however hint at the emergence of 'an alternative Eurasian vision' (Bhambhri 2005, 386), which is closely related to the narratives of the 'new great game' discussed in Chapter 4. In this context, the Central Asian label spans 'the region extending from the Caucasus and the Caspian basin to the Tienshan and Pamir mountains' (Kaushik 2007b, 281). Alternatively, other commentators proffer the term of 'Central Eurasia', which 'implies the inland areas of the Eurasian continent, which include the republics of Central Asia, Afghanistan, the Caucasus, the Xinjiang Uighur Autonomous Region, the Tibet Autonomous Region, and Kashmir' (Sharma 2004a, 275). In particular, the inclusion of Xinjiang in such discussions reflects the '*generations of closeness* between Xinjiang's non-Han populations and their ethnic brethren in Central Asia' (Chatterjee 2006, ix).

In this respect, setting the geographic ramifications of the Central Asian label exposes the particular strategic connotations that the region has acquired in India's foreign policy calculus. The reference to Central Asia therefore becomes shorthand for the complex challenges confronting New Delhi's decision making in the post-Cold War period. As. I.K. Gujral, the former Prime Minister, has indicated, India's external relations are increasingly constrained by 'an *encircling arch of anxiety* [which] stretches all the way from the Middle East to South Asia *via Central Asia*' (Gujral 2004, 88; emphasis added). Thus, Central Asia is not merely an area on the globe enclosing the five post-Soviet 'stans', it is also an epitome of the pervasive volatility and new security threats that endanger India's stability and show the potential to negatively impact its foreign policy making. The understanding of Central Asia simultaneously as a geographic region and an embodiment of the challenges facing New Delhi's external agency is central to the interpretation of its 'Look North' policy.

Thus, while drawing attention to the emergent complexity of

global life, the analysis of India's international relations with Central Asia reflects on New Delhi's post-Cold War encounter of Russia, China, and the West in the region. The contention therefore is that the understanding and explanation of the possible trajectories of India's interactions with other international actors are best deciphered not through the study of its bilateral interactions but through an examination of the character of New Delhi's associations with third parties. In this respect, in order to tease out the prospective climate in India's relations with Russia, China, and the West, this study does not merely engage in an analysis of India's bilateral interactions with these actors, but enmeshes such bilateral relations in a comparative narrative assessment of their involvement in Central Asia. The value added from such a contextualization springs from the multiplicity of the 'new great game' in Central Asia which involves the participation of actors not only external to the region, but also of those that are local to its environment. Thus, although Indian commentators tend to emphasize the 'commonalities' shared by Central Asian states, they also readily acknowledge that 'these are not so strong as to override specific national consciousness'.

> The future course of their development policies and relations, will be influenced by the specificities of each state including geographical location, composition of population, problems relating to restructuring of economies and immediate security threat perceptions of the ruling elites. (Shams-ud-Din 1997, 35)

The region, thereby, becomes an idiom, an intervening variable and a context (i.e. an enabling environment) for the confrontation both with the discursive modalities and the emerging patterns of India's foreign policy. The following section addresses the methodological approaches, which have assisted this mode of analysis.

Note on Methodology: The Framing of *Narrative Imbrication*
It has already been suggested that this book analyzes India's post-Cold War international relations, with a particular emphasis on New Delhi's policy formulation towards Central Asia. Such an investigation is undertaken from the standpoint of International Relations theory, whose analytical propositions form the conceptual map for interpreting India's 'Look North' policy. The investiga-

tion is guided by two mutually reinforcing approaches—the discursive study of foreign policy and the assessment of the logic of mythmaking. For the purposes of brevity, as both these approaches are detailed in Chapter 3, it has to be mentioned that (i) *the discursive study of foreign policy* perceives the public articulations of foreign policy as potent symbolic resources simultaneously reflecting and creating social processes through which meanings are exchanged—that is, the discursive processes of foreign policy making are embedded in specific political, social, and historical conditions (Diez 1999; Lak 2005; Wæver 1998a; Zolkos 2005); (ii) *the logic of mythmaking* reflects a conviction that the articulation of international strategies relies on 'mythmaking'—that is, myths are not only a means of expression, but also modes for the organization of hopes and fears which offer a shortcut to domestic policy-legitimation by providing a latent pool of malleable (*national*) symbols for validating foreign policy agendas (Snyder 1991). It is noteworthy however that both these approaches—the discursive study of foreign policy and the logic of mythmaking—contribute to the construction of an interpretative account resting on a third methodological approach, labeled here as *narrative imbrication.*

Narrative imbrication, as the term suggests, is a process of bringing together the articulations of analysts and commentators on a specific issue. The result is a narrative produced by collating relevant statements that reveal the external stance of a state by tapping into the discourses of its domestic legitimation. Thus, narrative imbrication engages in a textual process tracing which both uncovers *'the narratives within narratives'* context of external relations and exposes that what distinguishes the explanation of international phenomena are 'the ingredients used in the narrative accounts' (Suganami 2008, 347–355; emphasis original). Thus, narrative imbrication offers an opportunity of simultaneously experiencing and deducing *the ingredients* of Indian discursive formulations regarding the country's international agency and its experience in Central Asia. It is in this context that the ontologies of the discursive study of foreign policy making and the propositions about the logic of mythmaking informing a state's external affairs corroborate in the production of a narratively imbricated analysis of India's relations with Central Asia.

It has to be acknowledged from the outset that it was not my intention to engage in (let alone present the outcome of this project in the form of) a narratively imbricated collage. However, narrative imbrication gradually formulated itself in the process of my research. It appeared as a joint product of my frustration and curiosity! While examining Indian interpretations of New Delhi's policy towards Central Asia, I was struck by two overwhelming tendencies in their accounts: either to produce assessments that have very few (and very often *no*) references to other analysts or observers, or to refer only to well-established Western (mostly, North American) scholars and commentators. To me, such a practice seemed to both befuddle and obfuscate the 'Indian debates' on New Delhi's international interactions which I wanted to engage with.[2] In particular, such foreign policy accounts appeared to be hanging in an intellectual vacuum of their own which tended to frustrate my research endeavors. On the one hand, the frustration seemed to derive from my inability to discern any identifiable dominant themes in Indian accounts on the country's external affairs as they seem to produce a series of monologues on New Delhi's international stance but very little in the way of a conversation between commentators. On the other hand, this frustration stemmed from the realization that I have fallen in the age-old orientalizing trap of not being able to pin down the object of my research desire in a form palatable to my Western-trained gaze. While infuriated on both counts, the identification of (and, perhaps, reconciliation with) such annoyance allowed my frustration to be overwhelmed by curiosity about and interest in the style, grammar, and vocabulary of the Indian discourse on international relations. The more I buried myself in Indian accounts of the 'Look North' policy, the more I began to distinguish certain identifiable patterns zigzagging across their narratives. Thus, in an attempt to connect the dots, I began jotting together the pronouncements of Indian commentators that seemed to address a similar set of issues. Thus, by putting them in a conversation with each other, the narrative imbrication approach emerged.

Although new to me, and not intended for this investigation, narrative imbrication is a strategy which has been used oftentimes by researchers and policy-makers both on purpose and by accident. For instance—just to point to two recent examples—Sabrina Ramet's (2005) brilliant review of the scholarly debates on the Yugoslav dissolution and J.L. Black's (2004) examination of Russian foreign policy under Putin gesture towards the narrative imbrication approach. As these instances reveal, narrative imbrication demonstrates that narratives are *'constructs'* employed in the explanatory enterprise of International Relations theory. At the same time, such an approach assists in rising above (although not necessarily trouncing) criticisms that narratives present a deceptive (if not potentially pernicious) story that 'misguides the audience into taking the illusions for real' (Suganami 2008, 354; emphasis original). More importantly, in the context of India's foreign policy formulations, Steven A. Hoffmann has boldly stated that the perspectives represented in his analysis

> *should be considered those of Indian analysts, officials, and leaders, and not those of this writer.* This is so even though in this type of essay the words generally must be those of the author and even though the Indian views are described in broad or general terms that pull together a number of specific thoughts that may come from more than one person. *Expressions of the author's own opinions will be rare and will be made quite explicit.* (2004, 36; emphasis added)

Such a caveat seems pertinent to this study as well. Narrative imbrication is considered here to be a way of rendering the perceptions of Indian commentators on 'specific' issues regarding the foreign policy of the country. Although concurring with Hoffmann that *authorship* of these perceptions belongs to those who utter them, I contend that the *responsibility* for such collated texts rests with the one constructing the narrative imbrication. In this respect, while the register and style of articulation are distinctly the ones of the Indian commentators, the structure, organization, and narrativization of these accounts is my own. Thus, while the statements used expose the discursive emplotment of Indian articulations on Central Asia, the deciphering and the discernment implicit in their imbrication together both confers and conforms to the perceptions of this author. Narrative imbrication therefore does not merely *'tell the story'* of a country's external affairs (Singer 1989, 13; emphasis added), but it *tells the story collated by the observer/interpreter of foreign policy articulations.*

The claim here is that narrative imbrication extends the following trumps to the study of a country's international interactions. Firstly, and as already indicated, it allows the introduction to the discursive ingredients that go into the broth of foreign policy making without interfering in the actual voice of these articulations. Although structured by the one collating such utterances, the ability to retain the authenticity of domestic articulations allows for a large amount of noise to seep through. Thus, secondly, narrative imbrication does not impute, nor endow coherence on the story it tells. Instead, it facilitates a confrontation with the complexity underpinning seemingly akin propositions. Thirdly, such an approach makes it explicit that the creator of the narrative imbrication *is* or *has consciously decided to take* the position of an external observer. This acknowledgment is especially pertinent to the study of India, where the role of an external/Western observer has been inherently problematic. Thus, while not doing away with the controversies associated with 'the eye of the Western beholder', the self-professed and self-acknowledged subjective splicing of the narrative imbrication approach intimates that it neither attempts objectivity, nor intends the promotion of grand narratives. Instead, by presenting the cacophony of domestic articulation of foreign policy making, its collation illustrates the complex diversity encountered by the one conducting the narrative imbrication. Such an approach, thereby, derives its logic, content, and coherence from the warren of pronouncements populating the terrain of a country's international affairs.

Following Andrew Latham's prescient observation, the proposition of narrative imbrication suggests that

> while observers need to be cognizant of the powerful cultural forces shaping Indian approaches to security building, it is important not to reify these forces. Cultures—even 'security cultures'—are ambiguous, complex, and dynamic, and they can and do change over time. This is not to argue, of course, that India security culture is infinitely malleable or open to direct international manipulation. Rather, it is to point out that as Indian 'national' culture continues to evolve (as a result of both globalization and indigenous forces) it is likely that Indian security culture will also change. (1998, 133–134)

Narrative imbrication traces the complexity and trajectories of such changes in foreign policy making. Its collations offer flexible modes of 'narrative explanation/understanding' that render discursive contextualization 'fundamental' to the explanation of international affairs 'either because explanations are given in a narrative form or because they invariably contain narrative accounts within them' (Suganami 2008, 338–355). As already indicated, such an emplotment of the narrative imbrication approach benefits from the discursive study of foreign policy making and the propositions of the logic of mythmaking—both of which are detailed in Chapter 3. The following section provides a brief roadmap for the conversation in which this volume engages.

Structure of the Book

The formulation, practice, and study of foreign policy reveal the dynamic interconnectivity between domestic and international politics. Thus, the external relations of a state are inherently intertwined (in one way or another) with the patterns of popular legitimation—regardless of where on the spectrum between dictatorship and democracy the state in question is located. At the same time, however, international practices and trends also interact with and impact on the decision-making attitudes of a state towards the outside world. India is no exception to this framework. Its foreign policy environment attests to the growing complexity of post-Cold War international affairs. The volume problematizes prevailing notions of the country's external agency by engaging with the discursive formulations and pronouncements of change and adjustment through which the patterns of foreign policy making are actually evinced. The claim here is that the focus on New Delhi's relations with Central Asia offers an opportunity for a better illumination of its nascent international agency. Said otherwise, this study examines the values and strategies underpinning its normative and strategic culture. The point of departure for such an investigation is the exploration of the kinds of order that India promotes in Central Asia through the narrative articulations of the 'Look North' policy.

This analysis requires an assessment of the history of Indian foreign policy not only as an idea and an ideal, but also of the practices, categories, and logics on which its discursive assumptions rest. Chapter 2, therefore, sets off the exploration by examining the trajectories of India's post-Cold War diplomacy. Unlike other international actors, India did not appear to welcome the end of bipolarity, which further complicated the articulation of its international interactions. Consequently, for the better part of the 1990s, New Delhi seemed uncertain how to position its external affairs. The tensions and ambiguities that define this period have revealed both a lamentation for the passing of comfortable certainties and the (unwilling) recognition of the necessity to abandon well-entrenched practices and patterns of behavior. Thus, the dissolution of the Soviet Union, the perceived failure of nonalignment, and the increasing tension between 'moralism' and 'militarism' (i.e. an 'Ashokan tradition' and a 'Kautilyan tradition') have compounded the overhaul of India's strategic vision. Chapter 2 indicates that it was only in the context of the 1998 nuclear tests that India seemed able to indicate a sense of comfort with the changing global environment and its international identity.

The claim is that India's post-1998 international interactions demonstrate not a mere operationalization of an improved strategy, but a qualitatively different interpretation both of the country's role in international life and the character of the international system. *1998*, thereby, marks an important juncture in India's foreign policy, which identifies (i) the end of its post-Cold War ambiguity; (ii) the adoption of a more assertive foreign policy stance; and (iii) a discursive break with the imperatives of post-Independence moralism. It has to be acknowledged however that neither technologically, nor ideationally would the 1998 tests have been possible if the groundwork had not been prepared by previous Indian governments. Said otherwise, if previous administrations had not initiated a nuclear weapons program (and had not begun appropriating Hindu symbols for the purposes of popular legitimation of foreign policy making), the transformation associated with the 1998 nuclear weapons tests would have been impossible. Thus, 1998 can be described as 'an *overdetermined* conjuncture'—that is to say, a conjuncture in which multiple dynamics merge into one explosive unity (Menon and Nigam 2007, 5).

Such an interpretation is central to the analysis of Chapter 3. The proposition is that India's post-1998 foreign policy making is underpinned by a particular *logic of mythmaking*. Developed by Jack Snyder (1991), this approach suggests that mythmaking offers a shortcut for the domestic policy legitimation by providing a latent pool of malleable (national) symbols for validating the foreign policy agendas of states. In other words, Snyder's interpretation focuses on the interaction between domestic politics and international ambition. More often than not such mythmaking demonstrates a deeply entrenched belief that a country's security can be safeguarded only through aggressive posturing. Such an assertive stance, in turn, becomes a mode for rationalizing the domestic political climate. At the same time, the logic of mythmaking demonstrates that dispositions about international relations reflect foreign policy judgments based on narrow domestic beliefs and idiosyncratic interpretations of policy-making reality. The focus here is on tracing the narratives through which foreign policy is conjured up in popular imagination as a validation of the appropriateness of particular order—both social and international.

In identifying the mythmaking qualities of India's post-1998 foreign policy, Chapter 3 undertakes an innovative combination of Snyder's approach with the methodology of the discursive study of foreign policy. As already suggested, both methodologies are intertwined in the framing of this book's *narrative imbrication* approach. The claim is that foreign policy discourses construct narratives that weave images of the past into the concerns of the present. Thus, foreign policy making becomes an identity issue, which takes coherence through the articulations of and responses to national insecurities. In the context of India, this composite analytical framework reveals that the mythmaking of New Delhi's external relations is illustrated by four discursive constructs: (i) a geopolitical trouncing of India's perceived weakness; (ii) the development of a 'new' ideology of national strength (Hindutva); (iii) the seeming settlement of domestic political contestations; and (iv) the promulgation of a narrative of self-aggrandizement. Mythmaking, thereby, turns the formulation of foreign policy into a powerful ideology for the consolidation of a fragmented domestic political stage through the discursive three-step provided by the reinterpretation of the past to fit the promoted national myth, the assertion of an ability to overcome the uncertainties of a globalizing world, and the social production of external affairs. Thus, the post-1998 assertions of foreign policy independence articulate both India's disposal of the structural and cognitive constraints on its external relations and its willingness (and perceived increased capacity) to insert the formulation of its national interest on the agenda of world politics, regardless of the opinions and expectations of other international actors.

Chapter 4, therefore, unravels the mythmaking underpinnings of India's international interactions with Central Asia. The assessment of New Delhi's agency in the region takes into account the patterns, contexts, and analytical frameworks informing the formulation of its external relations. Such an examination reveals the diverse articulations contributing to the narratives of the 'Look North' policy. Most commentators maintain that India's relations with Central Asia are a function of the long historical experience that they share. Nevertheless, it should be remembered that such a discursive construction was made possible by the dissolution of the Soviet Union, which forced upon New Delhi the realization that Central Asia is simultaneously (i) a distinct region in global life; (ii) a region, which is in India's immediate vicinity; and (iii) a region, whose patterns of relations have an impact on and are impacted by developments in South Asia. In this respect, the discourses of the 'Look North' policy did not emerge in a vacuum, but were profoundly implicated in the post-Cold War trajectories of India's foreign policy and the narrative modalities of its mythmaking re-articulations.

Thus, the narratives of the 'Look North' policy assert the viability of India as an example to the Central Asian republics. In particular India's state-building project is proffered as an illustration for the successful management of a diverse society through the institutional arrangements of a secular and democratic polity. This discursive purposefulness has become a critical component of the 'crafting and marketing a national identity' through the articulations of foreign policy (Kale 2009, 59). Intertwined with these pronouncements, the proponents of the 'Look North' policy emphasize the significance of regional cooperation to the stability and prosperity of Central Asia. Chapter 4 then goes on to illustrate the mythmaking strands in India's engagement of the region. In particular, it points out the idiosyncrasies of New Delhi's bilateral relationship with Tajikistan, which forms a crucial aspect in the assertiveness of the 'Look North' policy. The background of this discursive emplotment offers a unique insight into Indian perceptions of the emergence of a 'new great game' in Central Asia. As Chapter 4 demonstrates, what is distinct about its patterns is the simultaneous proliferation of extra-regional and intra-regional agency. Thus, on the one hand, Indian commentators draft extensive lists of international actors with vested interests in Central Asia. On the other hand, and more significantly, they claim that such a contestation between international actors has allowed Central Asian states to engage in 'pick-and-choose' strategies and in bandwagoning-for-profit policies.

This understanding forms the context for engaging Indian interpretations of New Delhi's encounter with the dominant nodes of this networked pattern of the 'new great game'—Russia, China and the West. As already indicated, the dissolution of the Soviet Union sent shockwaves through the structure of India's foreign policy formulation, which forced New Delhi—somewhat unwillingly—to reconsider the norms, rules, and practices of its external relations. Chapter 5 engages this experience and its impact on India's encounter of Russia in the context of the discursive articulation of its 'Look North' policy. It reveals that unlike their bilateral relations (which more often than not seem to be treated as a linear progression of increasingly close viewpoints), India's framing of Russia's agency in Central Asia demonstrates the dissociation between New Delhi's and Moscow's strategies. On the one hand, such a divergence originates from the sense of trauma (and betrayal) after Russia's disengagement from the subcontinent in the early 1990s. On the other hand, the differences between India and Russia in Central Asia reflect New Delhi's new sense of its international identity in the context of its post-1998 foreign policy strategy. Thus, India's search for 'normality' in its relations with Russia demonstrates that Moscow continues to be a major influence on its external affairs not only in Central Asia, but also in global politics.

At the same time, the narratives of India's external strategy convey a belief in the growing prominence of Asian countries in global politics. Thus, as Chapter 6 indicates, it seems only natural that the discursive formulations of the 'Look North' policy would consider India's relations with its 'significant Asian other'—China. It has to be acknowledged that for Indian commentators, the complicated legacy of the bilateral relationship between New Delhi and Beijing forms the point of departure, the prism, and the bulk of their investigation of the Sino-Indian interactions in Central Asia. The ongoing border dispute between them as well as the bitter memory of the 1962 war, the issue of Tibet, as well as China's partnership with Pakistan and its economic and military support for Myanmar are just a few of the dilemmas that frame New Delhi's relations with Beijing. It is therefore not surprising that the encounter of China in Central Asia has produced a diverse set of perspectives within the narratives of the 'Look North' policy. These perceptions identify China simultaneously as a *partner*, a *threat*, and a *model*. Although not necessarily complimentary, all three representations are elicited by the discourses of the 'Look North' policy.

It has to be acknowledged that the discursive effects of the post-1998 nuclear tests suggest the trouncing of 'the profound sense of insecurity [vis-à-vis China] since the 1962 war'. In this context, commentators point that China was 'surprised by' India's successful tests and 'began to take notice of India', which allowed New Delhi to adopt 'a more confident mood' (Mohan 2007, 16). Chapter 6 also points out that the analysis of the Sino-Indian relationship in Central Asia points to a unique problem faced by the external agency of both countries—the difficulty of bracketing their roles in global politics within the labels, language, and practices developed for the explanation and understanding of 'conventional' Westphalian states. The proponents of the 'Look North' policy point to the tension between *civilizational and territorial* notions of statehood in New Delhi's and Beijing's agency towards Central Asia. Thus, according to this interpretation, owing to the idiosyncratic nexus of historical experience and current patterns of global interactions both countries find themselves donning the unfitting attire of state-like polities in their external relations. The mythmaking logic of these claims simultaneously participates in and contributes to 'the invention of India' as a 'distinct, integrated political unit, held together and delineated by its common and coextensive culture, institutions, and history' (Dutt 2006, 74).

This analytical context has a bearing on India's perception of Western involvement in Central Asia. Chapter 7, thereby, pulls together the disjointed literature on India's interactions with the EU, the USA, and NATO. All three are treated under the label of 'the West' because the discursive construction of the 'Look North' policy (i) treats them as a joint normative entity (if not a fully-fledged actor); (ii) does not seem to distinguish particularly between the agency of the three actors; and (iii) often mixes the effects of one for the other or treats them as stylistic variations. The point of departure in interpreting the roles played by Western actors in Central Asia appears to be the recognition of their legitimacy in Asian affairs. In this respect, it is the discursive construction of '9/11' in the foreign policy making of both Western actors and New Delhi that animates Indian *support for* and *opposition to* Western agency in Central Asia. Five topics seem to form the nodes around which Indian perceptions of the West simultaneously convergence and divergence according to the individual proponents of the 'Look North' policy. These topics are:

- the Western practice of realpolitik;
- the effects of the Western presence in Central Asia on regional geopolitics;
- the Western impact on the states of Central Asia;
- the consequence of Western agency on China's role in the region (as well as in world politics);
- the impact of Western involvement in Central Asia on the fight against terrorism and, in particular, on the governance of Afghanistan and Pakistan.

The conflicting interpretations of these five issue-areas indicate distinct perceptions of the effect Western actors have (and will have) on New Delhi's interactions with Central Asia, as well as the dynamics in India's own security environment. The perception is that—more than Russia's or China's—the post-'9/11' agency of Western actors has introduced an additional level of complexity to the already confounding patterns of relations in Central Asia. Thus, the narratives of the 'Look North' policy reveal that the discourses of India's intrication in the 'new great game' call upon potent symbolic resources that simultaneously reflect and create social processes through which meanings are exchanged. In this respect, foreign policy articulations are representations of a decision-making reality—i.e. the external relations of states are neither objective nor transparent. As in the case of India they are embedded in specific political, social, and historical conditions.

In conclusion, therefore, Chapter 8 assesses the discursive emplotment of the 'Look North' policy. It suggest that India's international agency lacks the power to *influence* others—that is, it lacks the ability to affect the decision-making of other actors through the capacity to make some policy choices more attractive than others (but without recourse to force or the threat of force). The claim is that India's relations with Central Asia evince that its international agency still has *no influence* in global affairs. Despite the narrative construction of the post-1998 foreign policy, the possession of nuclear weapons, and the concomitant assertive foreign policy posturing have not been able to enhance India's influence. In other words, India still has not been able to establish itself as a *model* in global politics. As the survey of the 'Look North' policy reveals, the discursive proclamations of its external agency in Central Asia have not been matched by comparable transformations in the ideational and institutional makeup of New Delhi's foreign policy formulation.

The claim here is that India has a number of influential individuals and businesses, but it, itself—as an international actor—does not have an *influential* foreign policy strategy that could establish it as an alternative to existing ones. Thus, despite the proliferation of discourses of India's nascent global grandeur, the absence of a readily available Indian vision of global politics—a *Pax Indica*, if you will—prevents New Delhi from living up to the expectations generated by such narratives. Such an assertion should not be misinterpreted as an allegation that India does not have a respected and significant historical and cultural heritage. However, the international recognition of this legacy (just like the recognition of its nuclear capabilities) does not amount to *influence*, which would be able to arouse a desire for emulation among other actors. As the discussion of the 'Look North' demonstrates, the narrative construction of New Delhi's external affairs does not project an alternative vision of world order that would distinguish it from or assist to supplant the agency of other participants in the 'new great game'. Consequently, the international identity of India does not seem to convey any specific attributes that Central Asian actors might want to emulate. The analysis seems to suggest that India would retain its relative position of no influence for some time to come.

2

TRAJECTORIES OF INDIA'S POST-COLD WAR FOREIGN POLICY

Introduction

As Chapter 1 has explained, this book traces the discursive formulations of India's international interactions with Central Asia. However, such an examination requires an understanding of the formulation, practice, and study of the country's foreign policy making. This chapter, therefore, unravels the discursive trajectories of New Delhi's post-Cold War international interactions. Its 'uncovery' (Bially-Mattern 2005, 5) forms the background for the subsequent engagement with the logics of India's external relations that (in turn) underpin the narrative modalities of the 'Look North' policy.

The chapter reveals that for the better part of the 1990s, India's foreign policy formulation has remained in the grips of conceptual tensions, strategic uncertainty, and geopolitical constraints. These diplomatic predicaments reflect New Delhi's difficulties with adjusting to the patterns of the post-bipolar world order. It will be explained shortly that this perception seems to have changed as a result of the May 1998 nuclear tests. Their detonations appear to reveal a discursive overhaul of India's international relations premised on a much more assertive (if not aggressive) foreign policy stance. In this respect, it is necessary to explain what makes the 1998 Indian nuclear tests such a momentous occurrence; especially since India had already detonated a nuclear device in 1974.[1] In other words, what was so different about the narrative construction of 1998 to warrant proclamations that virtually overnight India had been transformed from a dormant elephant into a roaring tiger (Kapur 2006, 194)?

Since the specificities of the tectonic shifts in foreign policy making provoked by the 1998 nuclear tests will be elaborated shortly, it is crucial to emphasize here that these detonations were linked directly to New Delhi's international strategy. In other words, they were constructed as part of India's new foreign policy toolkit. At the same time, the nuclear tests also (i) ended the policy ambiguity about the relationship between nuclear weapons and international relations; and (ii) asserted that nuclear weapons (just like any other military assets) are among the foreign policy instruments at India's disposal, which it would not hesitate to deploy if New Delhi deems it necessary (Kapur 2006, 180). In contrast, the nuclear test on 18 May 1974 was portrayed merely as a 'peaceful nuclear explosion', which displayed the advanced level of India's technological development (Sharma 1987, 223). A statement by then Prime Minister, Indira Gandhi offers an explicit indication for the lack of connecting the 1974 nuclear detonation to foreign policy making. She insisted that 'the peaceful nuclear explosion was simply done when we were ready. We did it to show ourselves that we could do it... We did it when the scientists were ready' (quoted in Datta 2008, 52).[2] It also appear 'to have confirmed New Delhi's premier regional position [by] demonstrating that India could become a nuclear weapons state if it wished' (Singh 2006, 76). In this respect, the explicit connection between nuclear weapons and international relations in the strategic rhetoric of the 1998 nuclear tests reveals New Delhi's newly discovered penchant for assertive foreign policy making.

At the same time, as will be demonstrated in Chapter 3, such assertiveness displays divergent constructions of India's international identity. Samina Yasmeen explains that the 1998 articulations of New Delhi's external relations have pitted the 'traditionally secular' interpretation of India's foreign policy making versus the conception of 'India as a Hindu state'—i.e. 'Hinduism is seen as the true reality of the subcontinent with its relevance to all aspects of the lives of its inhabitants'. In spite of their differences, both models appear to propound 'Indian destiny as a great nation. Its size, diversity, history, and tradition are seen as indicators of this destiny. By virtue of these attributes, India is viewed as a state capable and deserving of playing a major role at regional and international levels' (Yasmeen 2008, 34–35). From this point of view, it is not at all surprising that all political formations in the country—regardless of their ideological opposition and rivalry—'are ardent supporters of the hegemonic constitution of a great and strong India' (Ahmed 1993, 317). Bearing these attitudes in mind, the following sections trace the post-Cold War trajectories of India's diplomatic discourses.

Engaging with/in Foreign Policy Making

The understanding, explanation, and practices of foreign policy making among Indian commentators, scholars, and policy makers is as diverse and contested as that in any other national context. A number of them have indicated that the study of international relations defies any attempt 'to force the flow [of global politics] into predetermined theoretical patterns or preconceived logical grooves'—ultimately, the dynamics of world affairs 'will remain involuted, subject to wayward human behavior' and impossible 'to straitjacket in *a priori* generalization'; thus, the 'eternal challenge' for the formulation of foreign policy is the continuing adaptation to 'the unpredictability of inter-state and inter-societal relations' (Basu 2007, 199; Kachru 2007, 22). This confirmation of the complexity of global life is usually taken as a point of departure for distinct interpretations of international politics. On the one (more normative) end of the continuum, Muchkund Dubey (1993, 17), the former Joint Secretary of the Ministry of External Affairs, declares that 'the primary purpose of any country's foreign policy is to promote its national interest—to ensure its security, safeguard its sovereignty, contribute to its growth and prosperity, and generally enhance its stature, influence, and role in the community of nations. A country's foreign policy should also be able to serve the broader purpose of promoting peace, disarmament, and development, and of establishing a stable, fair, and equitable global order. This latter purpose may at times appear to conflict with the former, but in the medium and long run it too is likely to serve the country's national interest'. On the other (more geopolitical) end of the continuum, Jaswant Singh (1999, 34–35), the former Minister of External Affairs, has stressed the 'relentless pursuit of one's national interests'. The formulation of foreign policy in this context is perceived as:

> an interaction of forces within a country and outside its borders. The interaction is dynamic and constant and often there is a pattern, with a mix of polarities and friendly alignments between a country and its external environment. The external

polarities and alignments often change over time along a spectrum of hostility, competitive coexistence, neutrality, indifference and cooperative coexistence. The challenge for the practitioners is to mute a hostile relationship and to seek a cooperative one, but the general aim is to secure the best relationship possible under the circumstances rather than necessarily a peaceful one if satisfactory conditions of peace are unavailable. Thus, a student of foreign policy should estimate the interaction between domestic and external forces by examining a matrix of internal as well as external polarities (enmities) and alignments (friendships). They represent the parameters of a country's foreign policy system. (Kapur 2006, 74)

In attempting to reconcile the normative and geopolitical imperatives,[3] some observers of Indian foreign policy assert that the making of foreign policy 'is essentially an exercise in the choice of ends and means on the part of a nation-state in an international setting... It must be understood, however, that decision making in a foreign policy does not mean the formulation of a "grand design" by a few individuals in terms of their personal wisdom and their perception of the global environment. It is essentially an "incremental process" involving the interplay of a wide variety of basic determinants, political institutions, organizational pulls, and pressures of a bureaucratic-political nature, and the personalities of the decision-makers' (Bandyopadhyaya 2003, 1–2). The formulation of foreign policy reveals the complex interconnectivity between domestic and international politics—in other words, the foreign policy of a state is not at all divorced from some form of popular legitimation (regardless of where on the spectrum between dictatorship and democracy the state in question is located).[4] For instance, some commentators ascertain that

In India, as in all democratic countries, foreign policy can never be situated in isolation from the domestic environment. The formulation and implementation of foreign policy is the result of a wide variety of factors, attitudes, and circumstance, and action and interaction of diverse political forces inside the country. Foreign policy is inextricably linked up with domestic problems. It usually requires adjustment in domestic policy; similarly changes in domestic policy affect the conduct of foreign affairs. Thus, foreign policy is a projection of domestic policy in a wider field. (Pillai 1969, 2)

As will be explained in Chapter 3, the complexity of foreign policy making is 'directly linked to the multiplicity of ideas and views held in any given political unit about the appropriate ways of dealing with the other [...] Closely related to the notion of identity, it emanates from differing views in every state or society about the self, the other, and the extent to which cooperation with the other is possible and/or feasible' (Yasmeen 2008, 30). For instance, Chapter 4 will elaborate on the way in which the clash of identities between India and Pakistan structures the articulations of New Delhi's strategy towards Central Asia. B.M. Jain, therefore, argues that (despite his acknowledgement that foreign policy making is 'an exclusively legitimate right of a sovereign nation'),

at least in theory, every foreign policy is couched in normative terms. In practice, foreign policy makers are bound to consider a host of factors to safeguard the country's core national interests. [Thus] a foreign policy must reflect domestic strength as well as challenges emanating from the emerging patterns of power structures both at the global and regional level. It is essential, because short-term tactical gains as well as episodic treatment to crucial foreign policy issues tend to jeopardize long term national interests. (2008, 41)

In spite of the seeming agreement among different proponents that 'national security considerations' are the 'key factor in [foreign policy] decision making' (Perkovich 2000, 379), Sagarika Dutt (2006, 194–195) points out that 'defining India's national interest might not be such a simple task'. For instance, she suggests three sets of factors—(i) domestic, (ii) international, and (iii) ideological—which are relevant to the explanation and understanding of New Delhi's motivations in global life.[5] At the same time, others have discerned that there are 'two elements in India's national interest'—'the preservation of national freedom' and 'to lay firmly the social and economic foundation of her young democracy' (Pillai 1969, 5)—which appear to be continually invoked during the debates on the country's external affairs. Thus, the uncovery of a country's national interests involves understanding its 'national strategic culture'—that is, the formulation and execution of the 'national will' and its integration into foreign policy by 'preparing psychologically the foreign policy bureaucracy, the military, coalition partners, opposition parties, and the rest of the country to face strategic scenarios through debates, discussions, overhauls, and long-range intelligence assessments' (Chaulia 2002, 222–223; Singh 1999, 290). The claim is that 'like all cultures, which are little more than an aggregate of consistent behavior-patterns of a society, a strategic culture must be established and sustained in the overall national interest' (Bal 2004, 29). Consequently, 'the ultimate aim of India's foreign policy, like that of any other country, is the furtherance of its national interest. [It] should be mentioned that the concept of national interest is not a static one: its content changes with changing internal and international situations' (Pillai 1969, 5). Imtiaz Ahmed (1993, 82–83) has conceptualized India's external relations by zooming-in on two mutually-reinforcing dimensions: (i) 'the understanding of the composition of the state structure, i.e. the reaction between structure (social production) and superstructure (social ideas, social organizations, institutions, and ideological relations)'; and (ii) 'the understanding of foreign policy as an element of the superstructure, inextricably linked with the state structure'.

National interest, thereby, 'cannot be defined and defended simply on the basis of outdated ideologies and obsolete doctrines in the face of fast altering contours of the global political and economic order' (Jain 2008, 45–46). Likewise, Andrew Latham (1998, 129) has concluded that while the concept of national interests offers 'seductive ways' for constructing and interpreting foreign policy making, ultimately 'it is "too broad, too general, too vague, and too all inclusive" to provide a reliable guide to understanding India's actual foreign policy practices'. As explained in Chapter 3, the evocation of '*the* national interest' in the articulation of the *mythmaking logic* of India's foreign policy making suggests that its formulation

> is also closely related to a reading and re-reading of history with an inherent need to find data to validate the already held views about the self and the other. While operating broadly within a common perceptual context, therefore, groups in a state or society can and do differ on which end of the spectrum or space is most relevant to their interaction with anoth-

er state or society. The interplay between these different views determines the policies a state may pursue vis-à-vis the other. A predominance of geostrategic concepts, for example, could cause state A to opt for competitive policies toward state B. A shift in this balance may cause the same state to start preferring shared security instead of a geostrategic approach. At the same time, however, the multiplicity also creates conditions in which the debates are not resolved and the state pursues policies that reflect the difference of opinion and power balance among various groups. Effectively, therefore, a state may pursue policies that occupy different spaces along the spectrum of geostrategy and solidarity. They may sign agreements in some areas that reflect a commitment to shared security, while simultaneously pursuing competitive policies in other areas. (Yasmeen 2008, 30)[6]

In this respect, the analysis presented here concurs with the observation of Suryakant Nijanand Bal that

> any model [for the examination of foreign policy making] is actually little else than an approximation of reality, not always necessarily tallying accurately [with it]. However, as a template, it reduces the degree of uncertainty. Also, as new situations develop and fresh inputs are available, the model can be successfully modified to once again approximate realities. A model is thus not static but a dynamic entity and, where successively updated, a useful tool which helps in the formulation of policy. However, it becomes necessary to identify some constant elements or factors, which would form the base on which the model is to be built. (2004, 354–355)

Taking this perspective as a point of departure, Chapter 4 will illustrate that the narrative construction of India's agency in Central Asia explains foreign policy strategizing as a 'guiding principle on which complex problems [are] reduced to a deterministic pattern. It is based on a series of interlinked decisions regarding the selection, development, and deployment of resources and capabilities. The overall objectives are to realize a vision and achieve the desired targets in a comprehensive and changing environment' (Kachru 2007, 19). Despite this assertion, as Chapter 8 will detail, the survey of the 'Look North' policy reveals that New Delhi has 'no influence' in Central Asia, not least because the discursive proclamations of external agency have not been matched by transformations in the ideational and institutional makeup of foreign policy formulation. In this respect, even with the fall of the Berlin Wall and the dissolution of the Soviet Union, the patterns of New Delhi's international interactions appear to confirm the proposition that 'comprehensive reform is rare in India' (Rana 2007, 59). The following section details the main phases in India's post-Cold War international relations.

Dominant Patterns in India's Post-Cold War Foreign Policy

The somewhat unpredictable trajectories of India's post-Cold War foreign policy reflect not only the pervasive complexity of globalizing interactions, but also the perception that the external stance of New Delhi 'must change from time to time' (Prime Minister Manmohan Singh quoted in Jain 2008, 38; Gupta 1989; Mohite and Dholakia 2001). Some have claimed, therefore, that the period 'witnessed many seesawing foreign policies calibrated to changing times' (Chaulia 2002, 220). Other have taken such an ongoing evolution as a point of departure for innovative accounts of India's 'infinitely malleable' international identity, whose underlying 'national security culture' is subject to constant modification, manipulation, and adaptation ('with some traditions purposefully preserved while other are left to atrophy'); indicating that its foreign policy is not just a product of history, geopolitical context, and socialization, but also 'of political and social culture' (Latham 1998, 134–154).

Thus, the perceived affliction with 'with a general ambience of indiscipline and lack of national purpose' has been interpreted as an indication that in its foreign policy making India acts 'like a lady who has powerful suitors but is determined not to marry [any of them], because it is not in her interest to do so. A lady in this position has to play the game with considerable skill because every suitor is likely to feel that she is too inclined to the other party' (Basu 2007, 213). Such statements offer a smattering of the cacophony of voices involved in interpreting India's diplomatic formulations. For the purposes of clarity, the following sections analyze these proclamations in order to identify the main themes animating their discourses.

Post-Cold War Blues

As already indicated, the conceptualization and practice of India's external relations reflect the complex contingencies of its geopolitical climate. Unlike other international actors, however, India seemed not only unprepared for the changes triggered by the end of Cold War bipolarity, but it also perceived them as an unwelcome turn of events. In a nutshell, for India the crumbling of the Berlin Wall represented 'the loss of an entire world' (Menon and Nigam 2007, 166), because of 'the disappearance of the familiar contours of the postwar world' (Chiriyankandath 2004, 202). From New Delhi's point of view, the Cold War had a 'definite shape' and was 'well-organized', 'regulated', and 'predictable' (Budania 2003, 80; Sharma 2004a, 266; Gupta 1989). Thus, while it lasted the 'Cold War [had] provided an ideally stable environment: it allowed India to play an *exaggerated role* on the international stage for many years, where it could moralize about the inequalities of bipolarity and the "Cold War mentality" while still benefiting materially and politically from its ties to both the Soviet Union and the USA' (Singh 2006, 52; emphasis added). The 'collapse of the bipolar world and the radical transformations in the former Soviet Union' have therefore 'shaken the basic foundations and framework of India's foreign policy' (Muni 2003, 106). Consequently, for the better part of the 1990s, the Indian foreign policy elites seemed uncertain how to position their country's external relations. This setting reveals New Delhi's problems of coming to terms with the turbulence of post-Cold War order. It also displays the deepening sense of 'incoherence and indistinctiveness of India's foreign policy due to the absence of a well-defined and well-articulated policy framework' (Jain 2008, 42). The frustration with the contradictions and indecisiveness of India's post-Cold War foreign policy has led Barbara Crossette (1993, 11) to declare that New Delhi 'often produces muddled responses to international issues, as intense national pride and a sense of manifest destiny collide with the unwillingness to make bold policy moves. Wild allegations and abstractions are hurled around and sanctimonious speeches made, but concrete proposals or rational analyses rarely follow'. In this setting, the threat perceptions of New Delhi seem to suggest that

> India [has] moved from an organic to the critical period in its existence, from the ordained vision which dealt with a world

of certainties (to the extent that such certainties can be abiding) into an era of ferment which is compounded by uncertainties and doubts about our own reaction to the world around us. The validity of our orientations and perspectives, of necessity, stands questioned in the context of the end of the Cold War and the ideological confrontation which affected the international community for nearly seven decades since the end of the First World War. (Dixit 2001, 16)

The tensions and ambiguities that came to define this period indicate both a lamentation for the passing of comfortable certainties and the (unwilling) recognition of the necessity to abandon well-entrenched practices and patterns of behavior. The latter, in particular, seemed compounded by the difficulty in discarding 'certain habits of mind, deeply ingrained in the organizational culture of Indian foreign policy bureaucracy' (Jain 2008, 30). The turbulence of this policy ambivalence 'plunged India into a morass of political instability and uncertainty' (Chaulia 2002, 220). Policy-makers in New Delhi found themselves 'without markers to identify potential threats to [India's] way of life or reasons to be prepared. With the collapse of the communist regimes in Eastern Europe, followed by the dissolution of the Soviet Union itself, the global ideological confrontation that had serves so well to identify friend and foe vanished' (Woodward 2000, 19). Consequently, the 'twenty months between November 1989 and June 1991 witnessed three governments and two general elections [which left] foreign policy in shambles because of the preoccupation... with domestic issues and relations with neighbors, which precluded rapid responses to external challenges' (Jain 2002, 132). Thus, the former Indian ambassador to the USA, Abid Husain (1993) has offered one of the most revealing metaphors for India's foreign policy anxiety: 'One economist described India as a tiger in a cage. When the cage is open, the tiger would show its real strength. The cage is now open but the tiger refuses to come out of the cage'.

The title to this section—'Post-Cold War Blues'—is thereby intended as an indication of New Delhi's reluctance to venture out of the cage of Cold War politics. At the same time, it also suggests the central dilemmas facing the repositioning of India's foreign policy: (i) the dissolution of the Soviet Union, and (ii) the need to acknowledge the failure of non-alignment. These two mutually reinforcing dynamics evinced the third underlying predicament—(iii) the increasing tension between 'militarism' (i.e. coercive international stance) and 'moralism' (i.e. cooperative international stance) during the reevaluation of India's external relations.

Dissolution of the Soviet Union
A number of commentators have pointed out that there was 'nothing as traumatic' for post-Independence India as the collapse of the Soviet Union (Mohan 2004, 117; Sharma 2002, 110). The end of the Cold War 'robbed India of a long, time-trusted friend' (Jain 2008, 29–30) and 'brough about some [profound] soul searching' (Kaul 2007, 240). In spite of recent assertions that India had been 'under the thumb of the Soviets' (Rai and Simon 2007, xiv), the strategic partnership between Moscow and New Delhi had come to dominate the ideological, political, and security underpinnings of India's foreign policy (Shamsi 2004, 233). Therefore, some have ascertained that for India 'the shock [from the dissolution of the Soviet Union] was greater than for most outside the erstwhile Communist Bloc' (Chiriyankandath 2004, 199; Asopa 2007, 172). To an extent, this close partnership was 'forced upon' India by the gradual convergence between American, Chinese, and Pakistani interests during the 1960s and 1970s, which left New Delhi little geopolitical space for maneuver (Kapur 2006, 11).[7] In this respect, the Soviet-Indian relationship had been upheld as 'an example of cooperation and peaceful coexistence of countries belonging to different social systems' (Mishra 1996, 47). Thus, despite India's professed nonalignment, the Soviet Union had constituted New Delhi's 'most reliable fall-back option in economic terms as well as in political support' (Menon and Nigam 2007, 166). Consequently, the 'loss of Indo-Soviet relations to the inevitable march of history threw [New Delhi's] foreign policy into a chaotic situation' (Naik 1995, 173–175).

In this respect, the formulation of foreign policy was compounded not only by the unfavorable international environment, but also by its domestic impact—i.e. the disarray in India's economy in the early 1990s and the attendant social unrest (Cohen 2001, 299; Kapur 1997, 37).[8] In economic terms, the assertion has been that 'the collapse of the Soviet Union hit India the hardest' (Asopa 2007, 182). The beginning of 1991 saw India confronted with an 'economic crisis of exceptional severity'—the government's budget deficit rose to 8.5 percent of GDP, the inflation rate to 17 percent, the external debt soared over $70 billion, and debt-service ratio increased to 32 percent of GDP (Jain 2008, 49). According to Sumit Ganguly (2003/2004, 43) the 1991 financial crisis was an outcome of 'the Soviet collapse [which] undermined India's autarkic approach to economic development, which, in turn, had serious consequences with respect to its foreign policy options'. As O.N. Mehrotra (1997, 98) has explained 'the Indian foreign policy came in for a review because of mounting problems in the Indo-Soviet trade relations due to the erratic supply of Soviet goods'. Such developments seemed to reinforce the view that 'given the economic compulsions and the constitutional and political set-up, the only rational stance for our [Indian] diplomacy can be one of avoidance of war to the best of our ability. Peace is a minimum precondition for our economic development' (Bandyopadhyaya 1991, 63).

The Failure of Nonalignment
Nonalignment has been the most distinctive feature of India's post-Independence foreign policy. Conceived by Jawaharlal Nehru in the 1940s (Damodaran 1981, 204), nonalignment has pursued peaceful coexistence both at home and abroad. In terms of the former, Nehru stated that 'I do not want our country to be a victim of that narrow nationalism which is now to be found in almost all countries of Europe and Africa' (quoted in Seth 1993, 461–462). In terms of the latter, nonalignment advocated international cooperation among (primarily post-colonial) states disenfranchised and disenchanted by the Cold War order. It has been described as the 'ideological corpus', 'normative bias', and 'strategy' of New Delhi's external relations (Phadnis and Patnaik 1981, 223). Nonalignment has become the central feature for the strategic perception of India's foreign policy independence, revealing a 'mindset of operating autonomously [while] disregarding other models' (Rana 2007, 47). K.P. Misra (1981, 26–37) has argued that owing to its South Asian origins, the notion of nonalignment reflects 'the cultural psyche' and 'the ways of thinking of the Indian people'. As he points out, despite its negative construction (i.e. 'not an alignment'), nonalignment is not a negative concept, but a positive endeavor 'in favor of national reconstruction… [and] espousing to transform the present international order'. As Jawaharlal Nehru (1964, 381) himself declared in 1958 'when we say our policy is one of nonalignment, it means non-alignment with military blocs. You cannot have

a negative policy. The policy is a positive one, a definite one, and I hope, a dynamic one, but in so far as the military blocs today and the Cold War are concerned we do not align ourselves with either one [...] One has to lay stress on the fact that we are not parties to the Cold War and we are not members of, or attached to, any military bloc'.[9] Nonalignment, therefore, 'did not mean neutrality. [Instead], India wanted to prevent a third world war altogether, or at least, by holding its outbreak, till her economic plans were well under way, and also to keep herself in a position from where if a war occurred, she would not be obliged or faced to plunge into it' (Pillai 1969, 29). Some have even claimed that the practice of non-aligned peaceful coexistence was an *offensive strategy* 'directed primarily against the superpowers and China, with the intention of keeping them at bay and at the same time attracting their favor'— in other words, nonalignment was 'essentially a means to ensure India's independence under the circumstances of India's relative weakness vis-à-vis the superpowers and China' (Ahmed 1993, 226).

K. Raman Pillai has therefore pointed out that it is worth bearing in mind that by the time India attained its independence in August 1947, 'the polarization of a large part of the world into the Soviet Bloc and Western Bloc had [already] taken shape. Thus, India from the very beginning was confronted with the problem of evolving a foreign policy consistent with her national interest in the context of a world divided between the two contending blocs'. Pillai has emphasized that 'after decades of colonial rule [India] was eagerly looking forward to attaining her rightful and honored place in the world' through 'the exercise of her *independent judgment* on international issues' (Pillai 1969, 27–28). It is from within this conceptual constellation that Jawaharlal Nehru has articulated nonalignment as the underlying element of the country's external relations:

> We propose, as far as possible, to keep away from the power politics of groups aligned against one another, which have led in the past to world wars and which may again lead to disasters on an even vaster scale. We believe that peace and freedom are indivisible and the denial of freedom anywhere must endanger freedom elsewhere and lead to conflict and wars. We are particularly interested in the emancipation of colonial and dependent countries and peoples, and in the recognition in theory and in practice of equal opportunities for all races

[...] We seek no domination over others and we claim no privileged position over other peoples. But we do claim equal and honorable treatment for our people wherever they may go and we cannot accept any discrimination against tem [...] If by any chance we align ourselves definitely with one power group, we may perhaps from one point of view do some good, but I have not the shadow of doubt that from a larger point of view, not only of India, but of world peace, it will do harm. Because then we lose that tremendous vantage ground that we have of using such *influence* as we possess (and the influence is going to grow from year to year) in the cause of world peace [...] Therefore, it becomes all the more necessary that India should not be lined up with any group of powers which for various reasons are full of fear of war and preparing for war. (1961, 2–24; emphasis added)[10]

Thus, in pragmatic terms, it was the disintegration of the Soviet Union that turned nonalignment into an irrelevant foreign policy stance (Menon and Nigam 2007, 167). The loss of Cold War bipolarity as the governing logic of the international system immediately did away with the need to pursue a nonaligned path in global politics. In this setting, 'India found itself [confronted with] a deep dilemma—how to adjust its non-aligned policy to the imperatives of a geopolitical shift in the post-Cold War scenario' (Jain 2008, 30). At the same time, the obsolescence of nonalignment posed an unexpected challenge to the long-standing Nehruvian tradition in Indian foreign policy making. The long shadow that Nehru has cast over the formulation of India's external relations, on the one hand, owes much to the fact that he was among a handful of leaders at the time of Independence who were experienced in international affairs; and, on the other hand, reflects his stature among international actors in contrast to other Indian political leaders at the time (Dutt 2006, 195). Furthermore, Nehru—the '"architect" of India's foreign policy' (Pillai 1969, 5)—seemed gripped in 'the fervent belief that he alone could steer India to its destined international status' (ibid. 217).

This assumption of indispensability in external relations sprang from Nehru's undisputed monopoly over the Congress stances toward overseas issues before independence and the absence of contenders with his kind of 'broad world perspective'... Nehru the democrat nearly epitomized his much dreaded specters of 'Caesarism' and dictatorial behavior by turning the Cabinet into a rubber stamp on important international questions, and jettisoning the principle of Collective Responsibility. (Chaulia 2002, 217)

Thereby, India's policy-making anxiety in the immediate post-Cold War environment attests to the challenge of addressing the gaping fissures at the very core of the country's international identity.

Tension Between 'Militarism' and 'Moralism'
The context provided by the disintegration of the Soviet Union and the failure of nonalignment underscored the need for a 'basic change of philosophy' (Lal 2006, 98) in India's foreign policy making. Yet, while the agreement on the need for transformation has been nearly universal, its content and direction became a subject of contestation for the better part of the 1990s. At the heart of the debate has been the friction between 'Kautilya and moralism' (Cohen 2001, 307) or between a 'Kautilyan tradition' and an 'Ashokan tradition' (Ahmed 1993, 216–226):[11] the former refers to the model of regional geopolitics codified in the ancient text by Kautilya, *Arthashastra* (Bhagat 1990; Boesche 2002; Jog 2005; Kangle 1963; Kohli 1995; Mehta 1992, 91; Modelski 1964; Sharma 2005; Spengler 1969; Subramanian 1980; Upadhyaya 2009, 73); the latter (is a modified version of Nehruvian idealism, which) emphasizes that India is 'the world's most important democracy' (Mohan 2004, 57) and that its foreign policy should be an extension of 'cherished domestic values' (Cohen 2001, 307). The moralist position asserts that India is a force that is 'committed to looking for and speaking the "truth"' in world politics—a standpoint whose ideational origins can be traced to 'a *Mahabharata* story where a special envoy indicated the importance of showing the world the correctness of his position while emphasizing the incorrectness of his opponent' (Latham 1998, 144).

Thus, the choice for New Delhi seemed bifurcated between aggressive foreign policy behavior and an apprehensive international agency preoccupied with the protection of the country's volatile borders and precarious social order. The inability to address this issue in the immediate post-Cold War period underscored 'the continuing contradictions [of India's foreign policy making] between the amoral realties of world politics and the moral norms which we aim at' (Basu 2007, 222). Daniel Lak offers a good summary of the seemingly irreconcilable differences underscoring these propositions:

> The soft state is one that believes it exists on a moral footing and that wants its interlocutors, neighbors and enemies to realize this. If only everyone appreciates India's essential goodwill then peace and prosperity will be the inevitable result. Opponents of this point of view argue that a nation as important and strong as India should be confident and single-minded about its national interests. There has to be political and public consensus when the country is slighted, challenged, or attacked. The response must be quick, decisive, sharp, and effective. Israel (often) and the United States (occasionally) are cited as models of such behavior. These are countries not to be trifled with, and, it is believed, India should emulate them. (2008, 240)

In particular, the 1990–1991 Gulf War against Saddam Hussein's invasion of Kuwait pitted these two visions and 'served as a catalyst for a re-assessment of Indian foreign policy and a recognition of the realities of the post-Cold War era' (Hardgrave and Kochanek 1993, 405). Many were quick to assert that the idealistic underpinnings of New Delhi's moralism 'do not make for a practical foreign policy' because they 'show a lack of realism and a lack of awareness about Indian interests' (Basu 2007, 183). Therefore, in the immediate post-Cold War environment, New Delhi's attempts to construct a foreign policy in accordance with the shifting climates of international life seemed frustrated by the inability to meaningfully accommodate the desire for a more assertive role on the global stage and the concerns over the defence of its territorial integrity (Mohan 2004, 208).[12] Formally, however, majority of commentators have insisted that 'since the geopolitical bases of India's role in foreign relations have largely remained constant [despite the end of the Cold War], so have the goals of policy since Nehru's time' (Rajan 1998, 75). Thus, official policy discourse continued to rehearse the threat of nuclear proliferation and the danger of escalating regional rivalries (Mishra 1996, 43; Pannikkar 1995).

Thus, for the better part of the 1990s, India's foreign policy continued to be guided by the norms of 'peace, harmony, and coexistence' and the twin-belief (i) in the essential equity and justice of the international system; and (ii) that other states will not seek to change the international order by force (Mishra 1996, 5–9). In its attempt to 'learn to live with the uncertainties of the [post-Soviet] era', India—'without making any significant headway'—has endeavored to develop a 'two-track approach that was, on the one hand, aimed at resurrecting the vital elements of its economic and military relations, and, on the other, searching out alternatives in the West' (Jha 1997, 76). It is most likely these attempts to pursue a 'business-as-usual' pattern of behavior (with as little alteration from accepted practices as possible) which sidelined the ambiguities, contradictions, and inconsistencies of New Delhi's international agenda that have underpinned the lack of focus in India's external relations in the immediate post-Cold War period.

1998 and After: Nuclear Assertiveness

The testing of nuclear weapons is never a small affair. However, the actual event tends to grow in magnitude when the state undertaking the test has refused to formally accede to the nuclear non-proliferation regime and is in a nearly permanent state of attrition with one of its (equally-armed) neighbors. The five nuclear devices detonated by India during 11–13 May 1998 at the Pokhran range confirmed this point. The tests set off an international controversy and widespread criticism and, at the same time, prompted concerns about a nuclear arms race in South Asia. The latter's fears seemed confirmed by Pakistan's nuclear tests during 28–30 May 1998 at its sites in the Koh Kambaran mountain and in the Khoran desert. More significantly, however, the geopolitical discourse of India's nuclear tests indicated a marked departure from its previously largely conciliatory and non-committal attitude. In a nutshell, *they were aimed to provoke*. Said otherwise, by flaunting its ability for 'pre-emptive response', New Delhi publicized the alteration in foreign policy making which had to ensure India's 'survival' in an anarchic world (Basu 2007, 207–222).

The reverberations of these detonations displayed India's embrace of its 'comprehensive national strength'—an approach that reveals New Delhi's belief that the strategic combination of enhanced economic and military power 'would enable India to influence international rule-making in its favor and prevent infringements on its right to make sovereign decisions in its national interest' (Lal 2006, 103). In this setting, the 1998 nuclear tests have become an important cut-off point in India's post-Cold War development. They indicated its progress toward 'a more focused sense of itself in the world' which formed the backbone of 'a more aggressive and self-confident foreign and security policy' (Lak 2008, 245). At the time, the Indian Foreign Minister, Jaswant Singh (1998, 44) has proclaimed that 'nuclear weapons remain a key indicator of state power. Since this currency is operational in large part of the globe, India was left with no choice but to update and validate the capacity that had been demonstrated 24 years ago in the nuclear test of 1974'. This assertiveness seems to have been borne out of a long-standing frustration with New Delhi's marginalization in the international system: 'Indian official believe that they are representing not just a *state* but a *civilization*. Believing that India should be accorded deference and respect because of its intrinsic *civilization* qualities, many Indian diplomats and strategists are aware of having to depend upon *states* that do not appreciate India's special and unique characteristics' (Cohen 2001, 52).[13]

1998, thereby, becomes a cornerstone for the identification of the central features of India's new international identity.[14] In other words, it was 'India's perception about itself' that 'impacted on its foreign policy making' (Basu 2007, 159). As will be explained in Chapter 3, such perceptions ('encouraged by the state structures and reinforced by the media and educational institutions') come to dominate popular, policy, and scholarly 'myths' about external affairs (Yasmeen 2008, 31). It needs to be reminded that the emergence of such a stance was not decoupled from historical patterns. In fact, the symbolism of *1998* has been discursively embedded in the context of India's strategic perceptions. As Prime Minister Vajpayee proclaimed at the time, the nuclear tests responded to 'a regional and global reality that has evolved over the past fifty years. [...] We live in a world where India is surrounded by nuclear weaponry. No responsible government can formulate a security policy for the country on abstract principles, disregarding ground realities. Nor can policy be based on anything but *the supreme consideration of national interests*' (cited in *The Statesman*, 15 May 1998; emphasis added). This interpretation of India's strategic interests has been provoked by the perception that the country 'cannot afford to forgo its nuclear option when everyone around is arming themselves to the teeth' (*Hindustan Times*, 12 May 1998b). Such articulations claim that 'India was left with no option [in the face of] the collaboration [between] China and Pakistan in missile development and nuclear technology'; thus, proving that 'the international community [has] legitimized [the proliferation] of nuclear weapons when it indefinitely extended the nuclear nonproliferation treaty' (*Hindustan Times*, 12 May 1998a).[15] In this respect, the claim here is that India's post-1998 foreign policy indicates not a mere pragmatic operationalization of 'improved tactics' premised on 'learning from past experience that might help India achieve what it has fought for throughout the past half century: its rightful place in the world' (Narlikar 2006, 74), but a qualitatively different interpretation both of the country's role in international life and the character of the international system. Thus, post-1998 foreign policy making represents *'a decisive break with India's past commitments'* (Mehta 2006, 17; emphasis added).

A critical aspect of the message sent by the 1998 nuclear tests is that 'Indians are finally emerging from the mindset of dominated people, staking a claim to their rightful place in the modern global village' (Rai and Simon 2007, 242). The discourse on and the desire for foreign policy independence has long been part and parcel of New Delhi's international relations. Yet, Indian policy-makers have seemed reticent to engage in a behavior that might be (mis)interpreted as the escalation of tensions in already conflictual relations.[16] Moreover, the Cold War provided an additional layer of structural constraints which limited India's room for independent foreign policy making. According to some observers, this context turned New Delhi into 'the object of external pressures up to 1998. It was a field of power politics that produced a system of competitive coexistence of Pakistani, American, Chinese, and Russian influences in India' (Kapur 2006, 36). The nuclear tests (at least discursively) appear to have lifted the perception of such constraints, which, in turn, has ushered in the confidence that 'India can now negotiate from a position of strength' (*Business Line*, 12 May 1998). Said otherwise, in 'the post-Pokhran II period', the narrative modalities of 'India as a state with nuclear weapons' have allowed New Delhi to be *'more assured of itself'* on the global stage (Budania 2003, 83; emphasis added). In this respect, the assertiveness underscoring the 1998 nuclear tests reveals both the disappearance of such structural constraints and India's willingness to insert its national interest on the global agenda (regardless of the opinions and expectations of other international actors).[17] The following summarizes the main features of this post-1998 agency.

End of the Post-Cold War Foreign Policy Ambiguity
The 1998 nuclear tests have indicated an end in India's ambivalence between 'militarism' and 'moralism'. They reflected New Delhi's decision 'to rely more on power politics and less on morality and unilateral restraint in the pursuit of Indian interests' (Kapur 2006, 23). The contention is that the framework of post-Cold War international relations is 'confrontationist and anarchic in nature' and that 'the concept of balance-of-power has become more prominent' (Budania 2003, 81; Mohite and Dholakia 2001). Reinforcing this point, Prime Minister Vajpayee has reminded that 'neither my own statement of 15 May, nor the longer official text released later that day has characterized the nuclear tests as *"peaceful"*; thus, 'the capacity for a *big bomb*' impels the discernment that 'no one should have any illusions [about] India accepting any treaty that is discriminatory in character' (cited in *The Statesman*, 15 May 1998; emphasis added). Indian commentators have ascertained that the vacillation between 'a self-righteous pacifist approach [and] unilateral action does not take us anywhere':

> Any individual may face death bravely for his absolute principles. Can a country, or those who have the responsibility for its security, take a moral stand, on behalf of its people, which binds the future generations to an inequitable world order? This is where the nuclear option comes. There is no contradiction between working persistently and patiently towards a nuclear weapons free world and developing the nuclear option in the interim, *in the world as it is*. (Udgaonkar 2001, 1792; emphasis original)

The apparent choice of Kautilya's geopolitical agenda has indicated the seeming settlement of the domestic debates on the trajectories of post-Cold War foreign policy making. As Andrew Latham (1998, 137) explains, the 'Kautilyan tradition' depicts the system of world politics as 'an inherently violent place where conflict and violent competition [is] the rule, and where peace and stability [are] the (rare) exception'. Thus, the adoption of the 'Kautilyan paradigm' as the basis for foreign policy formulation reveals 'a powerful cultural expectation that, in the subcontinent at least, small states should subordinate themselves to the interests of larger powers' (Latham 1998, 137). The geopolitical stance of 1998 contends that 'a country cannot afford to be complacent and let down its guard on matters as important as national security. [...] It needs to be appreciated that the inescapable requirements of national security cannot be compromised. In international politics, the policy of mutual friendship and cooperation with one's neighbors has to be balanced with vigilance. A neighbor's capacity to damage India's security interests should never be underestimated, let alone disregarded' (Kenwal 1999, 1614–1615).

In this respect, the 1998 nuclear tests 'forged a powerful sense of unity' that the country is 'finally finding the confidence it needs to gain global influence and make its point of view known in global capitals' (Lak 2008, 245). At the same time, they also became an important 'sign of self-confidence' projected in an 'emphatic manner' to the rest of the world (*Hindustan Times*, 12 May 1998a). Such a shift in foreign policy formulation has to indicate that New Delhi 'can play its condign and productive role in global and regional affairs without being subservient to hegemonic powers' (Jain 2008, 220). At the same time, as will be explained in Chapter 3, this perception reveals a tendency 'to view international relations as a zero-sum game in which gain for one side means a loss for the other. The geostrategic approach with its emphasis on ideas of balance of power is often elevated to the status of a value that needs to be cherished and sought' (Yasmeen 2008, 29). Thus, New Delhi's post-1998 international relations emphasize the assumption of the paramountcy of 'a national consensus' for the formulation of a 'purposive foreign policy' (Basu 2007, 222).

Assertive Foreign Policy Stance
The resolution of the foreign policy debates that have plagued the formulation and practice of India's post-Cold War international relations has also facilitated an increasingly more confident external policy. According to C. Raja Mohan (2004, 205–207), a veteran Indian journalist and commentator, this development suggests the recovery of a 'forward foreign policy' approach pioneered by Lord Curzon. This 'Curzonian school' of Indian foreign policy re-appropriates the 'Indocentric' approach advocated by the former British

Viceroy. This strategic narrative displays the belief that '"strength respects strength" in foreign policy' (Chaulia 2002, 221). Confirming this view, Ashok Kapur (2006, 15–33) insists that such a policy-shift has allowed New Delhi to emerge 'as a catalyst in regional and international diplomatic and military affairs'. In his view, New Delhi's recognition of the 'conceptual and policy implications of the relationship between nuclear weapons and foreign policy made "escalate and negotiate" the new mantra of India's external relations'. Other pundits maintain that the nuclear assertiveness of such a forward foreign policy makes other states 'more willing to listen to what India has to say, to give our views some credence' (Lak 2008, 248).

As will be explained in Chapter 4, in terms of India's Central Asian policy, the Curzonian logic of its post-1998 assertive foreign policy appears to display appreciation for the British colonial ability to recognize 'the strategic significance of looking beyond the northern borders over the Hindu Kush and the Pamirs into the heartland of Central Asia and while clashing with Czarist Russia in the Great Game, finally checkmated it by creating the Vakhan Corridor' (Bal 2004, 28). The perception is that it was 'only under the British [that] India became a base for extensive foreign military operations and only under British tutelage was established a global strategic tradition based on the subcontinent' (Singh 2006, 50).[18] At the same time, Chapter 3 will demonstrate that the emphasis on India's strategic preponderance in its post-1998 foreign policy reveals the significance of nuclear weapons as *discursive intangibles*— 'such as prestige and stature'—'to materially affect a state's ability to thrive [in a global political order]'; in this context, 'many states acquire arms not for military-strategic reasons but to achieve the essentially political goal of enhancing their international status' (Latham 1998, 141–142). Confirming such a narrative explanation, one commentator has proclaimed that 'India has arrived on the threshold of superpower status, literally with a bang' (Chaulia 2002, 221). Pragmatically speaking, such an assertive stance reflects the discursive lock-in of the post-1998 foreign policy mythmaking. As J.N. Dixit, the veteran foreign policy official and commentator, has acknowledged 'if we do not [develop] arrangements for the operational deployment of our capacities' and, in this way, make 'our nuclear weapon capacity a factor in our defence preparedness, then *conducting tests* and *developing our delivery systems* would be *a meaningless political and strategic exercise'* (cited in *The Economic Times*, 23 June 1998; emphasis added).

Break with the Imperatives of Non-Violence

Perhaps, the central tenet of India's pre-1998 foreign policy has been the Nehruvian rejection of a 'balance of power approach' and the subscription to a perspective that 'looks at the world through the conceptual lenses of cooperative security' embedded in strategies for political, economic, and social development (Dutt 2006, 204).[19] In contrast, the shift indicated by the 1998 nuclear tests was 'the result of unilateral military-political actions' pursued on the basis 'of practical geopolitical considerations rather than the idealism of Nehru's peace policy' (Kapur 2006, 5; Mistry 2003, 2950). This change reflects the central element of New Delhi's threat discourse—the fear of (and a broad sense of historical vulnerability to) foreign intervention (Latham 1998, 139). As Chapter 3 will demonstrate, the narratives of the post-1998 foreign policy articulations targeted the perceived 'softness' of Nehru's 'pseudo-secularism', which 'twisted India's strategic culture into all kinds of absurdities' and ultimately led to 'enfeebling a once fierce nation' (Chaulia 2002, 220; Singh 1999, 13). In fact, Bimpla Prasad has revealed the emergence—shortly after Independence—of voices critical of the Nehruvian 'policies of neutrality and appeasement', which are 'based more on considerations of international morality than on those of national interests' (Prasad 1963, 438–439). According to Ashok Kapur (2006, 39–40) the synergy between diplomacy and military power evidenced by the post-1998 assertive foreign policy stance has overcome Nehru's 'fundamental conceptual error... [his failure to] understand that strategic action, often with the use of coercion or its threat, was the ruling law of the international drama'.[20] The espousal of nonalignment and conciliatory foreign policy behavior has undermined 'the rigor of realpolitik' (Lama 2005, 132).[21] Thus, by espousing 'power politics', Indian foreign policy elites have recognized that

> peace talk and peace diplomacy were insufficient, that military power was needed to back up Indian diplomacy, that India needed to demonstrate a capacity to escalate international conflict, to create a situation where something was left to chance that required the great powers' attention to alleviate Indian concerns. (Kapur 2006, 39–40)

This foreign policy transformation appears to have rectified the lamentation of some Indian commentators in the past that in 'post-1947 India, reference to Kautilya's work are scant. In his speeches Nehru did not refer to Kautilya's prescriptions about statecraft' (Kapur 1976, 77). In this context, the post-1998 assertiveness of India's forward foreign policy approach represents not merely break with Nehruvian principles of international relations,[22] but also with Gandhi's commitment to the imperatives of non-violence: 'I am not pleading for India to practice non-violence because she is weak. I want her to practice non-violence being conscious of her strength and power. No training in or collection of arms is required for the realization of her strength' (Gandhi quoted in Dixit 2001, 21). Imtiaz Ahmed (1993, 227) has indicated that 'Gandhi left no room for the development of the military in post-independence India since it runs contrary to non-violence. From Gandhi's position, therefore, India must forsake the military or violent basis of power, if it intends to remain morally free and contribute to the creation of a non-violent peaceful world'. From this point of view, the 1998 nuclear weapons tests 'represent a decisive break with the best moral intimations bequeathed by Gandhi and Nehru, who for all their failing articulated an idealism that could have been the basis of a more morally exemplary foreign policy' (Mehta 2008, 17). It is in this respect that the 1998 nuclear tests have become a symbol for the tectonic shift in the post-Cold War Indian foreign policy making. At the same time, they attest to India's idiosyncratic understanding of realpolitik—one, which intimates that national security can be achieved in 'essentially unilateral terms' (Latham 1998, 137).

Conclusion

This chapter has examined the discursive landscape of India's post-Cold War foreign policy. Initially, the breakup of bipolarity seems to have puzzled the articulation of New Delhi's diplomatic stance. Such a confusion reflects the difficulties in articulating a new international identity and new foreign policy roles for the country in what appears to be a constantly changing global environment. The chapter has illustrated that these efforts were compounded both by the disarray in India's economy in the early 1990s as well as by the emergence of unsettling social dynamics. Furthermore, the formulation of a coherent foreign policy had been challenged by the proliferation of geopolitical dilemmas and tensions. These security predicaments have undermined the very bedrock of New Delhi's diplomacy.

The chapter demonstrates that it was the strategic discourse of the 1998 nuclear tests, which shook off the narrative uncertainty of India's foreign policy making. The nuclear assertiveness of their emplotment has provided the facilitating environment for a more proactive and self-assured stance in international life. Thus, India's post-1998 foreign policy has been presented by commentators as a demonstration of a qualitatively different interpretation of the country's role in global politics. The following chapter engages the discursive articulations of this proposition and investigates the logics that animate its claims.

3

THE MYTH OF ASSERTIVE POSTURING AND INDIA'S POST-1998 FOREIGN POLICY MAKING

Introduction

The context provided by the discussion of India's post-Cold War foreign policy in Chapter 2 has identified the main trajectories in the formulation of New Delhi's external relations. As demonstrated, it is the discursive construction of the 1998 nuclear tests which seems to indicate a resolution to the conflicting conceptualizations of New Delhi's international interactions. This chapter, therefore, engages the discursive logics of this transformation by tracing the contextual circumstances within which the formulation of diplomacy is enmeshed. The claim here is that India's post-1998 foreign policy making reflects a particular contextualization of the country's external relations within the domestic articulations of national insecurities.

Foreign policy formulations, thereby, become discursive platforms both for the manifestation of national self-positioning in the international arena and the re-contextualization of historical narratives. As will be explained, such an emplotment uncovers the *logic of mythmaking* informing the domestic validation of New Delhi's foreign policy stance. As the following sections reveal, its mode of analysis suggests that the formulation of India's post-1998 foreign policy has morphed into a powerful ideology for the consolidation of a conflict-ridden domestic political stage. In this res-pect, mythmaking becomes a mode for the discursive trouncing of the insecurities, tensions, and constraints that have plagued New Delhi's external relations in the immediate post-Cold War period.

Coming to Terms with the Logic of Mythmaking

Resting on a 'domestic politics perspective', this chapter contends that India's foreign policy strategy—especially after 1998—has been informed by a particular *logic of mythmaking*. Developed by Jack Snyder (1991), the rationale of this proposition focuses on the interaction between domestic politics and international ambition. Since Snyder proffered this understanding of the domestic sources of international behavior in relation to actors with already established influence or 'Great Powers', it would be useful to consider the substance of his proposition in order to make it relevant to the articulations of India's external relations. In illustrating that foreign policy articulations offer a discursive platform for the manifestation of national self-positioning in the international arena, the following subsections outline the import of discursive analyses of foreign policy making and the *logic of mythmaking* informing the external relations of states. In other words, the claim here is that myths—such as those animating the formulation and maintenance of foreign policy—begin with 'a change in the function of language' (Cassirer 1963[1946], 282).

The Discursive Study of Foreign Policy

In spite of its alleged abstruseness, the study of foreign policy through discourses seems to have gradually gained prominence in the analyses of international relations (Diez 1999; Wæver 1998a; Zolkos 2005). In fact, as Roger Boesche (2002, 31) points out, the origins of this approach could be traced back to Kautilya's injunctions which stressed the importance of *language* to 'a science of politics'. Thus, the public articulations of foreign policy are perceived as symbolic resources which simultaneously reflect and create social processes through which meanings are exchanged—that is, the discursive processes of foreign policy making are embedded in specific political, social, and historical conditions. It can be argued, therefore, that foreign policy articulations are *representations* of decision-making reality—i.e. the external relations of states are neither objective nor transparent. Thus, the discursive study of foreign policy indicates that it is a narrative representation *through* and *for* 'someone'. This 'someone' is defined here as state-elites—understood as the decision-making authorities of states (Kavalski 2008, 53–54; Lak 2005; Pattanaik 2004). The discursive approach to the international relations of states considers 'foreign policy effects' as part and parcel of a rhetorical mode, which is intended to project a particular political agenda. For instance, in terms of India's foreign policy, it has been ascertained that such an approach points to the material effects of 'a set of widely resonating ideas that have evolved out of a long historical experience and are deeply rooted in the shared consciousness or "common sense" of the Indian political class' (Latham 1998, 132). Such discourses produce 'India's sense of collective self' (Basu 2007, 156). Thus, the discursive study of foreign policy asserts that the formulation of a state's external affairs is a function of the logic of language, 'not the relation between language and some extra-linguistic "reality"' (Williams 2005, 23). In this respect, it is 'the vocabularies' of international interactions and the particular 'language of [their] discourse' that exposes the dynamics of external affairs (Pattanaik 2008, 408). For the purposes of brevity, the following overview offers only a brief synopsis of the main propositions of the discursive approaches to foreign policy analysis.

The discursive study of foreign policy rests on the assumption that the examination of domestic discourses of 'we'-concepts—such as 'state' and 'nation'—offers crucial insights into understanding foreign policy developments (Wæver 1998a, 100). Thus, it is 'the very act of linguistic expression that our perceptions [for instance, about foreign policy] assume a new form' (Cassirer 1963[1946], 45). An instance of such a discursive evocation of the nation is offered by a 2002 statement of the former Minister of External Affairs, Yashwant Sinha at the Brookings Institution. In it, he proclaims that according to the objectives of India's foreign policy

> *We* must also work to spread democracy at the national and also the international level [...] Now, several decades after the creation [of multilateral institutions they] will require changes in their governance. *We* need to readjust the structures of decision-making in international bodies to reflect contemporary reality. *We* cannot hope to foster a democratic culture in the world until the principal international institutions are themselves democratized and made more representative. (cited in Gupta 2008, 108; emphasis added)

The claim here is that the discursive study of foreign policy reveals the ways in which 'culturally conditioned ideas, images, and "institutional scripts'" shape the notion and practices of India's international relations (Latham 1998, 129). This argumentative slant stresses that narratives 'can serve as [a] catalyst in foreign policy', because of 'the impact which the message may have on the general public' (Rai 2003, 24). In other words, the domestic articulation of foreign policy objectives contributes to the public 'participation in the *idea* of the nation' (Hall 1996, 612; emphasis original)—that is, the language of international relations 'glues' individuals together into a shared *national* pattern. Thus, foreign policy making becomes an identity issue, which takes coherence through the articulations of and responses to *national* insecurities. To paraphrase from a different context, the narratives of a state's external relations reveal nations as imaginary constructs that depend for their existence on an apparatus of discursively-articulated cultural fictions (Brennan 1990, 49; Ollapally 2005, 117). The claim is that foreign policy statements not only actualize, but also reflect a choice of particular national self-image; thus, they are predominantly aimed at domestic audiences rather than the alleged external target (Shih 1990, 125–139). As such, the discursive study of foreign policy 'is less an unmediated theoretical tool for describing the world than a culturally informed interpretative framework that actually *frames* and *creates* the world that state officials see and within which they make foreign policy' (Latham 1998, 136; emphasis added).

In this respect, the study of discourses scrutinizes the concomitant narrative constructions that underwrite the formulation of foreign policy (Diez 1999, 610). The inference is that foreign policy choices reflect particular state interests, which, however, are not independent of the discursive context in which they emerge. Said otherwise, the external affairs narratives of a state illustrate 'the implications of policy in terms of the impact on public opinion' (Rai 2003, 30). In this respect, foreign policy can be defined as 'a discourse of power which is global in scope [yet] national in its legitimation' (Campbell 1998, 70). By examining the manner in which foreign policy emerges, is defined, redefined, and becomes embedded in *discursive fields*, 'we can see how [its narratives] shape action and are likewise shaped by it' (Bell 2002, 345). Therefore, the narratives of a country's external relations are analyzed as systems or chains of meanings (Kavalski and Zolkos 2007, 379–380), which suggest that foreign policy articulations are (concurrently) *discursively enabled* and *discursively limited*. On the one hand, the policy-effects of discourse are exposed not as *causal*, but rather as creating the *horizon of the possible*. On the other hand, the structure of discourse does not have an independent existence, but is *knowable* to us through particular agency-articulations. It is contended that this discursive approach is integral to the uncovery of the logic underscoring India's foreign policy practices. As will be explained shortly, foreign policy discourses construct narratives that weave images of the past into the concerns of the present.

The Logic of Mythmaking

The suggestion that a state's foreign policy behavior draws on 'mythmaking' might sound outlandish to some; yet, according to Jack Snyder (1991, 14), this proposition reflects a conviction that the articulation of international strategies relies on 'stable belief systems [that] protect against the mental burden of constant fundamental reassessment'. Myths, thereby are not only a means of expression, but also modes for the organization of hopes and fears. According to Ernst Cassirer, the power of 'mythical thought' derives from the ability of its narratives to construct a 'system of identity', which tends to objectify 'man's social experience, not his individual experience'. He indicates that through this objectification of feelings, myths construct a perception of reality which 'cannot be rejected or criticized; it has to be accepted in a passive way' (Cassirer 1963[1946], 6–48). Mythmaking, thereby, offers a shortcut to domestic policy-legitimation by providing a latent pool of malleable *(national)* symbols for validating foreign policy agendas. Thus, domestically articulated 'strategic myths' gain their foreign policy currency both by *mobilizing* the solidarity of the national community and by *justifying* specific agendas under the 'cloak of nationalism' (Snyder 1991, 28). In this setting, dispositions about international relations reflect judgments based on domestic beliefs and contextual interpretations of reality. As already suggested, the discourses of foreign policy making indicate an important mode of simultaneously imagining and consolidating the nation around a dominant (usually homogenizing) narrative—one that sees the nation as a kind of organizing logic which frames the external relations of the state.

The logic of mythmaking, thereby, is premised on two inter-related ideas: (i) the discursive reliance on geopolitics (and its attendant strategic concepts); and (ii) their functioning as potent ideologies for the modulation of domestic politics (Snyder 1991, 1). The mythmaking which is produced as a consequence of these dynamics and goes on to underpin the external behavior of states attests to a deeply entrenched belief that a country's security can be safeguarded only through aggressive posturing. This also reveals that mythical narratives 'have a capacity for affective mobilization, for stirring individuals to action in ways that simple appeals to material self-interest are incapable of achieving'; hence, the rhetoric of their discourses makes 'it much easier to convince people to kill and to die for considerably less tangible goals—be they creed, religion, or honor; in short, for beliefs' (Williams 2005, 27-28). This conviction goes to the heart of the discursive practices of 'securitization', which further intricate the *meaning* of foreign policy making in the story of *national* responsibility. As Ole Wæver reveals:

> Security discourses are characterized by dramatizing an issue as having absolute priority. Something is presented as an existential threat: if we do not tackle this, everything else will be irrelevant... By labeling this a security issue, the actor has claimed a right to handle it with extraordinary means, to break the normal rules of the political game. (1998b)

At the risk of simplification, the belief in the requirement of 'extraordinary means' rests on the conviction that international relations are 'always power politics' (Carr 1989[1939], 145). Such conceptualization prompts the assumption that 'war may at any moment occur' (Waltz 1959, 232), which urges states to behave in a way that is most advantageous for them individually. From this perspective, coercive strategies allow states (in terms of utility-maximization) to enhance their position in the international arena (Keohane 1986, 113). Owing to the presumed anarchic character of global politics and the inability of states to 'operate within a common framework of moral precepts' (Morgenthau 1973[1948], 257), assertive (belligerent) posturing tends to be explained as a 'self-help' mechanism in an environment where closer cooperation and collective security are deemed impossible, because of the egotistic, self-interested, and suspicious-of-the-other attitude of each state. According to Andrew Latham such conceptualization reveals the 'mythical tradition' of realpolitik, which narrates global politics as a discourse of sovereign states, each keeping law and order within its own borders by the application of force from the center, and also using force to keep secure against other states. Relations between states are conducted by diplomacy, against a background of military preparedness and alliances, and within a limited code of international law of which states, not people are the subjects. (1998, 136)

According to Snyder, the myth of aggressive posturing (typically) reifies this 'mythical tradition' of world affairs in which security is scarce and flaunting a state's military capabilities is conceived as the best route to its safety. At the same time, this aggressive international stance becomes a mode for rationalizing the domestic political climate—in particular, when it is marked by ambiguity and political contestation (Snyder 1991, 31). Usually grounded in a 'Hobbesian' perspective of world affairs, the mythical tradition of realpolitik articulates an identifiable 'timeless wisdom' of its vision of world affairs 'centered upon the principles of power politics and the dictates of international anarchy' (Williams 2005, 2–3). Its *raison d'être* draws from the assumption that 'opponents are made more tractable by having their vital interests threatened'. In this view, indicating readiness and willingness for preventive aggression translates into critical 'offensive advantage', which is central to foreign policy narratives. Thus, the premium on military power (especially, first-strike advantage) belies the confidence that threatening behavior makes other states 'compliant'. Utilizing these strategic beliefs, state-elites construct powerful justificatory discourses for a foreign policy based on aggressive posturing. In the process, they tend to exaggerate the advantages of such an offensive international behavior by denigrating alternative strategies and underrating its costs (Snyder 1991, 2–6).

Illustrating this proposition, Ashok Kapur (2006, 3) reveals that the 'power politics' of post-1998 Indian foreign policy displays the strategic 'capacity to first inflict harm and then to negotiate restraint'. At the same time, the then external affairs minister Yashwant Sinha has extended the scope of India's nuclear strike capabilities by arrogating to New Delhi the right to preemptive action against states threatening 'the use of weapons of mass destruction'. He went on to declare that 'every nation has that right [...] It is not the prerogative of any country. *Preemption is the right of any nation to prevent injury to itself* (cited in Sharma 2004a, 273; emphasis added; Budania 2003, 85; *Hindustan Times*, 8 April 2003; Nautiyal 2004, 150). According to the former ambassador K. Shankar Bajpai such a stance reveals that an 'increasingly frustrated India, unable to develop graduated responses to [its geopolitical] challenges, feels driven to apply the ultimate sanction of full scale war' (cited in Vaughn 2004, 444). As will be explained shortly, the assertive posturing that underpins the 1998 nuclear tests has intensified both the social production of foreign policy and the use of international affairs as tool for the settlement of domestic conflicts—namely, the 'tests removed a feeling of "national weakness" among Indians [...] This is why criticism of the Prime Minister virtually ceased for a while after the tests: he was now praised, even by his recent opponents, for being courageous and decisive' (Mishra 2000, 231).

Snyder, however, points out that despite the rhetorical subscription to the notion and practices of realpolitik (as demonstrated by the statements in the previous paragraph), the logic of mythmaking animating such foreign policy articulations is counterintuitive (if not detrimental) to the tenets of geopolitical strategizing. He makes obvious that states engaging in aggressive international posturing are more often than not likely to undermine their relative power and security by provoking opponents to form defensive coalitions. In this respect, threatening foreign policy behavior contradicts one of 'the most powerful regularities in international politics: the balance of power', whose basic principles are held to operate in reverse. The discursive myths of aggressive posturing obviate the propensity to 'self-encirclement'—that is, 'the most aggressive states make most enemies' (Snyder 1991, 5–7). Confirming this proposition, Ravinder Basu (2007, 13, 158) suggests that the assertiveness of India's post-1998 foreign policy has increased the 'suspicions not only of Pakistan—its traditional enemy—but of Bangladesh, Sri Lanka, and Nepal'; this anxiety has led them 'to create regional equations against potential (real or imagined) Indian hegemonic tendencies'. Consequently, the confusion of 'nuclear attack capacity' with 'nuclear deterrence' underscores *'the delusion of grandeur'* informing New Delhi's assertive foreign policy—namely, India 'already had nuclear deterrent capacity from 1974 onwards. The new tests prove India can flatten Pakistan cities five times over instead of twice over. That makes *no strategic difference;* a foe can be killed only once. All we have achieved is the ability to increase mutual losses' (*The Times of India*, 17 May 1998; Mistry 2009). Thus, rather than mitigating the effects of international anarchy, mythmaking tends to enhance its perceived negative consequences (especially in terms of rising the levels of insecurity among neighboring countries).

Unsurprisingly, the question arises why (despite the evidence of its detrimental effects) do states (i.e. state-elites) continue to engage in aggressive foreign policy posturing? Snyder (1991, 10–11) elicits the 'logical difficulty' of explaining such foreign policy behavior from a realist standpoint. Strategies steeped in the threat of pre-emptive offense (even if only discursive) impact international affairs. Such a behavior, therefore, violates 'the basic principles of international politics that Realists themselves have articulated' and the exigencies of a state's position in global politics. One needs only to remember Hans Morgenthau's opposition to the Vietnam War and John Mearsheimer's opposition to the 2003 US-invasion of Iraq as instances of the 'realist' challenge to the myth of aggressive posturing. Snyder (1991, 10–11), therefore, delves into the domestic political scene in search for an explanation. He discovers that aggressive posturing is usually promoted by narrow-interest groups, whose proponents gain access to decision-making by 'joining in logrolled coalition, trading favors so that each group gets what it wants, while most costs are diffused to society'.[1] The dynamic politics of this *quid pro quo* exchange allows the promoters of aggressive foreign policy access to the propaganda resources of the state.

> Selling myths is easier for coalition members... because the instruments and credibility of the state can be exploited for the task and because self-serving strategic arguments become less traceable to the parochial interests that benefit from them. Moreover, coalition leaders have their own need for mythmaking, since they must justify the over-commitment that is endemic to logrolling. (Snyder 1991, 17)

Snyder's observation hints that in a climate of policy ambiguity—when interests are uncertain, and information is monopolized—ideological convictions tend to enhance the domestic exposure of narrow-interest groups. In particular, given that the penchant for 'militarism [is] typically more concentrated than the interests opposed to them', the nature of coalition politics is inherently more apt to produce support for aggressive posturing (Snyder 1991, 18–19). Myths, then, are understood as scripts which regulate and legitimate foreign policy making—i.e. they provide 'the cultural and political *imaginary* (set of mythical narratives)', which play an important role in shaping the external practices of the state (Latham 1998, 133–135; emphasis original). In this respect, Ernst Cassirer (1963[1946], 37, 15) has noted down the paradox that myths—the 'most incoherent and inconsistent of all things in the world'— become the expression of a desire 'to live in an ordered universe, and to overcome the chaotic state in which things and thoughts have not yet assumed a definite shape and structure'. Consequently, he observes that

> modern political myths appear indeed as a very strange and paradoxical thing. For what we find in them is the blending of two activities that seem to exclude each other. The modern politician has had to combine in himself two entirely different and even incompatible functions… He is the priest of a new, entirely irrational and mysterious religion. But when he has to defend and propagate this religion he proceeds very methodically. Nothing is left to chance; every step is well-prepared and premeditated. It is this strange combination that is one of the most striking features of out political myths… myths made according to plan. The new political myths do not grow up freely; they are not wild fruits of an exuberant imagination. They are artificial things fabricated by very skillful and cunning artisans. (1963[1946], 281–282)

Therefore, since foreign policy elites are a heterogeneous (not a unitary) group (which constrains their ability to adjust policy) the narrow interest in aggressive behavior not only 'hijacks' state policy, but also its 'strategic myths come to *capture* those who invent them: because myths are necessary to justify the power and policies of the ruling coalition, the leaders must maintain the myths or else jeopardize their rule' (Snyder 1991, 17; emphasis added). It is often overlooked, however, that mythmaking begun for the purposes of gathering the domestic political dividends of social mobilization 'can spin out of control'. More often than not, the militarization of foreign policy accrues electoral profits through stoking up nationalistic claims (Snyder 1991, 15–18). In this respect, the logic of mythmaking draws attention to the fact that dispositions about international relations reflect foreign policy judgments based on narrow domestic beliefs and idiosyncratic interpretations of policy-making reality. Thus, to borrow from a different context, myths have the ability to dull an individual's power of judgment:

> What characterizes them is not so much their content and their objective meaning as the emotional atmosphere which surrounds and envelops them. This atmosphere must be felt; it cannot be translated nor can it be transferred from one climate of opinion to an entirely different one... The effect of these [myths] is obvious. Nothing is more likely to lull asleep all our active forces, our power of judgment and critical discernment, and to take away our feeling of personality and individual responsibility that the steady, uniform, and monotonous performance of the same [myths]. (Cassirer 1963[1946], 283–284)

The Logic of Mythmaking in India's Post-1998 Foreign Policy

Chapter 2 has indicated that the nuclear tests of May 1998 marked an important juncture in India's foreign policy making. As was explained, the main features of such a transition to a militarized international behavior have become (i) the end of the post-Cold War ambiguity of New Delhi's external relations, and its substitution with (ii) a more assertive foreign policy stance, indicative of (iii) a significant break with the foreign policy imperatives of post-Independence moralism. However, it often remains overlooked that what is significant about these changes is the *thing changing* (i.e. the character of Indian foreign policy) rather than *change*, per se.[2] Too often, therefore, analyses of the post-1998 period tend to take as their point of departure the claim that India has 'earned *international respect* and *influence*' through its booming economy, IT revolution, and nuclear capability (Lak 2008, 260; emphasis added); however, such declarations (although indicative of a particular change in mood and perceptions) only seem to acknowledge these transformations without problematizing their nature and the dynamics within which they originated (and on which they continue to draw).

In this respect, by focusing on the *thing changing*—the narrative construction of India's international relations—the following study uncovers the discursive mythmaking that came to dominate New Delhi's foreign policy narratives. The contention is that the 1998 nuclear detonations set off the myth of aggressive posturing, which spins the story of India's rise to global prominence in relation to its nuclear capabilities. While confirming the 'explosion of [seven] nuclear myths'—(i) 'the nuclear tests make India a full member of the nuclear club'; (ii) 'by testing a missile warhead India's security has increased'; (iii) external sanctions will cripple the burgeoning Indian economy; (iv) 'India need not worry at all about economic sanctions since the West desperately needs the Indian market';[3] (v) 'India has a principled objection to the nuclear apartheid implicit in the Non-proliferation Treaty which allows five powers to have nuclear arsenals, but not others'; (vi) 'the BJP is now bound to win the next election'; (vii) 'now that India has proved it is a nuclear power, the world will give it more respect' (*The Times of India*, 17 May 1998)—the proposition of assertive posturing operationalizes their implications and structures their contextual effects both to the narratives of India's external relations and its agency in Central Asia. As will be explained in the following sections, the rise of an increasingly assertive Hindu nationalism has promulgated

> the belief that India is a special nation with a glorious past and a vocation for future greatness… An auxiliary proposition associated with this belief in Hindu greatness is the widely shared view that historically, India's Hindu civilization was defeated and subjugated only when India was divided and weak. These self-perceptions support a powerful consensus that India must be a military great power—one that is dominant regionally and influential globally. Increasingly, this set of beliefs, refracted through the policy lenses of the Indian political and security establishment, defines the basic contours of Indian strategic thinking. (Latham 1998, 132)

The benchmark for foreign policy effectiveness set up by such mythmaking is that India 'be taken seriously as a player who could inflict unacceptable military and diplomatic costs' (Kapur 2006, 199). It is assumed that such an acknowledgement enhances India's 'rightful place in the world' (Lak 2008, 248). It has been observed that consequently the formulation of India's external affairs has been 'more openly aligned to self-interest' and to 'safeguarding its right to independent judgment' (Rana 2007, 60). Such foreign policy articulations encompass four narrative attributes—(i) a geopolitical trouncing of India's perceived weakness; (ii) a 'new' ideology of national strength (Hindutva); (iii) a settlement of domestic political contestation; and (iv) a narrative of self-aggrandizement—which are going to be addressed in the following sub-sections.

Geopolitical Trouncing of Perceived Weaknesses

As already indicated, the analyses of the post-1998 period have tended to take the nuclear tests as an indication of the emergence of more convinced and coherent international policy premised on power politics. For instance, one commentator insists that the 'Pokhran II nuclear tests symbolize violence, hatred, and the capacity to inflict destruction on presumed enemies, internal and external. They are emblematic of a new kind of aggressive and belligerent Indian [foreign policy]' (Vanaik 2007, 381). This shift towards the precepts of realpolitik has been provoked not merely by an aspiration to overcome the decision-making ambivalence that came to dominate the immediate post-Cold War period, but also by the intention to exorcize Indian foreign policy from its underlying flaw—its *evasiveness* and *indecision*. As revealed in Chapter 2, the 'art of governance' during the better part of the 1990s 'lay in postponing decisions rather than in taking a political risk' (Jain 2008, 35). Corroborating this stance, Kapur contends that the lack of military backup for India's claim to global power status exposes that 'a desire without a decision and a commitment is just talk'. In this respect, the narrative constructions of the post-1998 foreign policy have consciously targeted 'the distortions introduced in Indian strategic thinking and practices as a result of the use of a Nehruvian state apparatus that has been committed to the agenda of the Nehru dynasty rather than an agenda to engage effectively hostile external alignments' (Kapur 2006, 41–182).

The infusion of 'new realism' as a substitute for the failure of past foreign policy regimes gives a polarizing picture of Indian foreign policy making, which is alleged

> to have had no real strategic vision or well-developed strategic sense, being too prone to a moralistic form of posturing

as a substitute for pursuing a hard-headed and self-serving foreign policy perspective. Furthermore, the lack of a 'strategic culture' and inadequate recognition of the importance of power accumulation and power politicking was put down to an underlying historical deficiency enabling 'outsiders' to repeatedly invade and defeat India over the centuries. (Vanaik 2007, 390–391)

In this context, the mythmaking narratives accompanying the 1998 nuclear tests have relied on the discursive construction of a sense of security, confidence, and trust that 'the world is what appears to be', which conjure up the feeling of protection against future threats and dangers (Kinnvall 2006, 30). Thus, it would be useful to think of the convictions underpinning the proclamations of the post-1998 changes in New Delhi's international stance as *geopolitical prescriptions* for the foreign policy imagination that envisage aggressive posturing as the only viable way for India's external relations. As will be explained in the following section, it was the emergence of a particular form of Hindu nationalism that cast the formulation of foreign policy 'in the realist mode of power politics' (Manchanda 2007, 361). Borrowing from a different context, such a discursive justification of foreign policy making within the mythmaking narrative of Hindutva reveals that it 'is much more violently expressed where the anguished misfortune has taken a grip on the present: in those places, where, rightly or sometimes wrongly, identities feel threatened. In such cases, the past returns under a myriad of shapes, coming together to create a monstrous form derived of myth and fervid fantasy—a regressive utopia— derived of a past in which religion, race, nation, are mixed' (Morin 2006, 136).

The Ideology of National Strength—Hindutva
In introducing the framework of foreign policy mythmaking, Jack Snyder has indicated that a central feature of its discourse is the propagation of (and reliance on) a powerful unifying ideology that intends to consolidate a fragmented domestic political stage. Confirming this model, India's post-1998 decision-making has been infused with a renewed sense of national consciousness informed by the politics of Hindutva. A number of commentators have grappled with the implications of this ongoing phenomenon (Hasan

and Nakazato 2001; Gandhi 2003; McGuire and Copland 2007; Sarkar 2002; Stuligross 2006; Vohra and Dixit 1999). Although originating in the pre-Independence period and associated with the life and work of Vinayak Damodar Sarvakar, Hindu nationalism burst on the post-Cold War Indian political stage with the destruction of Babri Masjid in Ayodhya on 6 December 1992 (Noorani 2003). The militancy of the over 100,000-strong mob seemed motivated by the myth that the 400-year-old mosque was built over the ruins of a temple consecrating the birthplace of the Hindu god, Ram (Thakur 1993). According to Sreeram Chaulia (2002, 220), Hindu nationalism reveals an agenda for the rediscovery of 'India's Hindu genius and restoring the nation to its superior Hindu glory'. The contention, thereby, has been that Hindutva has 'an assimilationist program in which all non-Hindus are to be "brought back" into the Hindu fold. This is not considered as conversion, but as "re-conversion", the assumption being that everyone in India is naturally Hindu' (Menon and Nigam 2007, 37).

The significance of Hindu nationalism might have remained the subject for academic debate were it not for the meteoric rise of the political avatar of Hindutva—the Bharatiya Janata Party (BJP). In this respect, the transformations of Indian foreign policy tend to be associated with the two BJP-led governments which governed India continuously between March 1998 and May 2004 (Hansen and Jaffrelot 2001; Thakurta and Raghuraman 2004). According the Andrew Latham (1998, 146), Hindu cultural norms have had two crucial effects on the formulation of foreign policy: first, the highly-stratified and caste-dominated nature of the Hindu society reinforces the view that the international/global society is also rigidly hierarchical; second, the Hindu tendency toward moral relativism can lead to contradictory international initiatives. Furthermore, some have argued that the rule of the BJP has demonstrated that 'Hinduism is not a religion but a political ideology' (Rajshekar 2005, 63).

Thus, the trajectories of Hindutva in the post-Cold War period have positioned it not merely as an incredibly successful discursive platform (trumping all kinds of other identities), but have also confirmed (i) that nationalism 'first and foremost is about the nature and proper mode of constituting the state'; and (ii) that its narratives constitute discursive formations that shape and influence a state's orientation in 'the international order' (Kinnvall 2006, 5–62; Malkani 1994, 13). Thereby, the post-1998 geostrategic shift in

India's international identity towards an aggressive foreign policy posture became closely 'entangled with [BJP's] commitment to Hindu nationalism' (Datta 2008, 5). In fact, the 1998 tests have been qualified as 'the Hindu nuclear bomb' (Arundhati Roy cited in Gandhi 2003, 291). In this setting, the mythmaking features of Hindutva underscore three mutually-reinforcing narratives of national strength: (i) reinterpretation of the past; (ii) overcoming the uncertainties of globalization; and (iii) the social production of foreign policy.

Reinterpreting the Past to Fit the National Myth
It seems like a truism to assert that the re-interpretation (or perversion) of historical narratives has been the hackneyed rallying cry of nationalistic rabble-rousing. In particular, the obscurity of the period when a nation was allegedly *born* has turned history into an easy prey for ideological propaganda—that is, once 'the premises projected onto this period have been accepted, political leaders can draw out policy implications to suit their political agenda' (Geary 2002, 9; Sarkar 2002). Thus, nationalism has become 'a consequence, rather than a first cause of political outcomes. As often as not, it is governments that create nationalism rather than nationalisms that create nation-states' (Olson 1990, 23). In line with these propositions, the historical and spatial strategies of Hindutva-informed governance have produced political narratives that

> tie an imagined space to a real place in such a way that these ties also bind the people addressed by the strategy to particular identities, and the political/practical consequences that they entail. But the important point about them is that they have to operate in a resistant medium—they must engage in ideological battle with rival (or prior) strategies that may have already established a different set of links between spaces and places. (Deshpande 2003, 76)

In this process, according to Chetan Bhatt (2001, 18), the invention of a uniform Hindu religious tradition, especially 'the idea of revelation and the literal word of God embodied in a text (accurately speaking, itself foreign to Hinduism), the infallibility of sacred books, a singular already written truth and one organizational structure ("the Vedic Church") were seemingly borrowed from the "Semitic" religions'.[4] Bearing this in mind, Hindutva can be read both as an ideological project questioning the 'Nehruvian model of secularism and multiculturalism' and as a policy platform according to which 'minorities would have to accept a formulation of "national culture" in which their contribution is not recognized and is either assimilated or accorded very limited rights [...] Religious majoritarianism then should be seen as a political project for state power' (Manohoran 2003, 332).

In this context, the formulation of foreign policy simultaneously stresses that India is 'one of humankind's supreme civilizational accomplishments', reminds of 'the active nature of the conflict between civilizations', and reiterates that 'India's dominant Hindu culture is still under attack from other hostile civilizations' (Singh 2006, 46).[5] *'Hinduization'* therefore engages not merely in the 'revision of history', but in its rewriting for the purposes of constructing a narrative of an 'unending war' (Rajshekar 2005, 65–75). As a result, the formulation of New Delhi's external relations becomes subject to a 'peculiar chauvinism' (Narlikar 2006, 59).

In this context, the militarization of the post-1998 Indian foreign policy becomes the crux for the discourses on national responsibility. Catarina Kinnvall argues eloquently that the narratives of Hindutva provide a feeling of 'ontological security' for foreign policy making. In this respect, mythmaking becomes a story which maintains a sense of 'psychological well-being', while avoiding 'existential anxiety'. Kinnvall goes on to assert that the sense of certainty underscoring Hindutva's discourses *re-nationalizes* India's external relations by establishing an essentialised connection between 'the present, the future, and a re-created past' (Kinnvall 2006, 29–56). Such a re-articulation of international agency has gradually supplanted the foundational story of India's international identity which constructs its 'tremendous capacity for accommodating the interests of diverse communities without any prejudice or self-interest' (Manohoran 2003, 320). Thus, while Hindu myths provide powerful narratives invoking 'a historically derived sense of identity for the members of "the nation"' by forging 'a national "imagined community"' on the premise of 'some foundational event in the nation's pre-history, which establishes its origins and (mythic) nature', their appropriation in the expressions of India's foreign and security policy becomes a potent discursive guide for the shape and conduct of New Delhi's external relations (Latham 1998, 134).

Overcoming the Uncertainties of Globalization
The second narrative of the post-1998 discourses on national strength addresses the challenges posed by an ever growing globalization. Indian commentators have noted that globalization is 'intimately connected' with the practice and process of international politics because, on the one hand, it 'accentuates the interwovenness between countries and leads to increasing mutual interdependence' and, on the other, it 'breaks the conventional boundary between foreign and domestic affairs and *transforms all manner of external issues into home concerns'* (Rana 2007, 1; emphasis added). Upendra Kachru captures the complexities and anxieties provoked by this unpredictable dynamism through the notion of 'extreme turbulence'. He asserts that

> Extreme turbulence impacts everything: be it politics, be it civil society, be it the environment, or be it business. It has changed the paradigm [of global politics]. [Such] turbulence is caused by a series of factors: by the forces of change in various fields; by scientific discoveries; by social, economic, and political restructuring; by the impact of globalization; and by the inability of the environment to sustain our needs, as [well as] changing lifestyles and values. These irregular and random changes are becoming more and more frequent, resulting in a continuous churning of our immediate environment. And when change happens with such frequency and rapidity, it results in extreme turbulence. (2007, xiii–3)

The pervasiveness of such an extreme turbulence confronts Indian foreign policy makers and commentators with the 'uncertainty and complexity' that has substituted the 'predictability of the Cold War' (Budania 2003, 80). Chapter 4 will demonstrate that this perception has important bearing on New Delhi's engagement with the world and, in particular, on the formulation of its Central Asian agency. Thus, the discursive study of foreign policy discloses the 'increase in "message velocity"', which distinguishes the 'intensity of interactions [and] the response of actors' in a post-Cold War context (Rai 2003, 25). In this respect, 'the logic of globalization' reveals that international interactions need to be re-positioned within a framework established on the 'widest meaning of economic, political, cultural, and communicational security in an uncertain global system':

It is almost unquantifiable as an aggregate of many factors [including] the behavior of a great number of smaller and bigger, global, national, and sub-national actors. It is conceptually explained within the parameters of 'Chaos Theory', which deals essentially with the concept of 'order within disorder'. The world of chaos will increasingly compel a number of Asian countries to manage a kind of a permanent internal crisis due, at least partly, to their increasingly unfavorable conditions in the global polity and economy. [Thus], the global order is a 'World of Chaos' [...] Much of the contemporary international system is turning turbulent, despite the presence of long-established global mechanisms and emerging institutions, which are designed and dominated by the global powers to promote their chosen values. While democracy is projected as a cherished value, there is a global democracy deficit at the same time. There is an enormous concentration of power from the economic realm to the cultural sphere. This has given rise to dissatisfaction worldwide. (Sharma 2004a, 266–270)

Consequently, the turbulence of complex global interactions has provoked a 'schizophrenia' in India's international identity that ranges 'from pathos through pathology to pride' and which indicates a 'sense of incongruity which invariably inflects the description' (Deshpande 2003, 57). Addressing the complexity of such conceptualization, some have insisted that the character, content, and contours of India's international relations has been challenged by two simultaneously contradictory and complementary dynamics of world affairs—globalization and regionalization (Jain 2008, 1). Others have ascertained that the post-Cold War flux forces New Delhi to deal with 'the complexity of human emotions, the involutions of human motivations, and the ambiguities and uncertainties of the political and socio-economic impulses which underpin them' (Basu 2007, 199). Capturing the disturbances, anxieties, and, at the same time, the possibilities inherent in the growing global interdependence, James Rosenau has originated the term *fragmegration*. It points to the pervasive simultaneity between fragmenting and integrating processes in global life; as such, fragmegration 'serves as a constant reminder that the world has moved beyond the condition of being "post" its predecessor to an era in which the foundations of daily life have settled into new and unique rhythms of their own' (Rosenau 2003, 11). Instead of its celebration, globalized fragmegration has produced large scale concern, anxiety, and unrest. As one Indian commentator has discerned:

> The genesis of a unipolar world can be traced not to the crisis of the communist world due to its inability to face the task of the post-industrial society, but to the growth of a global crisis produced by the current stage of development threatening human civilization with self-destruction. The crisis arose due to the failure of the existing international economic mechanism to cope with the increasing rate of consumption of non-renewable natural resources and environmental degradation and social stratification. The path of development available to one billion people of the affluent West was not available to the teeming billions of the developing world. Such a situation was fraught with risks and compelled the West to work out a strategy which would change the power balance by eliminating the socialist USSR. (Kaushik 1997, 48)

In India, in particular, the loss of geopolitical bearings in the immediate post-Cold War years has provoked decision-making uncertainty and social anxiety. The pervasive complexity of 'amorphous and highly unpredictable world politics' has befuddled the articulation of New Delhi's external relations (Jain 2008, 30). The insecurity of the period has produced 'emotional traumas of alienation, loss of self-esteem, and images of lost objects such as territory' (Kinnvall 2006, 60).[6] In this context, the logic of nationalism provides powerful mythmaking narratives that help either dispel or make sense of such an awareness of insecurity by (re-)asserting the mutual sovereignty of a community in the form of a nation-state. Yet, defying a simple uni-dimensional model of the relationship between globalization and nationalism, the conceptual fuzziness of Hindutva makes its discourses pliable for intertwining with the narratives of globalization.[7] To borrow from a different context,

> the muddle about the meaning [of nationalism's abstractions] reflects a strange inversion of the proper and usual relations between concepts (labels), objects, and subjects... Normally, one begins with observation or ideas (or both). Concepts are used to make statements about them: 'messages' that convey

information. In making statements, difficulties may arise. More or less misinformation, or 'noise,' may be conveyed. Unless conventional language has been seriously abused, the fault can hardly lie in the words. Messages will be unclear to the extent that observations or ideas are crude or fuzzy. To achieve greater clarity, it is usually not to the point to revise the definitions; the obvious remedies are more exact observation and more lucid thought. (Eckstein 1992, 231)

In this respect, Andrew Latham has argued that in India's case the discursive buttressing of the integrity of the nation reinforces the drive to prevent the fragmentation of the state under the conflicting pressures of globalization. Such an intertwining of both distant and current history in Hindutva's take on foreign policy reveal Indian longings for certainty in a fragmegrative world (Latham 1998, 140). The narrative malleability of Hindu nationalism has allowed its ongoing re-definition as 'a "historical short-cut" to development' (Deshpande 2003, 55-56; Sarkar 2002). Its appropriation in foreign policy, therefore, becomes a platform for the domestic discourses on national greatness and importance. In this setting, the 1998 nuclear weapons tests have been 'greeted with overwhelming public support in India, because they seemed to represent the fact that despite the fragmentation of its politics, the country was still capable of carrying out a national project of some technological sophistication' (Mehta 2006, 21; Chengappa 1998; Shukla 2005).

Such proclamations have set in motion the myth of India's ability to overcome the uncertainties of globalization and impose its framework in world politics through its achievements in *science*. Commentators have indicated that 'whatever the political and economic fallout of Pokhran II, the Indian scientific and technical community that was *engaged in the project against the odds* deserves all the credit. [...] Conducting explosions of the kind conducted by India calls for technical knowledge of the highest order. The Indian scientific establishment has demonstrated precisely such a capability' (*Business Line*, 12 May 1998; emphasis added). Raja Ramana, the former chairman of India's Atomic Energy Commission, has proclaimed that '*We no longer need to quote our ancient literature to feel proud.* I am elated that our scientists have not only got the material, but have made those devices and exploded them. [...] The domestic reaction to the nuclear explosions has proved that our country stands united, cutting across all regional boundaries. *We were a great country and we are a great country*' (*The Times of India*, 16 May 1998; emphasis added). This sense of national pride has been reinforced by the awareness that such a scientific achievement has been made possible despite the '*technological apartheid* accompanying the nuclear apartheid practiced against India— namely, 'embargoes on the acquisition of various technologies, equipments, instruments, components, [and] materials [to which] India has been subjected for over two decades' (Udgaonkar 2001, 1782–1790; emphasis original).

Other commentators, however, have pointed to the limitations underpinning the myth of India's ability to overcome the uncertainties of globalization and form a platform for unifying the nation. Such criticisms have usually targeted the utilization of scientific knowledge as a legitimating discourse for state-sanctioned violence. Partha S. Ghosh, the then Director of the Indian Council of Social Science Research, has remarked that on the 'background of an uncalled-for national euphoria over our nuclear tests one can easily discern the nexus [between] science and violence. It is not only politicians who are agog congratulating the scientists who have made the tests possible, even the scientists concerned arrogate to themselves the right to make political statements on behalf of the state'. Quoting Shiv Viswanathan, a sociologist at the Center for the Study of Developing Countries, Ghosh argues that 'such a macabre enthusiasm can only be understood by focusing on the internal structure of science as a mode of cognition, where violence is justified in the objective pursuit of knowledge' (Ghosh 1998; Singh 1998b; Udgaonkar 1999). The condemnation of the myth of national hubris through scientific prowess reflects a 'feeling of disbelief at the moral bankruptcy and intellectual idiocy of a nation grown mindlessly euphoric about the acquisition of weapons of mass destruction':

> For the time being in India there is only a cacophony of 'patriotic' fervor that equates the Bomb with national pride. People dance on the streets as if it is Diwali in the astounding belief that their world has become more secure. Newspapers roar 'Bravo India' and 'The Buddha Smiles'. Young men sign messages of congratulation in blood. It would not be so disturbing if all this were being orchestrated by those who took pride

in the killing of Mahatma Gandhi and those who distributed sweets when the Babri Mosque was demolished. But when almost every political party and even some 'Gandhians' join in to demonstrate their 'patriotism' and when press, politicians, and people unite as one and the common man takes leave of common sense, there is little choice but to take refuge in the wisdom of children. (Patwardan 1998)

In this respect, the mythmaking of the post-1998 Indian foreign policy reaffirms the *national* ramifications of New Delhi's external relations in the context of a fragmegrative world marked by extreme turbulence.[8]

The Social Production of Foreign Policy
The third theme within the narrative articulation of India's post-1998 national strength alludes to the *social production of foreign policy*.[9] Foreign policy in this context encompasses both concrete external strategies and abstract domestic/national desires. In other words, the 'foreign policy of a state is not at all divorced from the population. Rather, the state pursues it by gaining the consent of the masses, both with respect to national and national-international dimensions' (Ahmed 1993, 93). Nationalist discourses, therefore, translate foreign policy objectives into 'matters of patriotic faith' (Deshpande 2003, 74–76). In terms of foreign policy, such mythmaking furnishes resources to 'manufacture the nation itself' (Geary 2002, 18). The claim is that the 'popular euphoria over the successful detonation of nuclear devices' (*Business Line*, 12 May 1998) should be read in this context. The adoption of aggressive posturing thereby becomes a critique of the alleged repression of political Hinduism until 1998. According to Ashok Kapur (2006, 17, 129–207) 'politicized Hinduism' has suffered three successive waves of marginalization and suppression—first, by the Mughals, then by the British, and, finally, by Nehruvian 'secularism'. Kapur avers that all three assaults share an 'anti-India trend' in foreign policy. In particular, he blames the rhetoric of secularism for misleading the international relations of New Delhi (Kapur 2006, 17, 129–207).

The articulations of 'Hindu nationalism' infer a project of 'cultural homogenization' that seeks to create a unified and uniform international security identity for India (Shani 2007, 120). In fact, it has been argued that traditionally 'in the international dimension of the state of India, the ruling class would advocate and reconstruct traditions that are relevant to, and also easily understood by, the Hindu majority' (Ahmed 1993, 216). Thus, some commentators have made the poignant observation that during the leadership of both 'Indira and Rajiv Gandhi, a weakening Congress *morphed into* a party less staunch in its commitment to secularism and more willing to exploit intensifying Hindu nationalism for political gain. Thus, *it was the Congress itself that legitimized the resort to religious sentiments and symbolism that previously characterized the tactics of only marginal opposition parties'* (Hagerty and Hagerty 2005, 34; emphasis added).[10]

According to Satish Deshpande (2003, 83) the social production of foreign policy through the ideology of political Hinduism reflects the 'competitive de-secularization' and 're-sacralization' of state policy-making. As such, 'de-secularization is directly dependent upon the strategic deployment of essentialism. It is in the name of religious essences—un-analyzable, un-contestable claims that are treated as self-evident truth by the faithful—that state secularism is denounced for its attempt to treat all faiths alike'. This dynamic comes to indicate that Indian foreign policy makers are not merely 'rational actors', but are 'constituted through, and embedded in, social and cultural systems that invest actors, actions, means and ends with meaning and varying degrees of legitimacy' (Lanham 1998, 129). Thus, the 1998 nuclear tests both *forged* and *expressed* a 'national consensus' on India's international identity—the formation of a 'natural and inevitable', 'new foreign policy based on aggressive national chauvinism' (Basu 2007, 93; Manchanda 2007, 365).

Such formulations reflect the social perception that 'the current international order [is] protecting the prerogatives of the five declared nuclear powers (Russia, the United State, China, Britain, and France), none of which has displayed a credible commitment to disarmament. And this order seems particularly incapable of attending to the security aspirations of emerging powers like India' (Mehta 2006, 18). In this respect, the social production of foreign policy contextualizes the 1998 statement of the BJP that it 'rejects the notion of *nuclear apartheid* and will actively oppose attempts to impose a hegemonic nuclear regime. We will not be dictated to by anybody in matters of security and in the exercise of the nuclear option' (cited in Hagerty and Hagerty 2005, 38; emphasis added). The myth of 'nuclear apartheid' has played a central role in the discursive articulations of India's post-1998 foreign policy. It ascertains that *'there is no logical basis for denying the "right" to nuclear deterrent to some states while according it to others'* (Udgaonkar 2001, 1776; emphasis original). On the day of the tests, Prime Minister Vajpayee explained that

> no price is too high when it comes to securing [the] *supreme national interest.* We must be ready for any eventuality [and] be prepared to face the consequences and overcome the challenge. [...] *The talk of sanctions does not stand the scrutiny of logic and fairness. Besides, it sounds hypocritical.* Some of the countries which have talked of sanctions or have otherwise criticized our action have themselves not only conducted more nuclear tests than we have done, but they have also built huge stockpiles of nuclear weapons and delivery systems'. (cited in *The Statesman,* 18 May 1998; emphasis added)

In this context, the myth of 'nuclear apartheid' is a reaction to the externally-imposed sanctions provoked by a deep sense of injustice.[11] Some Indian commentators have even argued that such measures are 'motivated by a desire to prevent a black state from joining the ranks of white and honorary white nations' possessing nuclear weapons (Subrahmanyam 1998). Others, however, have pointed to deeper insecurities underlying India's international and 'Asian identity' (Varadarajan 2005). From this perspective, the evocation of 'nuclear apartheid' is merely 'opportunist, not principled. [Even] if the big five [nuclear nations] give India the status of an honorary white and admit it to the club, India will happily practice nuclear apartheid against everybody else, even while maintaining the rhetoric of equal treatment. *Our real but unstated position is that as full-blooded Aryans, it is outrageous for us to be kept out of a white man's club'* (*The Times of India,* 17 May 1998; emphasis added). Such statements offer an insight into the imbrication of Hindutva's powerful unifying ideology with the social production of foreign policy as a strategy for national consolidation.

Foreign Policy Assertiveness as a Tool for the Settlement of Domestic Conflicts

As demonstrated, a motivating element for the mythmaking involved in buttressing aggressive foreign policy narratives has been the ambition to put an end to the fragmentation of the domestic political stage. The discussion of the post-Cold War trajectories of India's external affairs in Chapter 2 has proffered that a central feature of its 'globalization of diplomacy' in this period is the realization that such a dynamism has ended the 'myth that foreign policy is above home politics' (Rana 2007, 4).[12] In this respect, it asserts a particular version of politics as well as a state's international identity. According to Snyder (1991, 36–37), political formations supporting aggressive foreign policy posturing (because of their more concentrated interests and narrow agenda) tend to be more capable in utilizing state propaganda for 'selling their myths'; at the same time, the environment of fragmentation and uncertainty makes voters less receptive to the messages of groups with more diffuse interests. The contention is that the decision of the BJP to undertake nuclear tests during 1998 was part of such a strategy for asserting its authority over its coalition partners and imposing its dominance over the domestic political arena.

A number of commentators have, therefore, concluded that the mythmaking symbolism of *1998* was *not externally* determined (i.e. by geopolitical apprehension), but reflected the particular *domestic* political concerns of the BJP (Abraham 1999; Bidnai and Vanaik 2002; Parkovich 2000; Singh 1999). While the nuclear tests have 'indicated that the BJP-led government was firm on pursuing some of the issues that were close to its heart' (*Hindustan Times*, 12 May 1998b), it has also emerged that the BJP leadership had been considering conducting nuclear tests during its brief two-week stint in charge of India's government during May 1996 (Kampani 2000). In fact, the creation of a nuclear arsenal has been central to the platform of Hindu nationalism since 1962 (Chiriyankandath 2004, 203).[13] More significantly, however, the advent of weak coalition governments in the 1990s has meant that

> a challenge to the government on foreign policy was possible from outside as well as within the dominant party. By this time, the nuclear weapons program had come to be seen as an important symbol of Indian nationhood and identity. Advocates of an Indian bomb saw it as a way of projecting an image of scientifically adept, multi-cultural people, capable of achieving great things with a minimum of resources. [Thus], the medium range political calculations seemed to have made

it easier to reach a decision to go nuclear. Nuclearization now seemed capable of solving a wide range of national, cultural, and strategic problems. These suited an environment in which the decision to go nuclear was domestically permissible and, perhaps, politically essential for those on the Indian right. (Singh 2006, 120–121)

In fact, the settlement of domestic conflicts has been proffered as an explanation for India's 1974 nuclear test. Pankaj Mishra reveals that 'India's first nuclear test in 1974 came in handy for Indira Gandhi when she was facing a crippling railway strike (the first of the political challenges that eventually led her to suspend civil rights in 1975)' (Mishra 2000, 228; see also Gupta 1983). According to Daniel Lak (2008, 248), however, the timing of the 1998 nuclear tests was not to a little degree motivated by 'the worsening situation within the government'. Confronted with the task of keeping together a disparate coalition of conflicting interests, the then Prime Minister Atal Bihari Vajpayee resorted to foreign policy making as a tool for reinforcing the BJP's agenda on the political impulses of his coalition partners. Thus, 'striving to expand its social and geographic base and refurbish its image dented by bickering among the alliance partners, the BJP hopes to stoke the "nationalistic" feelings across different sections and buttress its political strength' (*Business Line*, 12 May 1998).

Such a strategy was facilitated by the general disinterest in 'the foreign policy and security domain' (as opposed to the preoccupation with the patterns of domestic politics) which has tended to turn the debate on external relations into a 'perfunctory' rhetoric with little substance on the 'tactics', 'conceptualization', and 'operationalization' of India's international affairs (Jain 2008, 35–44). In this context, by exercising the nuclear option, the BJP has *politicized* the formulation of foreign policy—that is, it has entered the discourses in 'the electoral and public domain as never before'— which has assisted the narrative constructions of the opponents of aggressive posturing 'as timorous and unpatriotic for "bending under pressure" to neighboring countries and big powers' (Chaulia 2002, 216). At the same time (perhaps, paradoxically), it might have been the very instability of Vajpayee's coalition that permitted him 'to act decisively without risking the survival of his government' (Chiriyankandath 2004, 204).

In this respect, the post-1998 belligerent external relations posture has assisted the BJP in claiming foreign policy distinctiveness in comparison to its predecessors—i.e. it has positioned itself as 'the *only force* capable of enhancing India's *national interest, national security, and national greatness*' (Kapur 2006, 389; emphasis added). In this respect, the BJP 'has upped the ante in the war of nerves between itself and its own problem allies, on the one hand, and with those who are firmly ranged against it in the Opposition, on the other. It is now fairly certain that most of the parties opposed to the BJP will hold themselves back as they evaluate the popular support for the achievement of Indian nuclear scientists. They would not want to swim against the seemingly strong nationalistic current, allowing the BJP-led government to benefit politically' (*Business Line*, 12 May 1998b). The tendency therefore has been to suggest that 'the present government, especially the Prime Minister, must be congratulated for having given his support and erased any doubt that may have lingered in the long years after 1974 about the competence of Indian scientists. These tests show that India's capability has been steadily growing since the first Pokhran test' (*Business Line*, 12 May 1998a).

Critics, however, have challenged this accolade and instead have ascertained that the main intention of the BJP leadership was 'to make electoral gains rather than the reconstruction of national identity or the promotion of a coherent national ideology' (Dutt 2006, 73).[14] Consequently, the nuclear tests were 'conducted more because of internal considerations and constraints rather than by pursuing the long run interests of the country' (Jain 2008, 35). Nevertheless, in terms of mythmaking, the inference here is that the contextualization of aggressive posturing into the narratives of political contestation reveals the intertwining (if not the discursive expansion) of Indian foreign policy making into the contexts of domestic politics, in the belief that the former could have effects on the latter. Thus, it is not surprising that the 'catalyst for change' behind the militarization of India's foreign policy became 'the new *nationalist leadership*' (Kapur 2006, 182; emphasis original). The claim, therefore, is that the BJP endorsed an aggressive foreign policy not merely for political expediency, but also as a result of the internalization of (cultural) narratives, which have impacted (through socialization) their assumptions about world politics and the *appropriate* mode for pursuing India's interests in international affairs

(Latham 1998, 130). For instance, Rita Manchanda (2007, 356–357) ascertains that the notion and practices of *appeasement* register as negative quality in 'the Hindutva lexicon' (and is usually associated with 'the failures of a "soft state"'). Positioned within this context, it is not surprising to uncover that Prime Minister Vajpayee has had a personal 'lifetime ambition' to lead India into 'the exclusive group of nations that openly possessed the capability to fight a nuclear war' (Lak 2008, 242). Such interpretations demonstrate that in consolidating a fragmentary domestic stage, the mythmaking involved in foreign policy formulation requires the validation of assertive proclamations.

'Chosen Glory'—Narratives of Self-Aggrandizement

Probably the most enduring reverberation of the 1998 nuclear tests has been the proliferation of exalted discourses on India's nascent rise to 'a major world power in the twenty-first century' (Prime Minister Manmohan Singh quoted in Walker 2006, 22). Proclamations declaring that a 'slumbering elephant awakens' (Vai and Simon 2007, ix) as a result of changes that have set in motion an 'unshackling of the imagination' (Menon and Nigam 2007, 85) and have ushered on the global stage an 'India unbound' (Das 2000) are indicative of the resilience of the mythmaking accompanying the post-1998 foreign policy (despite the change of government in the country). Some have suggested that the discursive dynamism of the myth of assertive posturing ensures that there will be little 'dramatic change' in foreign policy making (Vanaik 2007, 403). Others have argued that a major departure from the path charted during 1998 is less than likely because the impact of 'Hindu nationalism on the ideological base of Indian foreign and military affairs' is *'irreversible'* (Kapur 2006, 206–207; emphasis added).

Without contesting the relevance of such explanations, the claim here is that the self-exalting narratives of Indian foreign policy indicate (what Jack Snyder has called) a *discursive capturing* by the myth of aggressive posturing. This context illustrates Ernst Cassirer's assertion that political mythmaking is *invulnerable*—it is not intended to 'describe things or relations of things; it tries to produce effects [...] and to stir up certain emotions [...] charged with feeling and powerful passions'. In this respect, myths 'build up an entirely fantastic world' which is 'not only far removed from empirical reality; it is, in a sense, in flagrant contradiction to it' (Cassirer

1963[1946], 45, 283–296). Confirming these propositions, some commentators have suggested that the mythmaking narrative of New Delhi's foreign policy making can be extrapolated from India's 'exaggerated sense of self and unrealistic desire to be acknowledged as a leading nation', which seem to be detached from the posers plaguing the country's 'political stability' and 'economic development' (Basu 2007, 213).[15] Allegedly, such self-aggrandizing discourses boost up the national esteem by shattering the perception of 'an international order which confines India to an inferior position' (Mehta 2006, 21). As hinted in Chapter 2, the evocation of and the discourses on '*the* national interest' in India's (just like in any other country's) foreign policy making is 'more than an assumption about the sources of state action; it is a rhetorical device that seeks to use the political power of this concept to encourage a critical reflection and dialogue about interests and their relation to identity—to how a society sees itself and wishes to be seen by others' (Williams 2005, 169).

In particular, the mythic narrative of aggressive posturing offers a geopolitical expression of 'the socio-cultural syncretic identity of India' (Basu 2007, 157). This seems to be instanced by the 'ironic' and 'fatuous' indulgence that New Delhi's 'militarism' and 'miraculous economic performance' have catapulted India to the center-stage of world politics (Jain 2008, 223). Such a discursive capturing reveals that foreign policy myths act as *potent narratives* connecting 'the past to the present, not only helping to create a sense of shared (national) identity, but also providing examples of proper, acceptable, or ideal conduct' (Latham 1998, 135). *1998*, therefore, has become a major juncture in India's post-Cold War foreign policy because it gained its transformative significance as a *Chosen Glory*—a reactivating and (potentially endlessly) reactivated discourse bolstering a group's national self-esteem through the reproduction and re-articulation of historical representation (i.e. the '"verification" of history') as a means to assert the coherence and validity of a unifying collective identity (Volkan 1997, 81; Kinnvall 2006, 56–60; Sarkar 2002). This understanding indicates that nuclear weapons are being invested with enormous cultural capital (i.e. 'symbolically laden' arsenal) which must be viewed as 'an artifact of India's perception of itself as a global power'—said otherwise, the myth of aggressive posturing narrates the expectation that India is destined to play a dominant role in global politics only

(i) if it is military preponderant (i.e. maintains a decisive military edge); and (ii) if it is committed to a maximalist military posture entailing 'a three-full-and-three-half-war capability' (Latham 1998, 142–149).

Conclusion

This chapter has illustrated that the narrative construction of the 1998 nuclear tests has detonated an explosion of 'stories-in-common' about India's perceived (and almost palpable) global status, whose impact was largely unforeseen and unintended; yet, instrumental for inviting 'a vast and hitherto unaddressed audience' to partake in the myth of assertive international posturing (Deshpande 2003, 84; Ganguly 2006, 7). At the same time, it also confirms that the social production of foreign policy makes state-elites *more responsive to issues of national image*' in their formulation of international strategies (Rana 2007, 7; emphasis added). Thus, although primarily (and initially) it was '*the Indian leadership* [that] viewed their country as a potential great power and has, therefore, begun to articulate the type of regional and international order that *it* would like to exist within' (Gupta 2008, 105; emphasis added), these narratives have trickled down to the publics at large and have animated popular (and populist) imaginations and fervor. It is in this respect that Snyder (1991, 18) has issued his warning that mythmaking begun for the purposes of social mobilization 'can spin out of control'. Usually, commentators take this proposition to imply a particular normative position—i.e. *spinning-out-of-control* refers to possible negative results.

The claim here, however, is that what Snyder had in mind is the broader dynamic of *self-organization*, which does not (necessarily) entail a normative slant since it is difficult (if not impossible) to predict future outcomes—that is, assign normative values to them. In terms of the post-1998 Indian foreign policy it suggests that the logic of mythmaking is already out of the control of its originators and has taken *a life of its own*—in other words, 'when it comes to myths, history is never entirely in the past' (Latham 1998, 134). In this respect, the myth of 1998 continues to influence India's foreign policy identity. As will be indicated in the following chapter, the recourse to the logic of mythmaking in the domestic validation of India's post-1998 foreign policy making is integral to the discursive formulation of New Delhi's agency in Central Asia. The interaction between domestic politics and international ambition underwrites the narratives of the 'Look North' policy and as Chapter 4 will demonstrate, it also contextualizes the interpretation of India's involvement in the 'new great game' in Central Asia.

4

THE 'LOOK NORTH' POLICY: UNCOVERING INDIA'S DISCOURSES ON CENTRAL ASIA

Introduction

As suggested in Chapter 1, the evaluation of India's agency in Central Asia has to take into account the patterns, contexts, and analytical frameworks informing the formulation of New Delhi's external relations. Such a regionalization of India's foreign policy—i.e. the development of distinct external policies towards different global regions (and, thereby, indicating an important perspective on the distinct international identity of those regions)—reflects not only 'the change that has taken place in India's perception of [these] regions, but also the transformation of international relations in the contemporary world of globalization' (Kaul 2007, 240). It also confirms the strategic vision underpinning the narratives of India's post-1998 foreign policy whose agency rests on the dictum that 'geopolitics in relation to countries of the rimland has to work out other doctrines, which are more closely related to their development' (Panikkar 1955, 89; Vaughn 2004, 443)

At the same time, the focus on Central Asia acknowledges that from an Indian standpoint 'Asia is now the hub of terrorism, organized crime, and nuclear proliferation, and it is also the hub of global economic change' (Kapur 2006, 1). The securitization implicit in these observations indicates that for India such trends 'have a direct bearing on its vital interests' because Central Asia is '*its* strategic neighborhood' (Joshi 2003, 4; emphasis added). Therefore, the narratives of the 'Look North' policy indicate a perception that by 'becoming Asia's America, India [will be] less likely to fight wars. The country will quite simply be too engaged with trade and business and global affairs to assume the classic posture of the belligerent. [Thus], the world's largest democracy is thinking big' (Lak 2008, 277–278). Moreover, the propositions of the 'Look North' policy point to 'secularism', 'democracy', and 'literacy' as 'national strengths' that India and Central Asia share—an assumption underpinning the mythmaking that both of them are 'once again poised for greatness' (Sinha 2004, 6). This discursive engagement with the international relations of the region not only indicates that India has a 'strategic will', but also probes 'how [New Delhi] will manifest it in action' (Bal 2004, 35).

During a visit to Turkmenistan in September 1995, the then Prime Minister P.V. Narasimha Rao made it clear that 'for India', Central Asia is an area 'of high priority, where we aim to stay engaged far into the future. We are an independent partner with no selfish motives. We only desire honest and open friendship and to promote stability and cooperation without causing harm to any third country' (cited in Muni 2003, 110). Such a proclamation offers a glimpse at the discursive genesis of the 'Look North' policy. In fact, Rao's statement touches upon the main themes of its foreign policy mythmaking. The chapter proceeds by detailing the narrative outlines of the 'Look North' policy. Its assessment of India's role in Central Asia has taken into account the contexts and patterns of its engagement in post-Cold War politics. The examination identifies the implications emanating from the narrative juncture provided by the 1998 nuclear tests on the formulation of the 'Look North' policy. In this setting, the chapter details the idiosyncrasies of India's relations with Tajikistan. Consequently, this context becomes a point of departure for discussing the emplotment of the 'new great game' in the discourses of New Delhi's agency in Central Asia.

It has to be acknowledged, however, that despite the articulations of an integrated (if not necessarily coherent, let alone homogeneous) 'Look North' policy, there has been a parallel narrative, which (while endorsing India's more proactive involvement in Central Asia) has been critical of the treatment of the region as a self-evident (autochthonous) entity. For instance, J.N. Dixit has noted the erroneous perception of 'the collective socio-political identity of [the Central Asian] countries in an omnibus manner under the label of Central Asia' (Dixit 2004, 16).[1] The alleged 'homogeneity [of the region] is quite deceptive' and it hinders the comprehension of the 'large diversity, which is articulated in many different ways' in the dynamics of Central Asian politics (Sharma 2007, 123). The suggestion has been that India needs to develop not a regional, but a 'country-specific' approach to Central Asia (Dash 2007, 205). This understanding informs India's relations with Tajikistan, which are detailed separately in this chapter. Notwithstanding the qualifications underpinning these criticisms of a unified 'Look North' policy, the dominant narratives of New Delhi's relations with the region stress the conviction that 'Central Asia constitutes *a natural unit*' because of its 'geographical contiguity and shared history and religion' (Joshi 2004, 205; emphasis added). New Delhi's engagement with Central Asia is therefore buttressed by the 'similarities of geographical features, climatic continuity, common and contiguous borders [which] had given to the region an uninterrupted cultural affinity and visible homogeneity in its population and social arena' (Haidar 2003, 257).[2]

The Narrative Outlines of the 'Look North' Policy

Most commentators maintain that India's engagement with Central Asia is a function of the country's historical interactions with the region. Thus, the 'long-standing historical ties encompassing the political, cultural, economic, and religious dimensions' constitute the basis for the international relations between New Delhi and the individual Central Asian states (Bal 2004, 4; Asopa, 2006; Batabyal 2007; Chatterjee 2006; Haidar 2003; Mann 2001, 2047; Mukerjee 1996; Sinha 2004, 5; Patnaik 2003; Roy 2001, 2273). The experience of the past has 'constantly exerted a strong mutual influence in their interactions' (Chopra 1997b, 127) and has 'shaped the destiny of our peoples more than once in the past and continue to be of great interest to them' (Kaushik 1997, 52). The historical span of these contacts illustrate that the relations between India and Central Asia are 'multi-dimensional, deep, and continuous' (Kumar 2007, 3). Yet, alongside these proclamations of extensive historical associations, observers have point out that while 'Central Asia is closer to New Delhi then Chennai or Bangkok, Tashkent and Almaty ring a distant bell when the names pop up in casual conversations' (Bhattacharyya 2004). The strategic importance of Central Asian states, according to Rakesh Kumar, the Director-General of the Indian Council for Cultural Relations derives from the observation that 'they are closer to us [i.e. New Delhi] than many of our [i.e. India's] state capitals [and] they are sitting on a sea of crude oil and gas' (cited in Bhattacharyya 2004). In this respect, it was the breakup of the Soviet Union that altered radically 'the geopolitics' and the 'security scenario' of the region (Patnaik 2005, 207). In particular, it forced upon New Delhi the recognition that Central Asia is a distinct region in India's immediate vicinity and whose patterns of interaction impact on and are impacted by developments in South Asia. This realization seems to have been one of the underlying features in the transformation of India's post-Cold War foreign policy. The understanding that Central Asia is India's 'immediate and strategic neighborhood' (Sinha 2004, 7; Muni and Mohan 2005, 69) reveals an appreciations of the 'deep and vital interests at stake' as well as New Delhi's 'concerns and strategic thinking' (Joshi 2004, 204–209). As one commentator put it 'once again, the Old Silk Route from Central Asia [has become] the conduit for destabilizing factors' (Bal 2004, 3; Mohanty 2006).

In this context, a number of Indian analysts have proposed the articulation of a 'Look-North' policy (Bal 2004; Haidar 2004; Jain 2008; Joshi 2007b; Stobdan 2004; Vohra 1999). As Nirmala Joshi (2007b, 445) demonstrates, this discursive engagement with the roles played by India in Central Asia emphasizes the need for the development of a 'proactive and meaningful policy that accords top priority to the region'. Thus, the claim is that the narrative exploitation of the legacies of the past by Indian foreign policy elites discloses a strategy that aims 'to remind the new generation in Central Asia that India is not new to them but rather a very old friend if seen in the historical perspective. This creates a "love at first sight" situation exhorting these past civilizational entities to recognize each other' (Jain 2008, 210). Consequently, it is ascertained that the point of departure for the articulation of the 'Look-North' policy is the suggestion that 'past linkages [act] as a bridge to the present' (Joshi 2007b, 445) and, thus, facilitate the 'exploration of new avenues of cooperation' (Dutt 2006, 207). This conviction underpins the alleged strategic rationale of the New Delhi's engagement of Central Asia.

According to Suryakant Nijanand Bal, historical experience suggests that any political instability in Central Asia 'would only heighten regional tensions with the possibility of external involvement and would be detrimental to India's long-term strategic interests'. He, therefore, insists that the uncertainty characterizing the post-communist transition of the Central Asian states impels India to monitor closely their 'nature, pace, and direction' as well as 'the point at which the region's new identity will stabilize'. In this respect, Ball claims that a distinct 'Look North' policy would enable India 'to formulate proactive strategies, to minimize potential threats, exploit opportunities and influence the final outcome of the transition' (Bal 2004, 141–279). It therefore becomes an expression of India's desire 'to promote a secular, multiethnic order in the region' (Dietl 1997, 142). Consequently, India is presented as a model for Central Asian states. It is claimed that in their search for 'support and constructive cooperation',

> India stood as an attractive direction to relate to. India was not only a multiethnic, multi-cultural, [and] resilient society with vast experience of managing delicate intra-ethnic relations, but also a secular and democratic polity. [At the same time], India was geographically distant, but culturally and historically close, without any record of an intrusive or aggressive behavior towards the newly emerged Central Asian republics. (Muni 2003, 106)

These statements do not intend to deny the diversity, multiplicity, and idiosyncrasies of Central Asia. However, as Nirmala Joshi (2007b, 441–442) declares, from 'an Indian perspective', the region has several defining features: (i) the rise of religious extremism in the post-Soviet period; (ii) the increasing levels of trafficking in goods and people; (iii) the incomplete, erratic, and uneven process of political and economic reform; and (iv) the turbulent geopolitical location of Central Asian states (abetted by their natural resources) which makes them subject to the interests of a number of extra-regional third-parties. Such characterization informs the articulations of the 'Look-North' policy and reveals the specific interests of India in Central Asia:

> (1) to gain access to oil, gas, and other natural resources for its own energy needs; (2) to seek military bases as a conduit for the sale and acquisition of military hardware; (3) power projection in the extended neighborhood; (4) to counter terrorist threats, especially stemming from Al Qaeda and the Taliban; (5) to deny Pakistan 'a strategic hinterland'. (Jain 2008, 210–211)[3]

Borrowing from a different context, the discursive constructs of the 'Look North' policy suggest the 'the encouragement and support [for] continued economic reforms in [Central Asia] leading to faster and well-distributed growth. This would provide both expanded market and political stability—the two key elements of India's foreign policy dynamics. Economic relations in non traditional ways and sectors should be the focal point of India's engagement with the region' (Lama 2005, 152). The contention is that without 'strong trade and economic relations' it may be difficult for India to sustain the 'strategic and security objectives' of the 'Look North' policy (Patnaik 2005, 229). Such narratives (as will be explained shortly) rely on the understanding that from the perspective of Central Asian states, the 'large and nearby India does not breathe down anyone's neck in [the region]. No Central Asian country has a dispute with, or apprehension from, India' (Gandhi 1996). The discourses on the 'Look North' policy did not emerge in a vacuum, but were profoundly implicated by the post-Cold War trajectories of India's foreign policy and the narratives of its mythmaking re-articulations. The following sections sketch out these dynamics.

India's Engagement in Central Asia before 1998

As argued in Chapter 2, the 'post-Cold War Blues', which infected India's international affairs during the 1990s illustrated the ambiguities and tensions of its foreign policy making. On the one hand, the uncertainty that came to dominate New Delhi's external relations during this period has revealed the chagrin for the passing of comfortable certainties. On the other hand, it has demonstrated the (unwilling) recognition of the necessity to abandon well-entrenched practices and patterns of behavior. In this respect, India's relations with Central Asia became one of the most conspicuous aspects of the foreign policy ambiguity during this period. The uncertainty that has dominated this period had 'two important implications':

> One was that there emerged a new Central Asia, independent and sovereign, freed from the control of the former Soviet Union, and looking forward to a greater and dynamic engagement with the rest of the world, particularly Asia. The second was a sort of crisis of confidence in India's foreign policy perspective resulting from the collapse of the Cold War framework of global politics and the consequent erosion of the for-

mer Soviet Union as a source of foreign policy support. (Muni 2003, 102)

Several commentators have indicated that India's failure to engage Central Asia more convincingly is an outcome not only of the 'post-Cold War Blues' of its foreign policy making, but is also a testament to its Nehruvian legacy. In this respect, the former foreign minister, Jaswant Singh (1999, 111) has argued that it 'is truly astonishing that for India's political leadership, particularly Pandit Nehru, who was not simply a student of history but had a sense of it, the Central Asian factor was completely absent. It was forgotten that forces from Central Asia had repeatedly invaded India during the past many centuries and had altered the course of its history—perhaps on account of the then Soviet Empire stretching over Central Asia'. As will be explained shortly, this criticism intertwines with the myth-making narratives of India's post-1998 foreign policy making, which asserts that the 'expression of a "soft" Hindutva is relevant for the study of Indian politics as well as its external policies after the fall from grace of the Nehruvians' (Kapur 2006, 206).

Another feature of India's post-Independence experience that has affected its relations with Central Asia is the formulation of New Delhi's external relations *in reaction to* Pakistan's foreign policy strategies.[4] As was explained in Chapter 3, the memory and the construction of a historical narrative of independent Indian statehood has been profoundly scarred by the communal divisions that flared during the partition of British India (Butalia 2000; Murdian 1994; Pandey 2001). This discursive experience has been imbricated within the mythmaking sustenance of New Delhi's foreign policy strategy, which suggests that neither geography, nor economic interests maintain the state boundaries between India and Pakistan, but the 'enmity between Hindus and Muslims' (Hagerty and Hagerty 2005, 17). These sentiments are intimately intertwined with Indian perceptions of the post-Soviet transition of Central Asian states:

> Though the process of these changes is multidimensional, the main focus is on the rise of religious revivalism, ethnic strife, and territorial disputes. As these nation-states are coming out of their economic backwardness and moving out of the tribal, feudal, and semi-feudal structures, they are confronted with new problems, which are partly rooted in their past and

are being encouraged and promoted by external actors [such] as Pakistan. (Chopra 1997a, 26)⁵

In 'Indian perceptions', therefore, Pakistan has 'vested interests' in pursuing a 'quest for strategic depth vis-à-vis India in Central Asia' (Joshi 2007a, 150). The assertion is that the 'philosophy [of Pakistan's interactions with the region] appears to have always focused on a prescriptive approach as to what *should* happen in or to the Central Asian state within the overall backdrop of deep antagonism against India' (Bal 2004, 332–333; emphasis original). The 'Look North' has therefore been construed as a '*non-Pakistani* alternative' for Central Asia (*Hindustan Times*, 13 July 2008; Mann 2001, 2047). Chapter 7 will explain that crucial to this framing of India's involvement in Central Asia is the discursive modulation of the '*intermediate zone* comprised of Pakistan and Afghanistan [which] has compounded the connectivity [between New Delhi and regional states]' because of its endemic 'political instability and serious security risks' (Muni 2003, 111–112; emphasis added). Chapter 7 will also indicate that the 'renewed India-Afghanistan bonhomie [following '9/11'] is being deeply resented in Pakistan' (*Hindustan Times*, 30 April 2006).

However, Pakistan's efforts 'to befriend the Central Asian states bore no fruit [because the latter] were looking towards India for help and guidance [during] the transformation of their political and economic system as well as in managing the diversity of multi-ethnic and pluralist societies' (Joshi 2007a, 148). It is therefore 'foolish to talk of Islamic revivalism in Central Asia. The Central Asian republics are not interested in Islam [and] will not compromise on the free market, secularism, and democracy' (Dietl 1997, 138). As a result, New Delhi's 'overestimation of the role of Islamic countries in the Central Asian republics' prevented it from 'a proactive policy [toward the region in the pre-1998 period] to replace its reactive posture, dominated by competition with Pakistan' (Kaushik 1996, 238). Such a preoccupation with Islamabad's policies in the region explains the 'belated, slow, and half-hearted stand' taken by India during this period which (consequently) compelled it to 'catch up [and] compensate for [its] inaction' (Asopa 2007, 172–173). Instead, 'facts [have] proved that Islam [is] not a decisive factor in the relations between Pakistan and the Central Asian republics. Economic considerations overshadow the religious dimension of their relationship' (Dietl 1997, 138).

Thus, the 'ill-conceived [and] ill-executed treatment [of the region] as a counterpoise between India and Pakistan' (Singh 1999, 111) has tended to befuddle New Delhi's foreign policy making both during and, especially, after the end of the Cold War. Joshi (2007b, 443) has thereby inferred that the 'reactiveness' of India's approach to Central Asia for the better part of the 1990s has remained 'once again rooted in a policy focus on the activities of Pakistan in the region'. It has to be recognized that the hostility characterizing the bilateral relations between India and Pakistan would impinge upon New Delhi's strategy towards Central Asia. As Samina Yasmeen (2008, 31) points out the 'two states have fought three major wars in 1948, 1965, and 1971. They have come close to armed conflict on numerous other occasions, including the crises in 1986, 1999, and 2002. These historical experiences have engendered a sense of mistrust of the other. They have also created a perceptual blockage that impedes a real understanding of the neighboring state'. In this setting, the framework of India's 'Look North' policy appears unable to obviate both the legacy of mistrust as well as the very real barrier posed by the Pakistan-occupied Kashmir. The experience of India's engagement with Central Asia during the pre-1998 period illustrates that Pakistan 'remains an important obstacle to a more productive cooperation with the region' (Muni and Mohan 2005, 66).[6] At the same time, however, Indian commentators have noted that since 'neither India nor Pakistan is an immediate neighbor of Central Asia'—a geographic reality which should be a 'positive factor' for their relations in the region—the wrangling between New Delhi and Islamabad for Central Asia can be described as an 'avoidable small game' (Dietl 1997, 134). Such statements reveal the narrative oscillation underscoring India's interactions with Central Asia for much of the first post-Cold War decade.

India's Engagement in Central Asia after 1998

The post-1998 foreign policy perception of Central Asia seems to be informed by the realization that despite the proclamations of the region's 'historical belonging' to India's 'strategic neighborhood', New Delhi is 'not giving sufficient attention to Central Asia'; consequently, 'good intentions have not been converted into substantive relations' (Dixit 2004, 18–19). India has therefore been relegated to 'a mere spectator' of regional politics (Mahalingam 2004, 133) owing to the lack of a 'well spelled out policy towards Central Asia' (Asopa 2007, 181). Confirming this observation, Bal (2004, 35) describes India's engagement with the region as a practice of 'wait and watch—a policy of passive and benign neglect [which conjectures] to react to events as they occur and to hope for the best'. Likewise, Joshi (2007b, 440) infers that New Delhi's engagement with Central Asian states has been 'more reactive than active'. Such *ad hoc* policy pattern has urged some to declare that India has rendered itself *'somewhat marginal'* to the international relations of Central Asia (Dutt 2000, 106; emphasis added).

In this setting, the discourses of a 'Look-North' policy have come to reflect the broadening geopolitical scope of India's foreign policy articulations since the 1998 nuclear tests. As was explained in Chapter 2, the assertiveness that has become the underlying feature of New Delhi's external relations did not merely indicate a more pragmatic operationalization of improved strategies, but a qualitatively different interpretation, on the one hand, of India's role in global politics, and, on the other hand, of the character and dynamics of the international system. Thus, the post-1998 assertions of foreign policy independence reveal both India's disposal of the structural and cognitive constraints on its external relations and its willingness (and increased capacity) to insert its national interest on the agenda of world affairs, regardless of the opinions and expectations of other international actors.

In this setting, 'India's "forward" Central Asian policy' in the post-1998 period tends to 'be seen as an integral component of its growing military, nuclear, and economic power' (Jain 2008, 210). Confirming the mythmaking logic of its international agency (detailed in Chapter 3), the perception is that New Delhi's relations with the Central Asian states reveal 'the operation of a virtuous circle, with economic gains propelling an associated political push from India [which] produces both an improved country image and country's standing in regional and multilateral fora' (Rana 2007, 62–63). As already explained, the 'Look North' policy reflects New Delhi's strategic awareness of the proximity of Central Asia to India. Thus, the region has begun 'to be considered as part of India's external neighborhood' and 'an essential component of our national security' (Joshi 2007b, 440). Such a shift in New Delhi's external relations has to indicate a decisive break with the cognitive residue of 'an exclusively east-west orientation' that has dominated the formulation of foreign policy before 1998 and, at the same time, has also provided a 'conceptual "model", "window", "lens", or "frame of reference" through which Central Asia must be viewed' (Bal 2004, 354–355) and the need to establish 'a long-term strategic relationship built around energy security and transit arrangements' (Dutt 2006, 207).

As will be explained shortly a number of initiatives have come to be associated with this policy shift. New Delhi has promoted these initiatives within the context of 'mutuality of national interests' between the Central Asian states and India (Jain 2008, 210). As a result of this commonality, New Delhi 'enjoys immense goodwill in these countries' (Asopa 2007, 181), because regional actors perceive 'India as a friendly power with no hidden agenda' (Joshi 2004, 210). From here, the argument develops that Central Asian states are 'interested in strengthening [their] relations with India [because] in their view India could be a balancing factor in their relations with other large powers' (Dixit 2004, 19).[7] At the same time, by recognizing India's latecomer status in Central Asian affairs, the discourses of the 'Look-North' policy suggest the need for (if not the endorsement of) a more active and assertive involvement of New Delhi in the region by developing 'an appropriate "strategy of equilibrium" in its relationship with the immediate and extended neighborhood' (Jain 2008, 222).

In this setting, the stated overarching objective of India's 'Look North' policy is the promotion of 'peace and mutual prosperity' (Sinha 2004, 9). This intent, however, has been buttressed by the twin-ambition of: (i) maintaining 'the democratic and secular ethos' of the region, because it 'binds India and Central Asia together' (Joshi 2004, 210); and (ii) evolving 'measures that would safeguard the stability and integrity of Central Asian republics and save them from getting divided and opposing one another' (Asopa 2007, 188). The narrative construction of this twin-ambition is detailed in turn in the following sections.

Experience of Managing Diversity within a Secular and Democratic Polity
Indian commentators have noted that the (violence accompanying the) dissolution of the Soviet Union and the Federal Republic of Yugoslavia has 'eroded the legitimacy of multiethnic, multi-lingual, and multi-religious states' (Dixit 2004, 24). This observation informs

the (tacit) conviction that India is one of the few (if not *the* only) remaining countries that shares the characteristic features of the now defunct socialist federal arrangements of the Soviet Union and Yugoslavia (Kavalski and Zolkos 2008). Consequently, such a realization underpins the responsibility of its foreign policy making to assert the viability of India's state-building project by demonstrating the relevance and experience in successfully managing its internal diversity through the institutional arrangements of a secular and democratic polity. In other words, India is not 'multicultural by accident', but 'multicultural by design' (Manohoran 2003, 330). The assertion is that 'democracy matters' (Singh 2006, 258). Daniel Lak (2008, xvii–xviii) insists that 'democracy is one of India's great accomplishments, perhaps its greatest triumph as a nation. It may be flawed, chaotic, and corrupt, but democracy flourishes in India [...] Democracy thrives in India in part because it is the only way to run such a vast, diverse society. People who are denied the freedom to despise and criticize their government can be expected to revolt'. Consequently, India's objective is to 'work for the rise and consolidation of democratic and secular polities in Central Asia, because the spill-over of the rise of religious extremism may threaten India's own internal stability and security' (Muni 2003, 98–99).

The 'Look North' policy proclaims 'high stakes in retaining the secular ethos of Central Asia' (Asopa 2007, 174). This objective clearly indicates New Delhi's opposition to 'religious extremism and ethnic separatism' (Muni and Mohan 2005, 68). It also resonates the foundational narrative of India's secularism—its compliance with 'the ancient *religious* tradition of India', according to which 'no person should suffer any form of disability or discrimination of his religion' (S. Radhakrishnan cited in Manoharan 2003, 329; emphasis added). There is a profound sense that 'the trajectory of change in [Central Asia] is going to be determined by the dialectics of reform and resurgence' (Pant 2005, 181–182). Thus, in the 'power vacuum' left after the dissolution of the USSR, New Delhi saw an opportunity to use its 'political closeness to the Central Asian states' for leveraging its position in the region both by supporting the democratization process and sharing its own experience (Patnaik 2005, 207–227).[8] Indian efforts and expectations however have been frustrated by the realization that the Central Asian states 'were ill-prepared for independence' (Joshi 2003, 69). Although 'conversant in the art of governance' (Asopa

2007, 173), all countries in the region are believed to suffer from a pronounced 'democratic deficit' which hinders them to establish 'long-term political and strategic vision' for their development (Sharma 2007, 125). In this setting, 'state failure remains a concern in New Delhi' (Gupta 2008, 115).

Indian commentators list multiple (and, oftentimes, contradictory) rationalities in their explanation of the weakness of democratic practices in the region:

- Firstly, there is a near-universal agreement that independence 'was thrust upon [the Central Asian states] in 1991' with little warning and preparation which accounts for the revealing 'lack of experience [and] shortage of expertise [necessary for] the transformation of their socio-political and economic system' (Joshi 2004, 204–205). As one commentator noted 'the Central Asian republics were nonplussed [by independence]'; they did not know 'whether to celebrate their liberation from the century-old Russian yoke or to grieve the passing away of their protector and benefactor' (Shams-ud-Din 1997, 329). Thus, 'the newly emerged Central Asian states were internally and externally insecure' owing to their 'porous, *unnatural* borders and fragile security structures [which] had rendered them exposed [and] threatened by the Islamic fundamentalist/jihadi forces' (Muni 2003, 103; emphasis added; Patnaik 2003).[9] According to these assessments, the independence of Central Asian states was an outcome of 'the exclusively subjective ambitions of a group of political leaders and their scramble for political power'; thus, 'the demise of [Soviet] ideology [reflects] a decision arising from a collective state of mind among the ruling elite, which [did] not alter realities on the ground [in the individual republics] with respect to security, social, cultural, economic, and other aspects' (Bal 2004, 301–302).
- Secondly, despite their independence from the Soviet Union, the 'power structures [of the Central Asian states] are still dominated by personalities [from] the previous communist regime, which have assumed new national identities' (Dixit 2004, 15). The governance of Central Asian states is thereby 'dominated by the former communist party ruling elites who had adopted democratic pretensions' (Muni 2003, 103). This makes it 'difficult for [regional leaders] to appreciate something that their cognitive process had never experienced'; therefore, the outcome of their 'endeav-

or to embrace what they themselves are not—western democracies' should not be surprising (Dash 2007, 190). The proposition is that it is 'the ruling elites [that] are not ready for democracy' rather than the populations of the region (Sharma 2007, 127).
- Thirdly (and closely related to the previous point), the perception of nascent forms of authoritarianism in Central Asia has tended to be explained with long-standing indigenous forms, institutions, and processes of power relations. Thus, the alleged 'inherent tendency' towards hierarchical modes of governance (Bandyopadhyaya 2002, 7) has made possible the 'over-concentration of [state] power in the hands of political elites', which, in turn, has precipitated 'the collapse of democracy' in the region (Sharma 2004a, 264). For instance, the 'lack [of] democratic tradition and culture' in the region derives from local patterns in which 'challenging the established authority is alien' (Joshi 2003, 93–94). In particular, since 'none of the Central Asian peoples had any sense of national identity' has meant that the creation of 'national cohesion' and its 'translation into political forms has proved to be problematic' in a region, where there 'has always been an amorphous mass with multiple and contending identities' (Sengupta 1997, 271–287). Furthermore, the reference to the clan-mentality of Central Asian politics (Dash 2007, 191; Sharma 2003, 75) reveals the complexity of populations wanting 'the right balance between modernity and tradition' (Joshi 2007a, 147). It also points to the quandaries of a political process in which the dynamics of 'regional and tribal affiliations' trump the legitimacy of 'political vision and program' (Sharma 2004b, 429; Patnaik 2003).
- Fourthly, and finally, the post-Soviet transition of the Central Asian states has been profoundly disrupted by 'drug trafficking and organized crime' (Dwivedi 207, 240). Indian commentators ascertain that 'Central Asia is the hardest hit [global region] by the explosion of Afghan heroin' (Roy 2001, 2278). At the same time, the emergence of 'authoritarian and corrupt regimes [which] are only interested in holding on to power' has ushered in 'a situation, which is very conducive to the growth of extremism and instability both within and these [Central Asian] countries' (Sharma 2004a, 276). The confluence between these dynamics has turned the region into 'a new Golden Triangle', 'accounting for a major share of narcotic production and trade' (Raj and Mahapatra 2004, 280). This concern has become close-

ly intertwined with India's ongoing preoccupation with the 'various dimensions' of 'the extent and potential forces of religious extremism' in the region (Joshi 2007a, 147; Mohanty 2006).[10] Consequently, the claim is that the Central Asian states have not been 'capable of meeting these challenges on their own due to the lack of prior experience in managing such problems, paucity of funds, ill-equipped security services and the failure to arrive at a common strategy' (Mahapatra 2007, 168–169).

The multiplicity of these dynamics and the accidental nature of their interactions in Central Asian politics infer that 'domestic troubles and transnational influence will continue to stir political upheavals and to promote state and non-state violence. To the extent that internal troubles cross national boundaries or originate in the policies of neighboring governments, domestic troubles will lead to inter-state confrontations' (Bajpai 2000, 47). Indian commentators therefore expect 'little prospects for a radical departure from the present scenario' (Dash 2007, 204). In fact, the alleged 'stability' of the region 'can vanish in no time' as it 'rests on a quicksand' (Sharma 2007, 127). The convoluted dilemmas that characterize the Central Asian context facilitate the promulgation of 'tyrannical democracies' in the region—polities characterized by 'gross distortions of majoritarian type democracies':

> The tiny political elite have manipulated their parliamentary majority and refer to it for legitimation. The elites act as tyrants and refuse the necessary compromise in political and social life. They refuse to establish consensual democracy for the purpose of fundamental change. Consequently, the political system resembles an infantile disorder. (Sharma 2004a, 265; 2005, 35; 2007, 125).

This understanding is deeply engrained in the narratives of the 'Look North' policy.[11] The projection of India's secular and democratic politics as a possible model for managing the (oftentimes confounding) diversity of Central Asian trends confirms the myth-making modalities of New Delhi's post-1998 foreign policy making. At the same time, these discourses are not completely divorced from the conceptual and policy inconsistency that marked India's pre-1998 engagement in the region.

Encouraging Regional Cooperation in Central Asia
Intertwined with the narrative modalities of secularism and democracy, the 'Look North' policy stresses the significance of regional cooperation to the stability and prosperity of Central Asia. Owing to their location on the map of global affairs and the seemingly inherent propensity to instability, the 'geopolitical structure of the post-Soviet states may have greater influence over the entire Asia and the world at large' (Reddy 2007, 217). In order to prevent the potential threats to New Delhi that are likely to emanate from such a volatile context, the proposition is that Central Asia 'should remain integrated' and 'India should try [to] forge a collective security arrangement and a collective project for the development of all the countries of the region regardless of their policy slants in favor of this or that great power' (Asopa 2007, 173–188). New Delhi's call for 'greater political cooperation among the Central Asian states' (Gidadhubli 2007, 171; Sachdeva 2007, 264) tends to rely on the 'host of common specificities' shared among them (Sharma 2007, 123; Mann 2001, 2036).[12]

This insistence on maintaining the unity of Central Asian states reflects Indian perceptions of the pragmatic benefits from (even a rudimentary form of functional) cooperation which 'transforms conventional aspirations into more open, dynamic, and wider practices of peaceful coexistence, collective responsibility, and development' (Lama 2005, 134–135). The regional character of 'these flows' facilitates the 'forging [of] linkages and bonds of solidarity' among the participating states (Pant 2005, 181). Thus, from 'an Indian perspective', 'the idea of regional cooperation would incre-ase the prospects for stability in Central Asia' (Joshi 2004, 255). It has been pointed out that since the 'creation of ethnically homogeneous states out of the present day Central Asian republics [...] is hardly possible without large-scale bloodshed', 'regional integration is the only way to prevent the development of a Yugoslavia-like situation' (Kaushik 2000, 40–41).[13] The fear also is that without regional integration history might be repeated and Central Asia may lose 'its creative capacity [just like it did] during the sixteenth century, owing to its internecine warfare, internal instability, and external aggressive policy' (Haidar 2003, 260). Thus, 'looking beyond Pakistan, India has recognized the urgency of promoting regional economic integration' (Mohan 2007, 393). Some commentators have even asserted that because the Central

Asian states are 'divided by artificial borders created by the Soviets to contain the dream of *one* Turkestan', the 'Look North' policy needs to consider the eventual 'emergence of *the* Central Asian Republic' (Dietl 1997, 111–141).

In this respect, there seems to be a significant level of disappointment among Indian commentators that 'the political leadership of these countries has been unable to evolve a mind-set that could be truly characterized as [Central Asian]' (Behera 2003, 210), because regional state-elites 'do not trust each other' (Mohapatra 2007, 170). This failure tends to be explained through the pursual of narrow personal gains by regional state-elites, which (more often than not) are disguised under the narrative cloak of (ethno-) national interests. Thus—confirming the observed entrenchment of 'tyrannical democracies'—commentators have noted that the failure of Central Asian states to establish a robust framework for regional cooperation illustrates their 'poor governance' (Pillai 2004, 249). Although the lack of a robust framework for regional cooperation is a significant shortcoming and a source of instability, Indian commentators assert that 'Central Asia won't blow apart' (*The Hindu,* 18 April 2008).[14]

It has to be acknowledged that the preoccupation with the necessity of regional cooperation in Central Asia demonstrates the discursive modalities of New Delhi's regionalization strategies. Regionalization is understood both (i) in terms of a specific 'regional approach' by an international actor; and (ii) in terms of the quality of interactions that characterize certain global neighborhoods and zones. Indeed, 'the evolving architecture of regionalization' has become an indication of the ability of global neighborhoods and zones to act as regions (Jayasuriya 2004; Katzenstein 2005; Lake and Morgan 1998; Muni 1997, 1609; Pugh and Sidhu 2003; Solingen 1998). Chapter 1 has illustrated that this understanding reflects the unprecedented degree of regional integration featuring in global politics since the late 1980s. In this respect, India's promotion of regional cooperation in Central Asia follows the discursive modalities of the regionalization of global politics. These narratives derive from a long-held but rarely acknowledged view that India's security 'can only be maintained by the establishment of an "All Eastern or All Asian Federation"' and the development of 'a common Asian approach to problems of foreign policy and defence' (Prasad 1963, 439). In its current reincarnation, such a perspective insists that regionalism 'constitutes a practical foundation for Asian security and stability'—the 'Look North' policy, thereby, puts forward India's 'creative' contribution to the construction of 'an effective structure of Asian peace', which

> promotes a regional security system as part of an overall global security system. It is imperative to establish a network of regional institutions to address critical issues like ethnic relations, cross-border terrorism, reconciliation, transnational crime and illicit trade, environmental degradation, etc. This is likely to further the cause of regional security and integration. (Sharma 2004a, 267–277; emphasis original)[15]

The discursive modalities of regionalism reflect the mythmaking underpinnings of India's post-1998 foreign policy:

> [Thus] along with [the] new focus on regional peace and prosperity came the idea of 'open borders'. Although [Prime Minister] Gujral was often accused of romanticism towards the neighbors, Vajpayee, who succeeded him, turned out to be an equal enthusiast and was beginning to talk of a bolder agenda. By the end of 2003, Vajpayee was waxing about 'open borders and a single currency' in the subcontinent. Three years later, his successor Manmohan Singh was wistful about having 'breakfast in Amritsar, lunch in Lahore, and dinner in Kabul'. This new desire for open borders was clearly a structural development, not merely the passing fancy of one leader. As Vajpayee argued, there was pressure from the people for a fundamental rethinking of India's [international] relations. (Mohan 2007, 17)

Consequently, the regionalism implicit in the discourses of the 'Look North' policy exposes that 'it is our [i.e. India's] purpose to engage more vigorously with an independent Central Asia through cultural structures; we do not need [the] silken crutches [from] the "romance" of the Silk Road [which] in the post-Cold War realignment [has become] the *cultural complement to a strategic design.* [Instead, it is] the Shawl Road between India, Central Asia, and Russia [...] unlike the Silk Road' that should be the guide for India's foreign policy in the region 'if we wish to pursue sharp international rivalries wreathed in the perfumed elegance of cultural artifacts. [Thus] we could always pit the Kashmir shawls against the Chinese silks. Finally, if our global strategy requires a north-south axis, the Shawl Road, not the Silk Road, captures that purpose as a *cultural strategy* perfectly' (Palat 1999; emphasis added).

It is noteworthy that the regionalization expressed in the 'Look North' policy does not impel particular frameworks for *appropriate* Central Asian relations (regardless of whether it is framed in the discourses of the 'Silk Road' or the 'Shawl Road')—a discursive and policy pattern which is important for understanding New Delhi's 'no influence' in the region (which will be developed in Chapter 8). Instead, it indicates New Delhi's resentment of the regionalizing strategies of other international actors. The following chapters will elaborate these dynamics in greater detail, but it has to be remarked here that the narratives of the 'Look North' policy have been setting the 'Kashmir shawls' in opposition to the 'Chinese Silks'—i.e. comparing the Central Asian agency of New Delhi and Beijing and pillorying the effects of the latter. Indian commentators have been somewhat perplexed by China's increasingly sophisticated regionalization of the region, especially as evidenced by their response to the establishment of the Shanghai Cooperation Organization (SCO). As Chapter 6 will demonstrate, some analysts have welcomed the gaining of a SCO-observer status by India as one of the more significant indications of India's pragmatic post-1998 foreign policy approach (Rana 2007, 67). It appears to enhance New Delhi's ability to '*dilute* Chinese and Russian influence' in the region (Bedi 2002; emphasis added). At the same time, other observers have noted that 'New Delhi is not loosing sleep over the fact that it is not a full member of SCO [because] unlike the other observer states to SCO, India has chosen to maintain some political distance from the ambitious goals [that] Beijing and Moscow have for the organization' (*Indian Express*, 14 August 2007). It is claimed that such a critical attitude to SCO membership 'in no way diminishes India's commitment to regional and multilateral approaches to the challenge of political stability and security in Central Asia' (Muni 2003, 122). Chapter 8 will indicate that the ambiguity expressed by the proponents of the 'Look North' policy in regards to the regionalizing strategies of other international actors points to persisting insecurities regarding India's post-1998 international identity. The following section, therefore, surveys the narratives through which foreign policy mythmaking imputes coherence to the formulations of New Delhi's external affairs.

The Logic of Mythmaking of the 'Look North' Policy

As argued in Chapter 3, the recourse to mythmaking in the narrative justification of a state's external relations offers a shortcut to domestic policy-legitimation by providing a latent pool of malleable (and potent) symbols for popular validation of foreign policy agendas. The pervasiveness and ubiquity of India's self-aggrandizing discourses reveal the necessity from 'a big mental leap, given its traditional self-perception as a weak and developing country' (Muni and Mohan 2005, 57). Thus, dispositions about the patterns of international relations expose socially constructed judgments and attitudes on appropriate frameworks of external behavior. The perception is that 'backed with nuclear power' India can play 'a more influential role as a democratic balancer and stabilizer in Asia' (Budania 2003, 85). The narratives of the 'Look North' policy indicate the understanding that 'projecting [India] on a global canvas needs both a sound domestic base and rigorously articulated strategic objectives' (Rana 2007, 75). As has already been identified, the logic of mythmaking of India's post-1998 foreign policy encompasses four distinct (and mutually-reinforcing) themes: (i) a geopolitical trouncing of India's perceived weakness; (ii) a Hindu-centric ideology of national strength; (iii) an imposed settlement of domestic political contestation; and (iv) a resilient narrative of self-aggrandizement.

These mythmaking strands have been combined in numinous ways in the discourses of India's 'Look North' policy. The independence acquired by regional states at the beginning of the 1990s—or as some have put it, 'the return of Central Asia to the world'—has tended to 'generate considerable romance in New Delhi about rekindling the historic links between India and Central Asia' (Muni and Mohan 2007, 66). Echoing these romantic visions, the actor Shashi Kapoor has declared that 'India and the beautiful countries of Central Asia *share the language of the heart* and a centuries-old culture. We have more in common with Central Asia than [any other place in the world]. Our culture and outlook on life has a great deal of similarity'. Likewise, Rajiv Sikri, then a secretary in the Ministry of External Affairs, has acknowledged that India, 'as an emerging Asian power can use its cultural connections and its rising profile to promote stability in Central Asia' (Kapoor and Sikri cited in *Hindustan Times*, 15 April 2006; emphasis added). Such (re)visions of New Delhi's international agency have been intimately intertwined with 'the useful perspective [offered by] the glorious history [of] Indian cultural and intellectual achievement' (Kachru 2007, 207–231). In other words, the perception is that 'cultural diplomacy is rooted in geopolitics' (Bhattacharyya 2004).[16] Reiterating the contribution of the Curzonian 'forward foreign policy' to the formulation of India's post-1998 assertive foreign policy stance (which was outlined in Chapter 2), the proponents of the 'Look North' policy confirm that it is 'this British imperial thinking that continues to be reflected in India's desire to establish preeminence in its peripheral regions' (Singh 2003, 111).

In this way, mythmaking provides the facilitating environment for the consideration of New Delhi's external affairs as 'essentially a byproduct of geopolitical circumstances' (Jain 2008, 41). The proclamations of shared 'geo-culture' (Kaushik 2003b, 30) provide the 'permissive environment' (Chatterjee 2006, 41) through which the discourses of India's relations with Central Asia articulate foreign policy as a reflection and a projection of internal anxieties. Said otherwise, the formulations of external agency are underpinned by complex narratives of dislocation that employ domestic resources and institutions for their popular validation. Thus, to borrow from a different context, 'the lens through which [Central Asia] is viewed determines the way policy is framed. The framing of policy implies what is at issue and also what is to be done' (Jonson 2004, 11). For instance, 'the vision of Asian solidarity and India's leading role in it' that underwrites the narratives of the 'Look North' policy confirms New Delhi's 'growing self-confidence and capabilities' and its 'historical-cultural evolution' in a 'geostrategic reality' which is 'reinforced and realized in the changing contexts of Asian and world politics' (Muni and Mohan 2005, 55). Consequently, the challenge for the foreign policy engagement of India in Central Asia is 'how to nurture its historical and cultural bonds in a manner that its contemporary concerns and future aspiration are addressed constructively' (Muni 2003, 99).

For instance, Suryakant Nijanand Bal (2004, xii–xiii) claims that India's engagement of Central Asia since 1998 attests to New Delhi's 'judicious exercise of realpolitik [which is] dependent upon the national will to make things happen'. As he points out,

> Unless, a country's collective consciousness strives to make its own history with a clear focus, it may well have to be content

with having it written by *others* from *their points of view and to serve their interests*—not a happy prospect at all. Future history will be determined largely by the geopolitical environment created by a nation to ensure that its future interests are secure, and to direct energies toward those objectives. Any country content on having its history determined and written by others, need hardly aspire to a status higher than that of a vassal state that would condemn it to be relegated to the backwaters of history, if not total irrelevance in the comity of nations. The sheer size, civilization, and culture of India do not make it a candidate to aspire for such an unenviable status. [Thus], it is not only a question of whether we have to play the Great Game—that has already been decided by history and geography. Rather, the question is what part we choose to play—a conscious part, or be content with that assigned to us by others. We must play with the determination to win in the true spirit of *dharma niti* and *raja niti*. However, the options of *danda niti* and *kuta niti* must also be explored where necessary after all other options have failed. (2004, xii–xiii; emphasis original)

Thus, in a few sentences Bal brings together the four thematic narratives of the logic of mythmaking underpinning India's post-1998 foreign policy articulations. He, thereby, asserts that the 'proactive orientation [of the 'Look-North' policy] holds the key to India's meaningful contribution to a new era in the history between India and Central Asia. India must learn from history and not condemn itself to relive it *ad infinitum*' (Bal 2004, 37; emphasis original).[17] Thus, 'the best way to ensure steady progress [for India's international stature] is to take a step back and see how the road curves ahead. [History] aids in identifying patterns. Tracing the developments at different points in time helps calibrate our judgment with an understanding of the challenges that have to be faced' (Kachru 2007, 207). In this setting, New Delhi's proclamations on 'commonality of interests' with the region has given a 'contemporary focus to India's past historical and cultural links with Central Asia' (Joshi 2007b, 440). The claim has therefore been that the foreign-policy assertiveness displayed by the discursive articulations of the 'Look North' policy exhibits the conviction that 'the great powers [are] limited in their exercise of their power if a regional great power possesses a diplomatic and military strategy to alter the matrix of calculations or the variables at play in a regional conflict' (Kapur 2006, 16).

Confirming the assertive posturing of its post-1998 foreign policy strategy, the narratives of India's engagement of Central Asia reveal that 'the factors and forces' preventing New Delhi from 'playing its legitimate role in Asia have either been mitigated [or] redefined' (Muni and Mohan 2005, 55). At the same time, the current engagement in the international politics of Central Asia reveals that

> India will act as a liberal superpower, motivated by national self-interest, but with pluralist, democratic values at the forefront [as a result of] India's quest for development and status as a player in the contemporary world of politics and economics. This quest is based on qualities of character, toughness, problem-solving ability, and tolerance for diversity. Imported notions such as Western-style democracy, legal systems, free markets, and social activism only enhance Indian society's innate strengths. [Thus] India is well on its way to becoming less of a soft state and more of a superpower. (Lak 2008, xviii–xx, 241)

Thus, 'rethinking the country's immediate and extended neighborhood policy', which is implicit in the articulations of the 'Look North' policy, has corroborated the mythmaking narrative that purely 'by virtue of its size, history, culture, and geographical location, India would always occupy a central place in world politics' (Jain 2008, 219–222). Thus, the narratives of its foreign policy making in Central Asia assist 'the evolution of strategies [for] offsetting threats and exploiting opportunities towards the furtherance of its enlightened self-interest [which] encompasses [the] continued, meaningful existence and the protection of its culture, values, and the way of life of its citizens [in] international relations' (Bal 2004, 2).

New Delhi's Bilateralism in Central Asia: India's Relations with Tajikistan

This chapter has already demonstrated that the narratives of the 'Look North' policy are underpinned by a desire to encourage a framework for the regional cooperation of the Central Asian states. Such proclamations notwithstanding, India's engagement in the region has been paralleled by a significant level of bilateral relations between New Delhi and Central Asian capitals. In particular, Astana and Tashkent have been the subjects of India's courtship. India's relations with both Kazakhstan and Uzbekistan are not merely 'a matter of historical continuity' (Mann 2001, 2048), but also reflect a perception that either of them is 'well poised to emerge as a "core" country and assume the leadership of Central Asia' (Asopa 2003, 174; Stobdan 2009, 3).

Analytically, the bilateral approach rests on the assertion that (at least initially) 'the desired stability of Central Asia' will depend not on regional cooperation, but

> above all, on the success of *individual* Central Asia states [...] The ability of each Central Asian state to evolve a political system which incorporates political pluralism and includes power-sharing arrangements for their multiethnic populations will, in particular, curb existing ethnic tensions and prevent confrontation along inter-ethnic and intra-ethnic lines. (Sharma 2003, 97)

Pragmatically speaking, the development of strong bilateral relations with some countries in the region reveals New Delhi's attempts to overcome the constraints imposed by its latecomer status in Central Asian affairs, which has further compounded the effects from the lack of a direct physical access to the region (Kavalski 2007b, 854). Thus, as Chapter 6 will demonstrate, India has adopted an approach aimed at making up for lost time with respect to the Central Asian agency of other international actors—especially, China. The 'unstated national strategic objective' of such bilateralism is to restore parity between New Delhi and Beijing in the region (Mohan 2004, 150). The tactic of 'picking off' China's vulnerable friends and allies in Central Asia has (arguably) allowed India to contest China's agency in the region without necessarily confronting it (Cohen 2001, 264).

In this respect, it is Tajikistan that—to all intents and purposes—has become the posterchild of New Delhi's bilateralism in Central Asia. The construction of Tajikistan as India's 'gateway to Central Asia' (Asopa 2003, 153) is of complex provenance in the narratives of the 'Look North' policy. The usual point of departure seems to be the observation of 'millennia-old', 'civilizational relationship between Tajikistan and the Indian subcontinent' (Kaushik 2003b, 30–37; Bal 2004, 20; Singh 2003, 195; Sinha 2004, 7). At the same time, the closeness between New Delhi and Moscow during the Cold War has allegedly given India an 'edge' in Tajikistan both as a result of 'a large number of [Indian] technical cadres trained in the Central Asian republics during the Soviet period' and the concomitant 'immense popularity of Indian literature, music, and dance, and the high esteem India [is] held by the Tajik and the Central Asian people' (Singh 2003, 198). Furthermore, many commentators assert that Tajikistan is 'the first Central Asian republic [to] realize the importance of building a broader national identity based on institutions' and not on an exclusive ethnicity—a state-building strategy akin to that of India (Sharma 2003, 73; Dash 2004, 202).

Strategically speaking, however, it is the shared perception of external threats that appears to motivate India's bilateral relations with Tajikistan. Indian commentators explain that the civil war which ravaged the country during the 1990s has been '*caused* by a skillful exploitation of the inter-regional/inter-clan rivalries by forces of Islamic fundamentalism supported by the Pakistan-backed Mujahideen in Afghanistan'—i.e. it was 'a spill-over of the victory of the Mujahideen armed groups in Afghanistan. The jobless Afghan *jehadis* found employment both in Tajikistan and in the Indian state of Jammu and Kashmir' (Kaushik 2003b, 39–40).[18] At the same time, such explanations of the conflict in Tajikistan should not be taken as an inference of any 'expansionist designs' on behalf of Afghanistan, but 'should be seen essentially as an extension of its own civil war'; thus, it was not only Tajikistan that was impacted, but 'the Tajik conflict in turn had altered the power dynamics in Afghanistan itself' (Asopa 2003, 182). In this respect, from the point of view of New Delhi, India and Tajikistan having 'suffered a lot on account of onslaughts of the dark forces of religious extremism active in Afghanistan *must work together'* (Warikoo 2003, 151; Aneja 2002; Dietl 1997, 127; Muni 2003, 116).

In fact 'a new and active phase' in their bilateral relations has been initiated in the wake of the Taliban takeover (Singh 2003, 201; Patnaik 2005, 207). Thus, while demonstrating the balance-of-power attitude informing India's policy towards Central Asia, commentators tend to establish a link between New Delhi's logistic and military support for the anti-Taliban Northern Alliance through Tajikistan. This assistance was articulated as a strategy for 'strengthening Tajikistan's secular forces in their war against Islamic fundamentalism' (Asopa 2007, 173). For instance, there have been allegations that India's military outposts in the country have been set up as early as the mid-1990s (Bedi 2002, 17; Jain 2008, 212; Kavalski 2007b, 849). Framed as an offer of 'humanitarian assistance', in 2000 India has formally acknowledged the establishment of a military hospital on the Tajik-Afghan border at Farkhor and the widening of a military air-strip near Dushanbe for transport aircraft (Singh 2003, 201–202; Muni and Mohan 2005, 69). More recently, India—still 'quietly, very quietly'—has deployed at least one helicopter squadron at its 'Ayuni' air-base in Tajikistan to bolster its already existing rapid response capabilities (Pandit 2007; *Hindustan Times,* 20 April 2006). The discourses of the 'Look North' policy legitimize this military outreach through the explanation that 'the nation's strategic interests lie far beyond [its] borders'—a realization, which is 'compeling New Delhi to consider the possibility of sending troops abroad outside of the UN framework' (Mohan 2007b, 395).

The discursive accounts of these developments seem to indicate that the rise of the Taliban to power in Afghanistan has jolted New Delhi out of its post-Cold War stupor vis-à-vis its relations with Central Asia. Indian commentators therefore often stress that the emergence of a 'militarized form of Islamic extremism in the Central Asian republics is directly linked to the rise of the Taliban' (Warikoo 2003, 145). Consequently, the narratives of the 'Look North' policy suggest that 'Pakistan is thus going to be a constant irritant to Tajikistan' (Asopa 2003, 191). In this respect, the transformations of Central Asian affairs in the post-'9/11' period seem to demonstrate (at least to Indian commentators), the 'timeliness' and 'prescience' of the Indo-Tajik support for the Northern Alliance (Singh 2003, 202) and that their 'coordinated approach [has] yielded results' (Sharma 2003, 95). In fact, some have suggested the emergence of a strategic triangle between India, Tajikistan, and Afghanistan (Kaushik 2003b, 45). Others have indicated New Delhi's centrality to the emergence of an international coalition ensuring the security of Tajikistan (Asopa 2003, 192).

As Chapter 7 will explain, the accounts of India's role in post-Taliban Afghanistan participate in the narrative attempt to overcome the limitations of New Delhi's pre-1998 foreign policy making. Thus, the fostering of strong bilateral ties with Tajikistan reveals India's attempt to carve out a space for its stakes in Central Asia. This development suggests that India's post-1998 foreign policy stance can be termed 'revisionist' to the extent that New Delhi aims to *revise* the existing patterns in its international environment in order to facilitate the exercise of its own agency (Mohan 2004, 80; Kavalski 2007, 847). This understanding informs the engagement with the frameworks of the 'new great game' in the narratives of the 'Look North' policy.

The 'New Great Game'

An overwhelming number of the proponents of the 'Look North' policy are convinced that Central Asia has become the host of a 'new great game'. Kishan Rana seems to capture best the patterns of regional interactions intimated by this term:

> Visualize a three-dimensional, multiplayer chessboard, where a move by each protagonist produces eddies and backflows that affect all the others, and prompt counter-movements. Factor into this, the time as a fourth dimension, which takes this analogy beyond easy description. [Central Asia] resembles such a turbulent, volatile, and unpredictable scene owing to the mix of cooperation [and] contestation that marks virtually each bilateral relationship. The situation is all the more unpredictable because of the absence of fixed mooring points. [The region] thus offers a heady mix of bilateral, regional, and great power diplomacy, in which the players weave bewildering nets of connections and counter arrangements. Some of the emerging developments appear contradictory, understandable only in a fluid context. (2007, 211–213)[19]

The origins of this 'new great game' are traditionally traced to the end of the Cold War, which 'did not change [regional] geography', but its meaning—that is, it 'drastically altered the global geopolitics [of] Central Asia' (Bhattacharjea 2008, 11). At the same time, it has been fueled by the growing demand for and (the related) need to diversify the sources of energy resources (Mahalingam 2004, 125–126). According to the narratives of the 'Look North' policy, what is 'new' about this 'great game' in Central Asia is the simultaneous proliferation of external (i.e. from outside the region) and internal (i.e. regional) agency. Consequently, 'in these troubled waters, global and regional actors angle for the best deals not only in terms of natural resources, but for political and military influence as well' (Bal 2004, 278–279).

Thus, on the one hand Indian commentators draft extensive lists of international actors with vested interests in Central Asian resources. Usually, these include (but are not limited to) China, the EU, Iran, Pakistan, Russia, Saudi Arabia, Turkey, and the USA (Aneja 2007; Bagchi 2007; Bal 2004, xiv; Dixit 2004, 16; Dutt 2003, 149; Gidadhubli 2003, 166; Joshi 2007a, 151; Mahalingam 2004, 124; Mattoo 2003, 48; Muni and Mohan 2005, 67; Patnaik 2005, 207; Shams-ud-Din 1997, 330; Sharma 2005, 67; Singh 2003, 197). What distinguishes the involvement of international actors in regional affairs is that they do not appear to be interested in the 'control [of] territory for imperial expansion, but [the] control [of] Central Asia's energy and strategic mineral resources' (Muni 2003, 97–98). In other words, the 'new great game' is about the creation of 'niches of influence by neighboring countries' (Shams-ud-Din 1997, 340).

On the other hand, and more significantly, the Central Asian states are no longer 'pawns of great powers'—instead, the complexity of the international affairs of the region and the proliferation of external agency has allowed them to 'jockey for power and position' (Mattoo 2003, 49). The contestation between international actors 'has given unprecedented options for the wily leaders of Central Asia [to] rapidly figure out the art of playing all sides of the new great game' (*Indian Express*, 7 September 2007). In this setting, 'the Central Asian republics make a lot of noise about the need to join or form new geo-cultural and geo-strategic alliances' (Shams-ud-Din 2007, 331) and external observers should not 'belittle the importance of the Central Asian peoples as independent actors and masters of their national destiny' (Kaushik 2003b, 32). In other words, for the external agency of the Central Asian states, the existence of (and increase in) this contestation between international actors vying for their attention is not an entirely negative development. Such a competition offers a propitious environment for 'pick-and-choose' strategies and bandwagoning for profit policies (Kavalski 2007b, 856). In fact, all five of the Central Asian states have indicated their propensity and panache for this kind of engagement with international actors. The discourses of the 'Look North' policy emphasize that this attribute reveals the qualitative distinction of the 'new great game' from the nineteenth-century 'great game'.

In this setting, the dynamic of Central Asian politics reflects the interaction between the 'external environment and internal processes' (Joshi 2003, 69). Such a multiplicity of regional interactions observed by the proponents of the 'Look North' policy evidence that India is a 'lesser player in the "new great game"' (Asopa 2007, 146). At the same time, the recognition that 'India is the least powerful' from the main international actors engaged in the region does not seem to hinder the perception that New Delhi is 'seen by the principal Asian and non-Asian actors as a potential balancing influence with few threatening overtones of its own' (Rana 2007, 212). Although such a proposition seemingly contradicts the self-aggrandizing mythmaking of India's post-1998 foreign policy, it nevertheless (and perhaps paradoxically) asserts the discursive platform for India's engagement in Central Asia. The responsibility for this ideational topsyturvydom is deduced from the dynamics of the 'new great game', which will render 'obsolete the old categories of East and West, North and South, aligned and nonaligned, developed and developing. Traditional geographic groupings will increasingly lose salience in international relations [meaning that] competition for allegiances will be more open and less fixed than in the past' (Mohan 2007, 393). In this contest, the main hurdle 'to the competing great power interests arises from regional fundamentalist and terrorist forces that draw support and sustenance from diverse sources in and around the Muslim world' (Muni 2003, 98). To counter this challenge, internal actors have made Central Asia the 'testing ground for [contending] "new regionalisms"', which can help reduce both regional susceptibility and vulnerability to such threats (Bhadrakumar 2004).

In other words, the 'new great game' transforms the pattern of Central Asian affairs into one which is dominated by a complex network of overlapping *inter-regional* relations (Jayasuriya 2004; Kanwal 1999, 1614; Katzenstein 2005; Lake and Morgan 1998; Pugh and Sidhu 2003; Raj and Mahapatra 2004, 283; Solingen 1998). The international actors engaged in Central Asia are promoting their own, distinct, and, more often than not, incompatible regionalizing strategies. Such a shift underwrites the changing contingencies of the 'new great game'. Bearing this in mind, the proponents of the 'Look North' policy insist that

> if the [new] great game [for] Central Asia were to be compared

to a five-act Shakespearean play, we may say Act III, Scene I has just begun: On a Venice street, Shylock famously posits to Salarino the metaphorical relationship of intricate counter-balances: 'If you prick us, do we not bleed? If you tickle us, do we not laugh? If you poison us, do we not die? And if you wrong us, shall we not revenge?' The geopolitics of energy in the Central Asian steppes cannot have a better description. The interlocking trends are several. Russia remains the lead player, but the United State is aggressively striving to retake some of the territory it lost. Central Asian countries have become savvier in creating space for themselves as energy exporters. Meanwhile, an ancient traveler has appeared on the Silk Road leading from Kashgar. China has raised its head above the parapet. This holds the prospect for transforming the great game of energy into a 'multipolar' affair in the spirit of our times. (Bhadrakumar 2008)

Thus, in the process of narrativizing New Delhi's external agency, what was (originally) construed as a position of weakness has become articulated into an account of national strength, which advances India's interests in the international field. The assertion is that

India has [achieved] some sort of a middle position with fairly close strategic understanding with the US and Russia [and] China [...] For India, the present situation offers considerable flexibility and resilience, partly because of the US-Russian mutual understanding on specific issues and partly because bilaterally, India's engagement with all the great powers, including China is constructive and mutually advantageous. India would like a useful and constructive balance of forces to be retained in Central Asia that ensures greater autonomy and strategic space to the Central Asian countries themselves. (Muni 2003, 124)

Consequently, the 'fluid political and strategic context' of the 'new great game' (Dutta 2003, 142) provides the facilitating environment for asserting the validity of New Delhi's post-1998 approach. Thus, despite the realization that some of the participants in the 'new great game' have 'the advantage of direct overland access to Central Asia' (Patnaik 2005, 226), India is still 'poised to play a constructive role in [the region] regardless of the fact that it lack geographic contiguity, huge financial resources, and easy access to the region' (Asopa 2007, 189). The former external affairs minister, Yashwant Sinha confirms this observation in his declaration that India's lack of direct access to Central Asia—'the largest landlocked landmass in the world'—is 'both a challenge and an opportunity because in today's technology-driven world, it is not always necessary to transport material [which is supplanted by] the logic of investment abroad and organizing production facilities there' (Sinha 2004, 7). Such discursive positioning of India's external affairs reaffirms the assertiveness of its post-1998 foreign policy making. In this respect, while acknowledging the dynamics of the 'new great game' in Central Asia, the narratives of the 'Look North' policy validate the mythmaking logic of New Delhi's international agency in the region.

India and Central Asia: The Narrative Modalities of the 'Look North' Policy

The discussion of this chapter reveals that Central Asia provides a context for India's foreign policy interaction with other international actors. Thus, the region has become a facilitating environment for evincing more fully New Delhi's perception of their agency than their bilateral relations might suggest. The narratives of the 'Look North' policy have been simultaneously driven by the realization that 'it is the oil of Central Asia that [has] made India active in the politics of the region' (Asopa 2003, 185–186) and plagued by the understanding that India 'cannot make massive investments because of its financial constraints' (Asopa 2007, 184). Chapter 8 will make clear that such articulations of a dynamic 'Look North' policy do not necessarily equate and should not be mistaken for increased *influence* in the region. That is why—as evidenced by India's interactions with Tajikistan—New Delhi maintains bilateralism as an important feature of its relations with Central Asia.

Nevertheless, the construction of India's interactions with Central Asia bares that it 'would like to have both a set of general security objectives in place and to strengthen relations with specific regional powers' (Gupta 2008, 108). The discussion in the following chapters will reveals that New Delhi's engagement with both Central Asian states and other international actors involved in the region shows that despite the assertive posturing of its post-1998 foreign policy making, 'formulating nationally-accepted [and] precise strategic objectives of external policy is surely the biggest challenge that begs to be addressed' (Rana 2007, 75). Jain (2008, 128) has therefore argued that 'if India is to play a meaningful role [in global politics] beyond the Southasian region, it will also need to sustain a positive momentum in its ongoing political, economic, and strategic relations with [Russia, the EU], the United States, and China'. The remaining chapters address India's interaction with the dominant nodes of this networked pattern of complex interactions in Central Asia.

5

THE PEACOCK AND THE BEAR: SHIFTING NEW DELHI'S RELATIONS WITH MOSCOW IN CENTRAL ASIA

Introduction

Chapter 2 has already revealed that the dissolution of the Soviet Union caused a major shock to India's policy making, which forced New Delhi (unwillingly) to initiate the overhaul of the norms, rules, and principles underlying its domestic and external relations.[1] Stressing the uniqueness of this experience, T.N. Kaul (1997, 39) has pointed out that the 'relations between any two countries, specially those which are of considerable size and population, and have an ancient culture and history, with links spread almost all over the world are not usually susceptible to sudden changes, for better or for worse, unless they are directly involved in a clash or congruence of their respective national interests'. In this setting, India's 1998 nuclear tests have indicated clearly that New Delhi has recovered from the trauma caused by the 'sudden' passing away of the Soviet Union and the charting of an independent, singular, and assertive decision-making approach.

This experience is integral to the narratives of the 'Look North' policy. Indian commentators often point out that the 'legitimacy' of Russia's international agency in Asia derives from its 'continental landmass' (Rana 2007, 211). At the same time, some would point out that the dissolution of the Soviet Union is a direct outcome of 'the urge of the Russian pro-Western democratic elite to *offload the burdensome Central Asian republics* in order to achieve a speedy modernization' (Kaushik 2003, 19; emphasis added). In this respect, the analysis of this chapter follows the proposition that the post-Cold War international affairs between India and Russia 'has settled into a new kind of relationship partly based on the old friendship' between them and 'partly on the new situation existing between Russia and the Central Asian states' (Kaul 1997, 421). Prior to addressing individually the contexts of India's encounter of Russia in Central Asia, the following section offers an overview of the bilateral relations between New Delhi and Moscow.

India and Russia: Reviewing their International Interactions
It appears safe to say, that the 'time-tested ties' between Moscow and New Delhi have 'witnessed profound upheavals since the collapse of the Soviet Union, ranging from a steep decline at the beginning of the 1990s through a new political and strategic understanding in the mid-1990s, to the [current] mutually "productive" and "enduring" partnership' (Jain 2008, 109). Reflecting this experience, Indian observers have tended to divide the Indo-Russian relationship into six-distinct periods: (i) foundational stage—starting with 'the death of Stalin' and the emblematic visit by Nikita Khrushchev and Nikolai Bulganin to India in December 1955; (ii) the 'traumatic epoch' of the 1960s, which became the 'testing years of Indo-Russian relations'—this was a particularly 'turbulent time for India' since it had to come to terms with two successive wars (in 1962 with China and in 1965 with Pakistan), 'Nehru's death, the resultant political bickering within the Congress [Party], rainless years, and the consequent drought across the country'; (iii) 1970s—'the decade of consolidation'—formalized the Indo-Soviet ties with a far-reaching Treaty of Peace, Friendship, and Cooperation, which was signed in August 1971; (iv) the 'rejuvenating phase' of the 1980s witnessed the introduction of extensive projects for social, political, and economic reforms in both countries, which 'from the grueling realities of a world ridden with war and conflicts, [allowed them to] dream of a world free of conflicts'; (v) the struggle for a 'new beginning' during 'the most traumatic period in bilateral relations' following the disintegration of the Soviet Union; (vi) 'Strategic Partnership'—starting in 1993, it is claimed that during this period the relations between New Delhi and Moscow have grown more pragmatic (Dash 2007, 474–477; Bakshi 1999).

Despite such a checkered experience, the contention tends to be that history has scripted a 'positive legacy' for the 'special relationship' between the two counties (Mishra 1996, 87). At the same time, the interactions between India and Russia in Central Asia have confronted New Delhi with the realization that Kremlin's foreign policy making is always dictated by '*its* interest and priorities'—i.e. 'contrary to what is commonly perceived', Russia's attitude to India has depended on New Delhi's compliance with 'the "role envisaged for India" by Moscow' (Sharma 2002, 97). Relying on the periodisation of Indo-Russian bilateral relations above, the following subsections sketch out the main stages characterizing the interactions between New Delhi and Moscow in the post-Cold War period.

Gorbachev, the Dissolution of the Soviet Union, and the End of the 'Special Relationship'

Understanding the impact of Soviet disintegration on Indo-Russian relations requires a brief overview of their Cold War pattern. Many commentators have pointed out that India and the Soviet Union had a 'special meaning' in each other's external relations strategies during the Cold War (Jain 2008, 110). In particular, their 'friendship' was promoted as 'having an important positive influence on the international situation as a whole', because of their 'considerable experience in fruitful cooperation' (Banarjee 1977, 109). T.N. Kaul has interpreted the close Indo-Soviet relationship as an indication of the *respect* for 'India's policy of nonalignment [and] her impartial judgment based on the merits of each case as it affected her national interests'. In the former 'Communist Bloc' such an appreciation rested on the realization that 'independent India was not a country to be trifled with, dictated to, or dominated as a client state' (Kaul 1997, 40).

It has been observed therefore that 'from 1962 to 1991' India followed a policy of *'tilted nonalignment'* (Hagerty and Hagerty 2005, 41; emphasis original). An Indian commentator has explained the dynamism of such a policy by observing that 'Nehru may have been strictly nonaligned against the West and not so in the case of Russia' (Pillai 1969, 198). There are a number of reasons that can explain the *Soviet tilt* of India's foreign policy making:

- *Firstly*, both Moscow and New Delhi grew to perceive each other as countervailing forces to the 'Pakistan-Beijing-Washington axis'—i.e. seen from 'the Cold War paradigm' the interactions between India and the Soviet Union 'were guided by shared defence and security concerns, which became invariably

rooted in New Delhi's weapon dependence on Moscow' (Jain 2008, 109–111).[2] As will be explained shortly, such a perceived commonality of standpoints informs India's current engagement with Russia in Central Asia.
- *Secondly*, 'India's socialist orientation was a *critical factor* in the evolving relationship between India and the Soviet Union' (Jain 2008, 111; emphasis added). Others have noted that even if New Delhi's policy making was not informed by 'socialism', per se, it has nevertheless been following a 'largely unadumbrated non-capitalist path idea' (Banarjee 1977, 93).

Thus, both geopolitics and similar ideological perspectives became 'the basis of Indo-Soviet rapprochement, which no other force could defile' (Dash 2007, 475).

It is on the background of this narrative of 'natural allies' (Chopra 1997a, 15) during the Cold War that a number of Indian commentators tend to accuse the last Soviet President, Mikhail Gorbachev, and his 'new political thinking' for ending 'the era of "special ties" between New Delhi and Moscow' (Jain 2008, 112). Thus, it is claimed that while Indians 'were euphoric about the prospect for ushering in a new millennium of peace and prosperity for all nations as a result of the new policies initiated by Gorbachev', he had already been 'offering collaboration against the Third World to the West' (Kaushik 1997, 47–48). The perception is that such an 'involvement with the West' made Gorbachev 'indifferent towards Russia's traditional friends like India' (Naik 1995, 167). Therefore, 'Indo-Russian cooperation encountered many pitfalls, primarily due to [Gorbachev's] *perestroika* and *glasnost* taking a volatile turn' (Dash 2007, 476). Thus, rather than 'pursuing any coherent policy, Gorbachev simply continued to muddle through, evading complex issues and problems' (Kaushik 2003, 15). Indian commentators have thence labeled Gorbachev 'a stranger [who] by quirk of circumstances had become the ruler in the Kremlin to destroy it' (Naik 1995, 167) and 'a heretic [who] unleashed the raging storm of Soviet *perestroika*' (Dash 2007, 474–476). As argued in Chapter 2, these epithets attest to New Delhi's resentment about the disappearance of comfortable certainties. At the same time, the strength of these attitudes confirms that 'the Moscow-Delhi ties lost their *basis* with the end of the Cold War and the disintegration of the Soviet Union' (Mehrotra 1997, 99; emphasis added).

Immediate Post-Soviet Period

As already suggested, the collapse of the Soviet Union indicated that the Indo-Russian relationship 'no longer stands on the same footing' (Chopra 1997a, 19). In particular, it revealed that with the end of the Cold War 'Russian interests in India seem to have diminished' (Naik 1997, vii), that New Delhi 'does not enjoy the same importance in Moscow's Asian policy as it did in the past', and that it can 'no longer be able to expect the kind of "one-sided generosity" which earlier existed in Indo-Soviet economic relations' (Jayawardena 1993, 114–117). In spite of the 'visible credibility gap in Indo-Russian ties' (Sharma 1997, 66), a number of Indian commentators have insisted that while 'the Soviet Union may have broken into a number of independent states, Russia still remains a superpower with great military and economic potential' (Kaul 1997, 41). Thus (even though seemingly ignorant of 'the pragmatic commonality of strategic and diplomatic interests between India and the former Soviet Union'), observers acknowledged that 'it was [only] natural that the shift of emphasis in Russia's foreign policy goals was to considerably modify her attitude towards India' (Jha 1997, 77). Therefore, proponents of this view have insisted that 'Indo-Russian ties have remained exemplary despite political upheavals and the breakup of the USSR' (Mishra 1996, 87).

However, it became difficult to maintain the validity of such views in the increasingly random patterns of interactions between New Delhi and Moscow during the early 1990s. Indian commentators have asserted that between 1991 and 1993 'the relations between India and Russia *had gone adrift'* (Asopa 2007, 186; emphasis added). On the one hand, it has been noticed that Russian foreign policy 'lacked coherence and a precise approach for dealing with the seismic changes that were taking place at the domestic and external levels' and was becoming characterized by 'personal idiosyncrasies, "narrow egotistical interests", and erratic political decisions' (Jain 2008, 112). In other words, the formulation of the Kremlin's external relations during this period was 'caught up in a *morass* of conflicting policy options' (Mahapatra 2004, 129; emphasis added). It has been proffered, therefore, that 'both Moscow and New Delhi realize that this situation calls for a certain transitional period [in their interactions] during which conditions must be created for a painless movement towards a new structure of Indo-

Russian cooperation, preserving the essential elements of the old strategic partnership' (Kaushik 1997, 53). Yet, in line with its reactive pre-1998 foreign policy approach (outlined in Chapter 2), India decided 'to "wait and see" what Russia would do and how this would affect the relationship of the two countries' (Jha 1997, 76).

On the other hand, Moscow's desire 'to mend its relations with Pakistan' has tended to confuse New Delhi (Mehrotra 1997, 99; Mahapatra 2004, 134; Menon 1991; Shah 1993). Thus, the initial period of 'India's relations with post-Soviet Russia were marked by a good deal of uncertainty, inconsistency, lack of clarity and even *"unreliability"'* (Jha 1997, 76; emphasis added). In this respect, New Delhi has been expecting 'an indication of the continuity of the old Soviet interests in India [but] Yeltsin has neither the resources, nor even the desire' (Naik 1995, 187).[3] According to O.N. Mehrotra, the 'objective of the Russian foreign policy [at the time was] to break away from the former Soviet allies, clients, and friends' in the belief that 'by renouncing the former foreign policy priorities Russia could formulate a new foreign policy which would be appreciated by the West'. From an Indian point of view these attempts have helped to turn Russia into an 'unpredictable' partner, whose external relations are 'not based on [its] long-term national interests' (Mehrotra 1997, 97). In this setting, 'the Indo-Russian relations [have] become an unintentional victim of an intemperate leadership that [has] pursued an excessively West-centric approach [which led] Yeltsin and his cronies to neglect India' (Dash 2007, 473). In a nutshell, Russia was perceived as a state 'clearly pulled between a declining nostalgia for past relations with countries like India and growing proclivity towards cultivating relations with the West' (Jha 1997, 75).

The interactions between the two countries had not been helped much by the then Prime Minister P.V. Narasimha Rao's tacit endorsement of the August 1991 coup in the Soviet Union, who declared that 'the overthrow of Mikhail Gorbachev was an instructive example of an overenthusiastic reformer' (cited in Mehrotra 1997, 98). This might explain the 'element of contempt in Yeltsin's attitude towards the Indian Prime Minister, Narasimha Rao' (Naik 1995, 186). Thus, 'while the relations between Moscow and New Delhi were worsening, no serious political efforts were made to repair them' (Mehrotra 1997, 99).

Re-launching the Relationship

As the previous section outlined, the dissolution of the Soviet Union has ruptured traditional perceptions of each other in both India and Russia. Thus, in the immediate post-Cold War period, the interactions between New Delhi and Moscow were marked by uncertainty, frustration, and suspicion. As one commentator has pointed out, the Indo-Russian relationship had been threatened to become 'little more than a weapons supplier nexus' (Ganguly 2002, 364). P.L. Dash (2007, 476), however, points out that the reference to 'Indo-Russian trade' has always been a 'truism beyond the confines of defence, energy, and [the] power and steel sectors'. Nevertheless, in terms of Indian perceptions, there has been a major shift in Indo-Russian relations beginning in 1993. The essence of this change was that instead of treating each other with (at best) neglect and (at worst) disdain, New Delhi and Moscow began to engage each other in mutual initiatives and dialogues.

Usually, the start of this alteration in Indian perception of post-Soviet Russia is associated with the January 1993 visit by President Yeltsin in New Delhi and the reciprocal visit by Prime Minister Rao to Moscow in June 1994. Some commentators have proclaimed that 'Yeltsin's visit to New Delhi [has] injected some life into the hitherto stagnant bilateral relations' (Jain 2008, 113) and that it has opened 'new horizons' for interactions between the two countries (Mehrotra 1997, 102). Others have asserted that the 1993-1994 high level dialogue has 'ended the nagging uncertainty' in the post-Cold War relations between India and Russia and, thus, have indicated 'the revival of closer ties between two old friends, who had drifted apart' (Mishra 1996, 87). In this respect, the meetings between Rao and Yeltsin has both 'marked a breakthrough in the Indo-Russian relations' (Sharma 1997, 68) and has led them to 'assume a realistic character' (Jha 1997, 93).

Indian commentators have noted that the 1993 change in bilateral relations has resulted from Moscow's *rediscovery* of 'its old friends in Asia, such as India' after the disillusionment with Russia's pro-Western foreign policy idealism (Jain 2008, 113). Observers in the subcontinent have rejoiced that 'the "infantile pro-Americanism" which persisted as a predominant strain in Moscow's foreign policy is gradually giving way to a great diversification by upgrading relations with countries like India to a strategic level' (Kaushik 1997, 55). This shift in Moscow's foreign policy has been explained 'both' as a result of 'differing geopolitical perspectives' and an unbridgeable 'civilizational divide' between Russia and the West (Joshi 2007a, 151). Moreover, the narratives of the 'Look North' policy have ascertained that the 'realization of the limits of Russia's integration into the Western political economy and security system, and the rising economic and military profile of many Asian states has once again revived the debate on Russia's Eurasian identity' (Pandey 2007, 334). Consequently, as 'the Euro-centric drive in Russia's foreign policy started to lose its momentum [and] after its disappointment with Western policy and attitudes grew stronger, Russia began to look for partners in Asia' (Jha 1997, 79). However, the perception that India has been the second (if not third) best option for Moscow's foreign policy making did not seem to dampen the enthusiastic assessments of Indian observers that Yeltsin's and Rao's high level dialogue during 1993-1994 has confirmed the 'patterns of stability' which characterize the relations between the two states (Mishra 1996, 87).

Nevertheless, there was (at least) one issue, which has continued to 'vex' the rejuvination of Indo-Russian relations during this period—the 'rupee-ruble imbroglio' (Mehrotra 1997, 102). The 'problem' has arisen, first, from Russia's increasing reluctance to trade with India on the basis of the 'rupee-payment system' (Jayawar-dena 1993) and, second, from the 'utilization of the [existing] rupee reserves of Russia in India' (Kaushik 1997, 54). According to Rajan Mishra (1996, 88) the way in which Moscow has imposed its decision to auction a portion of the 'rupee debt' to Russian bidders in order 'to enable them to make commodity imports from India' has been both 'disturbing' and an indication that relations between the two countries 'have not returned to an absolutely even keel'. Thus, J.A. Naik has asserted that the rupee-ruble exchange issue was not merely an 'irritant' of bilateral relations, but that it

> should go down in [the history of] Indo-Russian relations as an instance of the ruthlessly exploitative Russian nature on matters concerning money and the poor negotiating skills of successive Indian rulers... The original amount [of the debt] was entered into Indian account books in [Soviet] rubles, but the repayment was done in its equivalent of Indian rupees through the export of goods from India. The exchange rate between rupee and ruble went on fluctuating and it is this

exchange rate that the Russians have all along manipulated to their advantage. The [Indian] debt is always mentioned in the rupee figure, which was always subjected to an inflated exchange rate. Thus [it is difficult to] know how much was the original loan in Russian rubles, how much was returned through the export of goods, and how much remains as an outstanding amount. One gets the impression that despite the repayment of the loan over the years, the loan amount goes on increasing because of the ruble's artificially manipulated exchange rate [which] benefits the Russians enormously in this transaction. (1995, 183–184)

In spite of the bitter aftertaste from the settlement of the rupee-ruble exchange issue, it seems that the strength of 'the positive images [that India and Russia have] of each other' has helped facilitate the rejuvination of their dialogue since 1993 (Jain 2008, 129). Acknowledging the dynamics of mythmaking, Mishra (1996, 90) has discerned that 'relations between India and Russia, and their friendship, have become part of the educational and emotional consciousness of a generation of Indians'. From this discursive point of view, it takes more than an economic issue to derail the ties between the two countries. Some have even noted that 'the imperatives of Indo-Russian friendship and cooperation [have] endured [because] they cut across political divisions and remain unaffected by the political fortunes of the ruling parties in the two countries' (Jha 1997, 83–84). In this context, the Moscow Declara-tion signed by Rao and Yeltsin in July 1994 has been praised for raising the relationship 'to a strategic long-term level' (Kaushik 1997, 55) and has been commended as an 'exercise in pragmatism, free from sentiment and ideological overtones' (Mishra 1996, 93). According to P.L. Dash (2007, 474) this document demonstrates that 'from the profligate state of subdued inactiveness [Indo-Russian interactions] have bounced back to the level of partnership that is poised to take wings into the future'. Thus, the 1994 Moscow Declaration has been interpreted as 'a clear indication of the growing mutual understanding between the two countries' (Sharma 1997, 69). It has stressed that 'the fight against terrorism' and 'the respect for the territorial integrity and pluralistic character of multiethnic states like Russia and India' are the cornerstones of the renewed dialogue between Moscow and New Delhi (Naik 1995, 187). Thus, both India and

Russia have declared 'their resolve to guard themselves against attempts to redefine norms of self-determination and sovereignty', and, at the same time, have also agreed 'to exchange experience of nation-building in plural states' (Mishra 1996, 87-91).

The Beginning of a Strategic Partnership

As was indicated above, the re-launching of the Indo-Russian bilateral dialogue during 1993–1994 has been commended for 'laying the foundation for a better strategic understanding' between the two countries, premised on a shared perception of 'pragmatic geopolitics' (Jain 2008, 109–114). From New Delhi's standpoint, the restored 'Indo-Russian relationship has to be based primarily on common business interests and balance of power' (Jha 1997, 77). The dialogue on these 'strategic commonalities' has indicated a 'sharp contrast' with the Cold War patterns of cooperation which were 'high on symbolism [but] short on specifics' (Mishra 1996, 88-94). Such a pragmatism has seemed to inform Moscow's reaction to India's 1998 nuclear weapons tests—it 'neither strongly condemned [them], nor imposed sanctions against New Delhi' (Jain 2008, 122). However, despite the significant revitalization of bilateral relations since 1993, Indian commentators detect a qualitative change of bilateral relations as a result of Vladimir Putin's ascendance to the Russian presidency. The changing of the guard in the Kremlin and its impact on Moscow's international identity has tended to confirm Indian projections that 'Russia is bound to regain its stature as a powerful player in international politics' (Sharma 1997, 71).

For instance, Jain (2008, 116) has commented that Putin's foreign policy has taken the 'Indo-Russian political and defense cooperation back to the stage of the good old special relationship between the two countries'. In fact, many have observed that 'Putin's eastern policy [is] far more complex and extensive than anything mounted by Yeltsin' (Black 2004, 71). Therefore, most commentators have welcomed the signing of a Declaration on a Strategic Partnership between India and Russia during President Putin's visit in December 2000. According to Dash (2007, 477), it 'has elevated political relations [between the two countries] to a higher plateau than ever before [and] has enhanced the possibilities for tapping the huge potentials that exist in both countries'. This declaration has thereby asserted the 'firm footing [of] India's ties with Russia' (Joshi 2002). The proclamation of a strategic partnership has asserted that India and Russia are 'natural partners and allies' in the creation of a multipolar world, which 'have no direct conflict of interest' (Jain 2008, 120–128).

Paradoxically, however, it seems that 'Moscow and New Delhi were [once again] thrown together by Washington, whose bellicose attitude towards Iraq and Iran worried India as much as it did Russia' (Black 2004, 318). In fact, some Indian commentators have long insisted that 'Asian countries together with Russia need to be united [against] and vigilant with the United States' (Chopra 1997a, 23). According to them, 'it was bad enough to live in a bipolar world, but a unipolar world, with the USA dominating and dictating to the rest of the world [is] even worse' (Kaul 1997, 41). The contention therefore is that 'the Indo-Russian strategic moves are aimed at countering the negative fallout of the deepening US military presence in Central Asia' (Jain 2008, 209). As would be explained shortly 'an essential ingredient [of the strategic partnership] has been the desire to checkmate the growing US presence around the two countries, especially in Central Asia' (Dash 2007, 477). In this context, the 'strategic' nature of the Indo-Russian partnership tends to be confirmed by New Delhi's increasing appetite for Russian weapon systems (Naik 1995, 180). Moscow's offer 'to sell sophisticated military hardware' to India has revealed that 'Russia's relations with New Delhi are acquiring a truly *strategic character*' (Kaushik 1997, 55; emphasis added). Thus, as 'Russia and India [are drawing] closer than ever before, the arms deals [between them] keep piling up' (Black 2004, 318; Bakshi 2006; Nayar and Paul 2003, 51; Pandit 2001).[4] According to Mishra (1996, 90), the growing arms trade between the two countries reflects not only the accrual of economic and defence benefits, but also (and mostly) India's and Russia's shared security concerns as two of 'the largest multi-ethnic, multi-lingual, and multi-religious states [in the world]'.

The overall traction of such a positive assessments seems to be confirmed both by the 'increasing frequency' with which Indian and Russian 'officials passed each in the air between New Delhi and Moscow' since 2000 and by Russia's 'extraordinary commitment' to 'support India "unconditionally" in the case of conflict' (Black 2004, 317–318). The latter, in particular, reinforces President Yeltsin's 1996 commitment that Russia 'will not enter into an arms supply relationship with any country inimical to India' (Mehrotra 1997, 109). At the same time, it needs to be pointed out that the logic of mythmaking informing India's post-1998 external relations (which was outlined in Chapter 3), places the discursive requirement for New Delhi's ongoing procurement and upgrading of its weapon systems in order to buttress the validity of India's assertive stance.

Encountering Russia in Central Asia

So far, this chapter has established that it was the simultaneity of perspectives which has tended to bring Moscow and New Delhi closer together both during and after the Cold War. The investigation now turns to Indian interpretations of Russia's engagement with Central Asia. It is noteworthy, that a number of commentators place the origin of the bilateral Indo-Russian relations in the region. For instance, V.D. Chopra (1997b, 128–141) has insisted that owing to their interaction with 'the Central Asian region, relations between India and Russia can be traced back for thousands of years. [Thus], it was on this edifice that cultural, economic, and political relations between India and Russia have been shaping'. In this respect, similar to the interpretation of their bilateral relations, India's perception of Russia's external relations with Central Asia have tended to be framed by the narratives of past experience.

At the same time, however, unlike their bilateral relations (which seem to be treated as a linear progression of increasingly close viewpoints), the Indo-Russian interactions in the region of Central Asia have also illustrated the emerging dissociation between New Delhi's and Moscow's external affairs strategies. Although contradictory, these trends are not mutually exclusive and offer a glimpse into the growing complexity of international life (Kavalski 2007a). The bifurcation of a state's foreign policy making between conflict and cooperation in relation to another international actor are merely simplified and generalizable models for rendering the external affairs of states more tractable. In practice, however, foreign policy making is a composite process comprising elements from both these alternatives. Prior to detailing the *convergence* and *divergence* in perspectives between India and Russia in Central Asia, the following subsection briefly outlines the context of Moscow's post-Cold War involvement in the region.

Russia's Post-Soviet Foreign Policy towards Central Asia

For the purposes of brevity (and, also, because Russia's external relations are not the main subject of this investigation) the following account offers only an overview of Moscow's agency in the region since 1991. It has been pointed out that Moscow's engagement of Central Asia reflects not only the thorny history of their interactions, but also the complexity of Russia's geography and demography—that is, while 'eighty-five percent of the Russian Federation can be said to lie in the East, eighty-five percent of its population lives in the West' (Black 2004, 275). Recognizing that 'geography [has] bestowed upon Russia the position of primacy in Central Asia', Indian commentators observe that 'it is not an easy job to eliminate Russian influence and its role in Central Asia'—in other words, 'Russia is thickly woven into the very fabric of [the] Central Asian psyche and way of living and thinking. Owing to its size, manpower, technological know-how, superior military power, and, above all, having perfect knowledge of the region and its people, Russia is well-positioned [to] protect the region against external encroachments' (Asopa 2007, 175–185). In other words, Moscow 'cannot just pack up and depart' from the region, because it has become 'a natural part of it' (Kaushik 2007b, 282). This is what makes it '*the* key player in the Central Asian republics' (Chenoy 2008, 52; emphasis added). Russia's territorial expansion into Central Asia has therefore been interpreted as 'a policy to secure long term resources for Russia' and also as 'a retreat to a more secure perimeter at a time when its influence in Europe was blocked' (Jonson 2004, 9). For Indian commentators, this has been a 'clear indication that Russia is determined to protect its historic, political, and strategic interests in the Central Asian republics' (Bal 2004, 309). After the dissolution of the Soviet Union, 'socialist ideology became irrelevant to Russian foreign policy [and] it was replaced by the [pursuit of] the national interest' (Gidadhubli 2007, 197).

In this respect, Parviz Mullanov has identified three main stages in Kremlin's post-Soviet Central Asian strategy: (i) 'democratic consolidation'—a period (starting with the collapse of the Soviet Union and continued until the end of 1992) during which Russia's foreign policy attention was directed towards the West and away from the former Soviet republics, which made Moscow's Central Asian policy 'uncertain, with different agencies and institutions holding conflicting points of view with regard to local issues'; (ii) 'return to geopolitics'—a period (stretching from 1993 to 1999) during which the main task of Russian foreign policy in Central Asia has been 'to ensure that local republics remain within its zone of influence and that 'governments in the region have a pro-Russian bias'; (iii) reinvigorated 'pragmatism'—a period (beginning with Putin's ascendance to the Russian presidency in 1999) during which Moscow's international agency in Central Asia has been 'shorn of any ideological pretensions' and subjected to the rules of commercial profit to the effect that 'basic norms and values [have been] disregarded for the sake of economic and political benefits' (Mullojanov 2008, 121–128).

Thus, for the better part of the 1990s, Russia pursued a policy in Central Asia 'which was very different from its policy in Europe'—i.e. Moscow did not allow international actors and organizations to participate in conflict management activities in the region and, instead, assumed for itself the roles of 'a security guarantor' and 'a leader with regard to economic cooperation' (Jonson 2004, 9). Also, owing to the 'intricate webs' of Russian print and electronic media, 'the Central Asian populations, no matter their ethnic origins, are grounded in a Russian interpretation of events' (Black 2004, 296). Some have even claimed that 'you can take the [Central Asian] Republics away from Russia, but you can't get Russia out of the Republics' (Dietl 1997, 128). Yet, until Putin's arrival to the Kremlin, Moscow's regional policy lacked focus and, in fact, oftentimes tended to be *ad hoc*. In fact, Indian commentators have asserted that prior to 'Vladimir Putin's leadership', Russia's diplomacy in Central Asia lacked any 'sense of direction' (Bhadrakumar 2008). According to Lena Jonson the policy change associated with Putin reflects: (i) the way Central Asian problems began to be defined—in terms of their security, strategic, and economic dimensions; (ii) the means by which Russia has responded to developments in Central Asia—by emphasizing not only the 'military-political instruments', but also (and increasingly) 'the economic and diplomatic levers of foreign policy'; (iii) the overall orientation of Russian external affairs—in particular, the centrality of Kremlin's assessment of other actors involved in Central Asia and whether Moscow would be willing to accept or counter their influence in Central Asia. In this respect, Jonson argues that a mixture of *external factors* (such as the international perception of Moscow's anemic agency in Central Asia at the end of the 1990s has compelled Putin to adopt a more forceful stance to the region), *internal factors* (such as the domestic perception that Russia's great power status in Central Asia has not been recognized, which provided the facilitating environment for 'consensus and unity' to be built around Kremlins assertive strategy), and *historical and cultural factors* (such as the impact of past experience on Moscow's preparedness both to commit foreign policy resources to Central Asia and to maintain long-term interest in the region) have contributed to Moscow's engagement in Central Asia in the post-1999 period (Jonson 2004, 10–15).

At the same time, J.L. Black (2004, 276–279) insists that with Putin's ascendance to the Russian presidency, 'the "struggle against fundamentalism and international terrorism" [have] become [the] buzzwords for Moscow's drive to consolidate its position in Central Asia' (such discursive articulations have assisted the establishment of a Central Asian Economic Community, Eurasian Economic Com-munity, etc.). In this respect, it could be argued that since the disintegration of the Soviet Union 'both security and economic considerations have driven Russia's policy towards Central Asia. While the former essentially puts Russia on the defensive, the latter presents it with new opportunities' (Trenin 2003, 128). Indian commentators have also acknowledged these patterns and their analyses of Russian interests in the region have tended to vacillate between those who support the projection of its 'enlightened self-interest' (Bhambhri 2005, 388; Singh and Krassiltchikov 2003) and those who are critical of Moscow's selfish desire to 'regain its great power status' (Gidadhubli 2003, 193). At the same time, as discussed in Chapter 4, there is a distinct belief that the problems, challenges, and unpredictability accompanying the trajectories of post-Soviet statehood in Central Asia are the direct result of an '*independence* [...] forced upon [regional states] by a Russia struggling to create its own national identity' (Dutta 2003, 162–163; emphasis added). With these perceptions in mind, the following sections detail the patterns of convergence and divergence in India's encounter of Russia in Central Asia.

Indo-Russian Convergence in Central Asia

T.N. Kaul (1997, 42) has pointed out that 'there is no basic conflict of national interests between India and Russia or [between] India and [the member states of] the Commonwealth of Independent States (CIS); on the contrary, there is much that draws them closer in the political, economic, and strategic spheres'. Such a commonality of interests underpins the convergence between New Delhi's and Moscow's positions in Central Asia. Some have even claimed that the 'convergence of Russian and Indian geopolitical interests in the peace and security of the Central Asian region [is] historical' (Kaushik 1997, 52). In this respect, B.M. Jain indicates that the legacy of the Soviet occupation of Afghanistan continues to structure Indo-Russian relations in the region. He, therefore, argues that President Putin's reassignment of 'strategic priorities' to India reflects Moscow's concern over Pakistan's 'close ties with the Central Asian republics' (Jain 2008, 119–125). The contention is that Islamabad's support for the 'rise of Muslim fundamentalism in Central Asia has a direct bearing on the unity and security of Russia' (Chopra 1997a, 26). Thus, 'the common threat posed by Islamic fundamentalism to their territorial integrity [has] called for active strategic cooperation between India and Russia' (Kaushik 1997, 53).

Some of the proponents of the 'Look North' policy have thereby ascertained 'the deep interest' of New Delhi and Moscow to promote 'peace and stability in the area between the borders of the Republic of India and the Russian Federation—[which] is clearly aimed at the Central Asian states of the CIS, including Tajikistan' (Mishra 1996, 92). Likewise, Shashi Kant Jha (1997, 83) has declared that 'Russia and India share an interest in stabilizing the situation in the interconnected regions of Afghanistan and Central Asia'. Such an 'equal concern for peace in the region' and opposition to 'international terrorism' impels both New Delhi and Moscow to 'support each other' (Asopa 2007, 187). In this respect, R.R. Sharma (1997, 72) has argued that the 'strategic partnership' between New Delhi and Moscow *serves* India's deep strategic interests in Central Asia. Such a convergence of perspectives in their cooperation in the region has long been framed by a desire to 'moderate resurgent fundamentalist challenges, which could threaten the secular identity and territorial identity of both states' (Jha 1997, 83). Consequently, O.H. Mehrotra (1997, 106) has even contended that 'Russia has expressed its willingness to launch a joint war with India against fundamentalist-religious and other ethnic movements'.

Thus, Indian commentators have noted that 'Russia appears to [have grown] quite aware of the common Indo-Russian geopolitical interests' in contrast with the 'infantile view' of Moscow's external relations in the early 1990s which neglected 'the threat from Islamic resurgence in Central Asia' (Sharma 1997, 67–70). Therefore, the provision of security to the region under Russian auspices has been deemed 'compatible with Indian interest' (Joshi 2007b, 443). At the same time, some observers have insisted that because of 'the commonality of interests which underpins their strategic alliance', Moscow has begun to act 'as a facilitator' for New Delhi's agency in Central Asia, because 'Russia would like India to become a big player in the region as a balancing factor for both American and Chinese presence' (Jain 2008, 214–215).[5] Furthermore, as Chapter 4 demonstrates, the narratives of the 'Look North' policy recognize that in Central Asia 'India finds itself competing not so much with Pakistan as with the West and China. In this competition, it has turned to an old ally, Russia, which itself has a residual influence in many of the Central Asian states. [Thus] India and Russia are likely to continue cooperating on a range of policies, balancing Chinese influence in the region and also countering Islamic extremist elements' (Singh 2006, 174).

Indo-Russian Divergence in Central Asia

The previous section has outlined New Delhi's and Moscow's 'common geopolitical relationship with the landlocked Central Asia' (Kaushik 1997, 56). Yet, despite this overwhelming perception of converging Indian and Russian interests in the region, a number of differences have also emerged. On the one hand (as already explained), such a divergence has originated from India's sense of trauma (and betrayal) after Russia's disengagement from the subcontinent in the early 1990s, which had forced New Delhi to adjust to the Kremlin's uncertain foreign policy objectives. On the other hand, the disparity between India and Russia in Central Asia has reflected New Delhi's new sense of its international identity in the context of its post-1998 foreign policy strategy (outlined in Chapter 2). A significant part of this disaffection with Moscow derives from the pervasive uncertainty of its foreign policy stance. Such a context made it difficult for Indian commentators to read Russia's international intents and 'the nature of its relations with Central Asia'—namely, they found it difficult to distinguish 'whether it continues to remain the hegemonic power [in the region] or it becomes just another regional actor with its influence gradually declining' (Shams-ud-Din 1997, 340). Thus, their interactions in Central Asia have revealed that the Indo-Russian connection 'is today very different from what it was in the Cold War era. Russia's main value to India is *no longer strategic but straightforwardly material*—it remains India's major supplier of military equipment [nothing more and nothing less]' (Vanaik 2007, 398; emphasis added).

For instance, in his discussion of 'the "new big game" in Central Asia', Jain has concluded that 'Russia is a major loser in myriad ways—not only has its politico-strategic grip over the Central Asian republics become tenuous, it has [also] been deprived of absolute control over its natural resources'. He therefore queries 'How can Russia assist India in the region'—the implication being that Moscow might no longer have the ability to affect developments in Central Asia (Jain 2008, 208).[6] Moreover, the realization that 'Russia will remain a relatively minor power for sometime to come' (Rajagopalan 2005, 308) has convinced Indian observers that 'Russia is unable to play a decisive role in [the] furtherance and protection of its interests [in] Central Asia' (Joshi 2003, 3). Owing to a multiplicity of (mainly) 'economic compulsions, [Moscow] is unable to assert itself as in the past' (Bal 2004, 303).[7] In this respect, the perceived weakness of Moscow's foreign policy towards Central Asia has clashed with the assertiveness of New Delhi's post-1998 external relations. The narratives of the 'Look North' policy indicate that 'creating a strategic partnership with Russia [has], therefore, be[en] a low priority for New Delhi' (Gupta 2008, 118). In particular, the reification of its self-perception as 'the largest democracy in the world' has compelled New Delhi 'to handle some complications of dealing with its old partner Russia' (Rai and Simon 2007, 134). The authoritarian, strong-hand mentality of the Kremlin's decision-making, in particular, has been perceived as hindrance to the creation of 'a security order in Asia' because its initiation requires a 'move in the direction of substantial democratization' (Sharma 2004a, 263). As Bal (2004, 309–310) argues, Moscow's 'deep-rooted belief of great power visions in Central Asia' should cause concern in New Delhi. Thus, the *'New Eurasianism'* of the Kremlin is not aimed at 'the creation of an alternative Russian national identity in socio-cultural terms, or to portray any cultural or social affinity with Asia, but to justify Russia's continuing significance and role in Asia and ultimately to rationalize the reassertion of its status as one of the region's great powers' (Pandey 207, 332–334). Consequently, Russia's attitude, strategies, and practices in the region confirm the perception that 'no one would describe Moscow as being even remotely liberal' (Lak 2008, 266). Indian commentators have been especially critical of Russia's 'pressure on the [Central Asian] republics to keep the pipelines running through *its* territories and shipments from *its* parts' (Dietl 1997, 129; emphasis added).

At the same time, it has been claimed that Russia's 'loss of its [Central] Asian republics' has impacted on its 'foreign policy [making], including its policy towards India'—that is, 'by virtue of its possession of the [Central] Asian republics, Soviet Russia had come to the neighborhood of India. Now Russia is no longer in India's immediate neighborhood' (Naik 1995, vii, 187). Such an alteration has affected the 'geopolitical perceptions, compulsions, and objectives of Russia's international identity' (Bakshi 1999, 313). Thus, the diminishing geographic proximity between India and Russia in the post-Cold War period has been used as an explanation for the growing distance between their foreign policy standpoints, especially as they relate to Central Asia. The acknowledgement that Russia 'has fallen behind because of its internal problems and its inability to emerge as a proactive international actor in the post-Cold War international environment' has prompted the proponents of the 'Look North' policy to suggest that 'beyond oil and arms sales, India finds little common ground with Russia' (Gupta 2008, 117). The perception of strategic distance as well as the realization that 'oil and gas' are the only 'elements' driving Moscow's 'political and economic relations' in the region (Gidadhubli 2007, 162) have urged some analysts to exclude Russia from 'the list of key Asian states' because of its 'one-dimensional' foreign policy (Sahni 2005, 93).

More importantly, however, the interactions between India and Russia in Central Asia have indicated that 'what was once a bilateral relationship is apparently making accommodative gestures at trilateral, triangular, angular, and multilateral ties' (Dash 2007, 473). On the one hand, the point here is that the complexity of post-Cold War international relations has revealed that the interactions between states are never only bilateral, but instead involve their simultaneous engagement with multiple actors, at multiple fora, and at multiple levels. On the other hand, from an Indian point of view, Moscow's willingness to involve third parties (in particular, China) in its Central Asian interactions with New Delhi has become the ultimate confirmation that the days of the Soviet 'special relationship' are indeed finally over. Already, during his landmark visit in 1993, President Yeltsin had proposed the development of a 'strategic triangle' and an 'axis for peace' between Moscow, New Delhi, and Beijing for the purposes of 'staving off crises' in Asia—an idea, which has been espoused and further developed by his successor, Vladimir Putin (Asopa, 2006, 211; Black 2004, 297–300; Kaushik

1997, 54; Khanna 2003, 351). Some Indian commentators have noted that a 'strategic triangle' of Russia, India, and China seems 'a fitting response to the threats [emanating from] the region' (Asopa 2007, 185; Bal 2004, 316-319) and that 'it is possible and indeed probable that the economic, political, and strategic interest of India, China, and Russia are likely to result in closer cooperation to the advantage of each and the detriment of any' (Kaul 1997, 43).[8]

Yet, despite such proclamations that 'multilateralism is the best solution' (Baruah 2004), New Delhi has remained wary of Beijing's agency in Asia and its potential domineering position in the region (Kavalski 2007b).[9] Thus, it has been suggested that 'the idea of the strategic triangle need not be dumped as futile', but as a 'fallacy', because 'it is Russia which would gain the most [from it]' (Bhattacharya 2004, 358-360). In this respect, it is the perception of Moscow's strategic weakness that informs its alliance with Beijing— i.e. 'Russia has no other alternative but to continue to seek good neighborly relations with all because of its much reduced economic and military capabilities and geopolitical clout' (Bakshi 2002, 83). At the same time, India seems concerned that 'China will not make the political and military accommodations that would make India comfortable with China's rise to great power status' (Gupta 2008, 123). Consequently, the growing ties between Russia and China in Central Asia (especially in the context of the Shanghai Cooperation Organization) seem to convince Indian observers that (i) both Moscow and Beijing 'share a common security perception as well as have convergence on the concept of a multipolar world order based on sovereignty and non-interference in a country's internal affairs', and that (ii) 'China is a more fitting partner for Russia's multifaceted interests in Central Asia than India, which automatically creates a larger political space for the strategic partnership between Russia and China' (Jain 2008, 126–127; Bhattacharjea 2008, 12).[10] In particular, 'the sale of sophisticated defence equipments to China has generated concern [in New Delhi]' (Gidadhubli 2007, 206) and appears to confirm the perception that for Moscow 'the financial lure of Chinese [investments] will most likely override any [Russian] commitment to India' (Gupta 2008, 117). According to Pramit Pal Chaudhuri, 'the truth is that on almost every economic issue, China is far more useful to Russia than India'. In this respect, the interactions between New Delhi and Moscow in Central Asia have illustrated that 'the Putin doctrine has little or no place for India. It may one day, but for now India is really just a place to make a quick buck through arms sales' (Chaudhuri 2002).[11] In this context, '*the least likely of possibilities* is some kind of serious movement towards an informal Russia-China-India axis' (Vanaik 2007, 398; emphasis added).

At the same time, New Delhi's attempts to gain access to Central Asia's natural reserves have clashed with the Kremlin's energy policy in the region. For instance, despite occasional assertions that Moscow is '*helping* [Central Asian states] to export their oil and gas to international markets' (Asopa 2007, 175; emphasis added), more often than not observers have tended to criticize the Kremlin for its ongoing attempts to maintain the region's dependence on 'pipelines passing through Russia' (Gidadhubli 2007, 162–163). At the same time, proponents of the 'Look North' policy have indicated that Russia is once again (just like in the nineteenth century) involved in the 'new great game' simply as a way to divert the attention of other international actors from its main foreign policy interests and focus (Bal 2004, 18–19). Moscow's proclamations are thereby perceived by Indian commentators as selfish, disingenuous, and insensitive to Central Asian concerns. Thus, the resurgence of Russian involvement in Central Asia since the beginning of the 2000s reveals 'a deeply rooted belief [in its own] great power visions that have not been abandoned' (Bal 2004, 310). Thus, the patterns of divergence in India's encounter of Russia in Central Asia reveal that owing to the exigencies of domestic and global politics, there is very little degree of certainty regarding the future trajectories of New Delhi's and Moscow's interactions.

Conclusion

The chapter has revealed that the post-1998 operationalization of India's diplomatic relations has not managed to overcome the tension—to put it simplistically—between friend and foe in the perception of Russia's international outreach. Such an interpretation notwithstanding, it seems that the encounter with the Kremlin's agency in Central Asia indicates a tendency towards the developments of 'normalcy' in their bilateral relations. Thus, Indian acco-unts of New Delhi's interactions with Moscow in Central Asia reveal the understanding that 'the heyday of its "special relationship" with Russia is over', and, at the same time (almost despite this realization) indicate an 'optimism about their firm and durable relationship in the political and strategic fields as well as in trade and economy' (Jain 2008, 120).

It has to be remembered, however, that India's encounter with Russia in Central Asia reflects only one aspect of the discursive construction of the 'new great game'. The following Chapter 6 and Chapter 7 will, thereby, position the agency of China and the West in the narratives of the 'Look North' policy. At the same time, however, the analyses of their case studies unravel additional aspects of Moscow's agency in Central Asia which have remained occluded from the individual assessment of Russia's involvement in the region. Likewise, this chapter has indicated aspects of the agency of Beijing, Brussels and Washington which are not accounted for in Chapter 6 and Chapter 7, respectively. This observation attests to the networked complexity of the 'new great game' in Central Asia as well as the discursive multiplicity of the 'Look North' policy.

6

AN ELEPHANT IN A CHINA SHOP: INDIA'S SEARCH FOR PRAGMATIC RELATIONS WITH CHINA IN CENTRAL ASIA

Introduction

As has already been suggested in Chapter 4, the awareness of a nascent 'new great game' in Central Asia forms an important aspect of India's engagement with the region. At the same time, the narratives of New Delhi's external agency reflect the belief in the growing prominence of Asian countries in global politics. Thus, it seems only natural that the narrative constructions of the 'Look North' policy would bring about a consideration of India's relations with its 'significant other'—China. As one observer put it, neither country has 'the option of visualizing their [external affairs] profile by ignoring the other side' (Singh 2003, 313). As a result, 'no book on India's [foreign relations] would be complete without a comparison with China' (Kachru 2007, xxi).

Indian observers often remark that India and China are gradually becoming the 'fulcrum of Asia' (Joshi 2005, 103). In other words, the 'two nations are set to recapture the places that they held in the world a few centuries ago—as the major producers of goods and services, with China as the world's factory and India as its back-office' (Muni and Mohan 2005, 52). However, despite such proclamations of a shared division of labor between the two rising Asian powers, a number of Indian commentators point out—with a discernible degree of admiration and envy—that, in fact, 'China has become the second most important country in the world [after the

USA]' (Bhattacharjea 2008, 1). Others claim that 'China's growing acceptance as the next global power' only provokes 'New Delhi's discomfiture' and the 'growing disaffection among India's leaders' (Singh 2003, 323).

It is in the context of such a multiplicity of voices that this chapter embarks on an analysis of the Sino-Indian relationship in Central Asia as recounted by the narratives of the 'Look North' policy. Firstly, it demonstrates the ways in which the complex interdependence between the Sino-Indian boundary conflict and India's relations with Pakistan, Tibet, and Myanmar has famed the bilateral relations between New Delhi and Beijing. Secondly, this context offers a point of departure for engaging the discursive modalities of India's encounter with China in Central Asia. Such an emplotment informs the constructions of Beijing as a *partner* in, a *threat* to, and a *model* for the 'Look North' policy. Thirdly, this chapter concludes with a discussion of the tension between *civilizational* and *territorial* notions of statehood revealed by the narratives of New Delhi's interactions with Beijing in Central Asia.

India and China: Bilateral Interactions

For Indian commentators of the Sino-Indian interactions in Central Asia, the complicated history of bilateral relations between New Delhi and Beijing seems to form both the point of departure as well as the bulk of their investigations. Thus, the acknowledgement that the two countries 'are the most ancient and sophisticated Asian civilizations' forms the hackneyed foundation for such analyses (Arora 1997, 235; Sandhu 1988, 17). The recognition of such a long history of bilateral interactions is then quickly transformed into a rhetorical ploy for validating a particular reading of the relations between New Delhi and Beijing, which consequently provides the legitimizing ground for championing a particular foreign policy agenda. In this context, many commentators have ascertained that more than any other of India's international relations, New Delhi's engagement of China 'suffers from the burden of the past, [for] history is like a millstone around the necks of the living [as] it is not made in isolation from the memories of the past' (Mishra 1996, 172). Thus, the *making of the history* of bilateral relations appears to be structured by New Delhi's and Beijing's ongoing *'misperceptions in foreign policy making'* (Mansingh 2000, 159; emphasis original). In this respect, the end of the Cold War has been interpreted as an 'enormous opportunity' that could push Sino-Indian relations 'in the direction of a "productive partnership"', free from the '*historic baggage*' of the past (Jain 2008, 135; emphasis added). In particular, the dissolution of the Soviet Union, and 'the emergence of a unipolar situation' has introduced the facilitating conditions for 'forging closer relations' between New Delhi and Beijing (Mishra 1996, 165). Some observers have even contended that the current environment of world affairs has impressed upon China that New Delhi 'has a similar foreign policy [to its own], which again enhances the possibility for a potential China-India cooperative relations in many myriad spheres' (Prakash 1997, 169).

Thus, the complexity of interpreting their historical record underscores the difficulty of forcing 'Sino-Indian relations into a Manichean straitjacket of friendship and enmity' (Mattoo 2000, 14). The experience of the past, however, informs the spectrum of Indian perceptions of China (Hofmann 2004, 51). Such a range of interpretations attests to the position of China as one of the main actors on the stage of India's external affairs, both because it 'fascinates, intrigues, and challenges the intellectual imagination and traditional categories of analysis like few other states in the international system' (Mattoo 2000, 13), and because India has 'its longest land border with China, [Beijing] looms large on the security and geopolitical environment of India' (Dutta 1997, 152). In line with the self-aggrandizing modalities of India's post-1998 foreign policy mythmaking, the two-step of such a framing of China's international agency reflects New Delhi's assertive strategic beliefs:

> A crucial self-perception is that India is a state of major potential and future international importance. It possesses a great power's worldview, even if its role in international security affairs has been modest. India is entering a new phase in terms of its world role as its power-related resources increase. India is surely a rising power and should already be entitled to a major power's international prominence. Resistance by the top-tier, nuclear-have nations of the world (China among them) to greater acceptance of India, both as a major state and as a legitimate nuclear weapons state, must be addressed actively via Indian diplomacy. (Hoffmann 2004, 33)

It is noteworthy that most Indian observers recognize that while 'in Indian eyes, the long-term Chinese threat is the most serious that India faces, for China the magnitude from the threat of India is relatively smaller' (Ganguly 2004, 104). Some have even pointed out that 'it does not take an expert on China to know that *India has never figured in China's threat cosmology in any serious fashion*' (Bajpai 1999, 157; emphasis added). Parallel assessments of the 'current strategic compulsions of both countries' tend to acknowledge that 'China remains relatively higher on India's list of foreign policy priorities compared to India's place in China's list of priorities' (Singh 2003, 158). Confirming the significance of the discursive study of international affairs, many observers emphasize the role of foreign policy rhetoric on the patterns of relations between New Delhi and Beijing—i.e. their dealings occasionally '"create a positive atmosphere" or "climate" that is "conducive to better relations" and that at other times will be employed to "cover up deeper tensions"' (Hoffmann 2004, 62). Thus, the competitiveness that seems to underpin the interpretations of Sino-Indian relations has been conditioned by their discursive framing (Clad 2004, 267). Some have even claimed that China and India appeared destined for rivalry 'from the moment of their creation as modern states' (Tellis 2004, 134). In other words, 'China should be India's primary long-term concern' because of 'the nature of the international power structure' and 'China's strategic culture'—both of which 'make India vulnerable to China' (Rajagopalan 2005, 306–307). Other commentators have proffered that the persistence of confrontational bilateral relations owes much to the *lack of consensus* on 'the "end" objectives' of New Delhi's engagement with Beijing (Srivastava 2000, 229), which underscores 'the stark debility of India's negotiating capabilities vis-à-vis China' (Ganguly 2004, 122).

In this respect, Sumit Ganguly (2004, 104–105) has asserted that 'finding the tensions in the Sino-Indian relationship does not require much researching'—that is, the 'discord between India and China is so deep-seated, and the memory of the 1962 war between the two so searing on the Indian side, that any dramatic improvement in the bilateral relationship is unlikely'. Provoked by a border dispute, the 1962 Sino-Indian war has preconditioned the framing of a set of intertwined and mutually-reinforcing issues—encompassing China's support for Pakistan and Myanmar, and India's hosting of the Tibet émigré community (Jain 2008, 135; Mattoo

2000, 23–24; Mishra 1996, 170)—that continue to plague bilateral relations. This list of issues strengthens Indian perceptions of Beijing's deceptiveness—i.e. 'while China professes a policy of peace and friendliness towards India, its deeds are clearly aimed at the strategic encirclement of India in order to marginalize India in Asia and tie it down to the Indian sub-continent' (Colonel Gurmeet Kanwal quoted in Tellis 2004, 138). Thus, the complex interdependence between the Sino-Indian boundary conflict and India's relations with Pakistan, Tibet, and Myanmar has structured the security environment of the bilateral relations between New Delhi and Beijing (Hoffmann 2004, 38). It also frames India's perceptions of China's Central Asian agency.

Border Conflict
As suggested, the demarcation of their joint boundary is the hub of New Delhi's and Beijing's confrontation.[1] The already well-over half-a-century long contestation has tended to unite Indian commentators around the conclusion that either 'a settlement of the border question still appears illusory' (Ganguly 2004, 124), or that the 'search for a resolution of the border issue appears to be elusive' (Kondapalli 2007, 414), or that the 'boundary dispute is likely to be prolonged indefinitely' (Jain 2008, 142). The main areas of contestation are Aksai Chin and Arunchal Pradesh (formerly known as the North East Frontier Agency). According to Indian observers, the crux of the dispute rests with the perspectives that dominated New Delhi's and Beijing's state-building strategies in the late 1940s, and in particular the views held by Jawaharlal Nehru and Mao Zedong (Sali 1998). For instance, while Nehru accepted the boundaries of British India as the legitimate ramifications of India's independent statehood, Mao viewed them as a colonial anachronism which required revolutionary rectification. In this respect, Steven Hoffmann (2004, 37) has demonstrated that Nehru's personal conviction that India possesses '"historical" borders' as opposed to (merely) '"British" [colonial] borders' became a central ingredient of the border dispute between the two countries.

Thus, 'the exploitation and domination by the imperialist and colonial powers that India and China experienced and their successful struggles against them, did not however bring them together' (Acharya 2000, 171). Sumit Ganguly has indicated that the divergence of perceptions reflects different interpretations of the post-colonial condition which informed 'Nehru's uncritical acceptance of inherited colonial borders' and Mao's drive to recover 'territory "lost" to Western colonizers'. Thus, India's willingness to subscribe to the rules, norms, and obligations that underpin the 'legislative worldview' of Western notions of statehood and international society, 'propelled the two countries down a path of confrontation' as China's position 'was largely shaped by considerations of power as well as notions of historical grievance', which questioned the legitimacy of Western notions of international order (Ganguly 2004, 105–111).[2] Such a divergence of opinions between New Delhi and Beijing at the time did not seem to permit a peaceful resolution of their border dispute and led to the 1962 war between them,[lxxii] which, in turn, has further solidified the intractability of New Delhi's and Beijing's position. Currently, New Delhi calls for 'finding a "pragmatic" solution' to the border dispute, while Beijing hopes for 'arriving at a "just" solution' (Kondapalli 2007, 415)—statements, which further reinforce the importance of discursive analyses of foreign policy making.[3]

The Pakistan Divide
Pakistan has become a factor in the relations between China and India only after the 1962 war and has been further framed by the deepening bipolarity of the Cold War world. As explained in Chapter 5, the increasingly pro-Soviet tilt of New Delhi's nonalignment was paralleled by Beijing's growing distance from Moscow. In fact, some Indian commentators explain India's closeness with the Soviet Union in the lessons that its leadership drew after 1962 (Ganguly 2004, 115). Thus, from an Indian point of view, the 'Sino-Pakistani nexus [is] aimed at India [and] arises from the need to counter Indian dominance on the subcontinent' (Chandi 2000b, 301).[4] In the wake of the 1962 Sino-Indian war, Beijing and Islamabad initiated talks on their common border, including the Pakistan-occupied territories of Kashmir. As Sumit Ganguly (2004, 118) has reminded 'interestingly enough, the settlement was announced on 2 March 1963, literally hours before Indo-Pakistani talks over Kashmir were about to begin'. The provocative nature of such an agreement aside, it demonstrated that New Delhi and Beijing have become 'not so friendly friends' (Deshpande 1985, 74). Since then, Pakistan has remained another dividing issue on the platter of Sino-Indian relations.[5]

Such a relationship has been reaffirmed by the Chinese military support to Pakistan. From 'India's perspective Beijing's arms transfers in the region are not always peaceful, commercial exercises, but they have a significant politico-military impact on its security environment' (Dutta 1997, 161). The Chinese 'military and strategic investments' in Pakistan have not only 'emboldened Islamabad to wage a "proxy war" in Kashmir without fear of Indian retaliation', but have also initiated 'an environment of "competitive psychology" among the ruling elites of India and Pakistan':

> First, it has prompted India indigenously to build new weapons systems as well as to procure sophisticated weaponry from diverse sources. Second, it has emboldened Pakistan psychologically to not only continue a proxy war in Kashmir, but also has hardened their attitude and approach to resolving outstanding disputes with India. (Jain 2008, 146)

In particular, the allegations of Chinese support for Pakistan's nuclear program tend to fuel India's anxiety and discontent. One commentator has pointed out that 'the true extent of Beijing-Islamabad nuclear collusion may never be revealed, but it is clear that Pakistan's nuclear weapons program has relied enormously on China's help, and Chinese nuclear engineers may even have designed Islamabad's nuclear weapons' (Mattoo 2000, 23). Indian commentators have therefore never taken seriously, the assertions of 'China's "peaceful nuclear cooperation" with Pakistan' (Kumar 2000, 152). Instead, Beijing's 'involvement in Islamabad's missile and nuclear programs are [treated as] serious issues for regional stability [which] compromise the global efforts at non-proliferation of weapons of mass destruction [...] India has lived with the reality of Chinese weapons increasingly being ever wary of its negative military-security, political, and diplomatic implications for the country. [Thus] the deep and ongoing collaboration between China and Pakistan *has made a mockery* of China's adherence to the Nuclear Non-Proliferation Treaty (NPT) and the Missile Technology Control Regime (MTCR). *Such a reality* cannot be wished away as it certainly *has the most direct implication for India's nuclear and missile policy*' (Dutta 1997, 161–163; emphasis added).[6] Such an effect on Indian sensibilities underpins the assertion that China's assistance to Pakistan's development of nuclear and missile technology to the extent of 'being Pakistan's biggest supplier of conventional military weapons is an obstacle to building trust between the PRC and India (Ranganathan 2002, 294). Thus, although 'India's relations with China [have been] improving, owing to historical factors, China's relations with Pakistan are friendlier' (Mishra 1996, 162). Such attitudes notwithstanding, Indian commentators have pointed out that from the mid-1990s onward China has gradually renounced its support for 'anti-India elements' in South Asia (Singh 2003, 127; Mansingh 1994, 289). In particular, Beijing's endeavor to be seen as a 'responsible power' has tended to 'moderate, if not end its proliferation activities' (Joshi 2005, 106). Thus, it has been argued that Pakistan's failure 'to curb the activities of Islamic fundamentalists who have been involved in [stirring] ethnic problems in China's Xinjiang province [has] earned [Islamabad] China's ire' and has also severely 'constrained what had once been China's flourishing "special relationship" with Pakistan' (Singh 2003, 203–345).

The Tibet Conflict
Tibet's arrival into the strategic calculus of Sino-Indian relations is closely intertwined with the border dispute between them. Although India (somewhat reticently) has accepted the Chinese takeover of Tibet, this does not mean that Indian commentators subscribe to Beijing's claim on the region (Addy 1984; Gopal 1964; Sharan 1996; Sharma 1988). On the contrary, there seems to be near unanimity that 'the Communist takeover of Tibet is strategic rather than historical. Historically, Tibet's relations with China in terms of the tribute-paying system were not much different from Korea's or Vietnam's. In other words, if we continue to believe in the Chinese historical claims over Tibet, we have to explain why other similar dependencies like Korea, Burma, or Vietnam were not "liberated" on the same historical ground' (Norbu 2000, 279). The contention is that Beijing's claims have achieved some traction owing to the nature of its relations with the region—for instance, while 'India's links with Tibet had existed since ancient times, these contacts have remained confined to culture and commerce', 'China's contacts were never as ancient as that [of India], yet they had been predominantly territorial, administrative, militaristic, and political in their nature with culture and commerce staying at the margins' (Singh 2003, 43; Arpi 2007, 91). These observations reflect not only suspicion about the accuracy and validity of Chinese

claims, but also the understanding that Beijing's claims to Indian territory are based 'on the assumption that in the past [the contested regions] had been conquered and ruled by Tibet' (Prakash 1997, 183). Beijing has also 'argued that local Tibetan authorities had no legal right to conclude any border treaty with the British' (Jain 2008, 137; Lal 1998, 449).

The issue of Tibet became a crucial ingredient in the concoction of contingencies that led to the 1962 Sino-Indian war. The shelter provided to the Dalai Lama after the 1954 revolt seems to have fortified Beijing's suspicions of New Delhi's collaboration with the insurgents.[7] In the subsequent decades India both provided shelter to the Tibetan émigré community and, at the same time, attempted to distance itself from collusion with calls (and activities) for overturning Chinese rule. The end of the Cold War, however, 'has particularly weakened India's ability to sustain an ambiguous Tibet policy' (Stobdan 2007, 421). Nevertheless, Indian observers assert that 'the seeming lack of interest that New Delhi now shows in the Tibetan question should not be misunderstood as a lack of strategic appreciation of Tibet; it is more a diplomatic posture of accepting the Chinese reality in Tibet in the face of Chinese military might' (Norbu 2000, 275). Thus, some Indian commentators have been concerned by 'the growing takeover of Indian monasteries by Tibetan Lamas—a fact that may later help the Chinese to strengthen their claims [to Indian territory] and assist with [their] consolidation efforts in the Indian Himalayan belt' (Stobdan 2007, 422). In this setting, although Tibet is gradually becoming a 'factor on the decline' in relations between New Delhi and Beijing, Indian commentators insist that 'Tibet's Indian connection continues to haunt [Chinese] imaginations' (Singh 2003, 147–365).

The Myanmar Hurdle
The emergence of Myanmar as an obstacle to Sino-Indian relations is of fairly recent provenance and does not seem to be directly related to the border dispute between the two countries. Only occasionally, some commentators would remind that 'a 128-kilometer stretch' of the border between India and Myanmar still remains undemarcated owing to its entanglement in 'the Indo-China boundary dispute' (Pillai 2003, 258; Kapur 1997, 88; Devare 2006, 179). Many, however, point out that 'India shares a 1,643-kilometer [long] border with Myanmar' and the 'the boundary dispute [is] very

minor as only nine border pillars [are] points of contention' (*Times of India* 2006; Banerjee 1997). India's foreign policy attention to Myanmar has intensified in the post-Cold War period, especially in the context of New Delhi's 'Look East' policy.

Indian concerns have been provoked by the growing economic and (mostly) military ties between China and Myanmar. For instance, the report of the 'construction of a Chinese naval facility on the Coco Island' (Mattoo 2000, 23; Ganguly 2004, 23) appears to confirm New Delhi's suspicion that Beijing is bent on the strategic encirclement of India in order to constrain its rise as an Asian and global power. In particular, Indian defence planners seem anxious that 'the leverage and influence that China has with the regime in Myanmar' would allow it to gain unchallenged access to the Indian Ocean and a strategic foothold to keep an eye on India's missile testing in the Bay of Bengal as well as to monitor Indian naval communications' (Chandi 2000a, 98–99). Vinod Khanna, however, has argued that commentators 'should not exaggerate the security threat to India from the Sino-Myanmar military links'. He contends that the anxiety caused by China's assistance is premised on a decontextualised interpretation of its Southeast Asian policy. Khanna insists that if 'Myanmar [is] leaning towards China, this is primarily because other countries, including India [have] inhibitions in dealing with the Burmese military junta. [Thus], China [has been] the only source of military and political support' (Khanna 2008, 89).

Therefore, 'symbolic of the pragmatism of India's [post-1998] foreign policy', New Delhi has been increasing its interaction with the military junta in Myanmar—in November 2004, Myanmar's head of state visited New Delhi and in 2006, the President A.P.J. Abdul Kalam became the first Indian head of state to visit Myanmar (Jain 2008, 38). On the background of this renewed political dialogue, India has supported the construction and maintenance of several infrastructure projects (Allison 2001). These have also paved the way for enhanced military-to-military cooperation, which has led to regular meetings between the chiefs and the general staff of the two countries, as well as regularized joint exercises. Indian commentators have been eager to note that 'true to the assurances of General Than Shwe [Myanmar's head of state] during his visit to India in October 2004, the Myanmar Army has conducted operations against Indian insurgents operating on its territory' (Kuppuswamy 2006).

The complex interaction between those four sets of dilemmas—the border dispute, the Pakistan divide, Tibet, and the Myanmar hurdle—and their contextualization within the broader palette of bilateral relations delineates the different stages in the relations between New Delhi and Beijing.[8] The following sections outline those stages in order to offer a better sense of the context of India's encounter of China in Central Asia.

1949–1962: Ambivalent Neighbors

This period is framed by the modern establishment of both countries in the post-World War II period and the formative experience of the 1962 Sino-Indian war. Most Indian commentators assert that there have been few indicators that might have suggested such a violent rupture in bilateral relations. In fact, prior to 1962, 'India did not harbor any fears of direct military confrontation between the two countries, which have been sharing common historical experiences, civilizational values, as well as similar socio-economic conditions' (Jain 2008, 135). These similarities together with the fact that both India and China faced 'identical problems' of development seemed to indicate that both of them would solve their disputes peacefully (Arora 1997, 235). Thus, although 'initial interactions between independent India and liberated China did not begin, and could not have begun in an amicable and smooth fashion' (not least, owing to Beijing's perception that New Delhi was 'virtually a "semi-colony" under the "control of American imperialism" and that Nehru was characterized as a "stooge" and "running dog" of the British'), India's mediation in the Korean War (1950-1953) has helped in establishing its image as an 'honest peacebroker', which 'brought the desired break in Indo-China relations' (Acharya 2000, 173; Gupta 1987, 107).

In the consequent warming of relations during 1954–1955, both India and China signed the *Panchsheel Declaration*, which has articulated their mutual commitment to the principles of peaceful coexistence (Dhanapala 1985); Singh 2003, 362–363). More importantly, New Delhi engaged in conciliatory diplomacy, which was intended to allay Beijing's apprehension and also ensure its cooperation on the resolution of the border dispute. Thus, India has formally 'recognized the Tibet Region of China, removed Indian military personnel from Gyantse and Talung, against compensation gave up rest houses and communication facilities, and conceded China's right to have trade agents in Calcutta, Kalimpong, and New Delhi' (Prakash 1997, 174). These interactions produced the slogan '*Hindi-Chini Bhai-Bhai*' (the Indians and the Chinese are brothers).[9] However, the Indian hopes and expectations of mutually beneficial coexistence have been shattered by the 1962 Sino-Indian war. With the benefit of hindsight, some commentators have suggested that the 'euphoric bonhomie of the early 1950s proved superfluous to deal with their [India's and China's] colonial legacy of disputed borders and mutual suspicion' (Singh 2003, 123).

Thus, the 1962 war has been variously described 'a psychological trauma' (Mansingh 2000, 159), 'a great shock' and 'a crushing defeat' (Jain 2008, 137). The high-pitched emotion invested in these qualifications notwithstanding, many Indian commentators emphasize the difficulty in coming to terms with the facts about one of the most formative events in the country's history (Prakash 1997, 179). Rajan Kumar Mishra has bemoaned the fact that there is 'no official account of the conflict from the Indian side [because of] the specious argument put forward by the External Affairs Ministry that [such an account] will spoil Sino-Indian relations'. Mishra has retorted that 'if this is the criterion than the publication of the official history of any war will be impossible'. He therefore, describes the difficulty of finding 'what really happened in 1962?', when, on the one hand, Indian commentators have tended to 'cultivate an image of Chinese perfidy' and, on the other, Western accounts tend to 'put the entire blame on India' (Mishra 1996, 172–173). In this context, a couple of factors are usually evoked as an explanation of India's defeat in the war: Nehru's decision-making naïveté and the military ineptitude of India's arms forces.

Nehru's Decision-Making Naïveté
Indian commentators have contended that Nehru's unconditional acceptance of Beijing's claim on Tibet without securing 'Chinese endorsement of India's border claims and special rights in other Himalayan states inherited from the British [was] an act of supreme self-delusion and wishful thinking' (Ganguly 2004, 109). Commenting on India's conciliatory stance during 1954–1955, another observer has pointed out that 'India's attitude towards China was determined in large measure by her unrealistic assessment of the Chinese leadership. In Nehru's eyes, the supreme need of the moment was peace, particularly in Asia. The only power that might disturb

Asian peace was China with her irredentist ambitions. Once those ambitions were satisfied, China, it was believed, would settle down to peaceful internal development. Unfriendly policies would merely antagonize the Chinese Communists and make them belligerent' (Chakravarti 1962, 59). Attesting to the preponderant misreading of Beijing's intentions, Nehru, himself, has, in fact, gone as far as to admit that India's defeat in the 1962 war was the result of an 'artificial atmosphere of our own creation' (cited in Jain 2008, 137).

This reflection points to the underlying difficulties of correct interpretation and appropriate response, which implicate the inherent complexity of the security dilemma between two confrontational actors (Booth and Wheeler 2008). Thus, Swaran Singh has argued that Indian decision-makers have consistently failed to comprehend that their attempts to assert Indian sovereignty over contested regions has reinforced Beijing's perception of the 'continuity' of 'British imperial thinking' in New Delhi's foreign policy by carrying on the practice of expanding into 'peripheral regions' (Singh 2003, 111–124). At the same time, Singh also insists that while 'the colonial experience was bound to exacerbate [India's and China's] post-liberation difficulties, the key to understanding divergences in policy lay in the fact that irrespective of their shared anti-colonial sentiments and common post-liberation challenges of nation-building, their national liberation movements had opted for different kinds of political institutions and ideologies, which were to play a crucial role in their respective interpretations of their history, ethos, and legacies [as well as] their mutual perceptions and policy priorities' (Singh 2003, 307–308). Thus, acknowledging the complex determinants of the security dilemma between India and China, Indian commentators have acknowledged that New Delhi's decision-making naïveté attests to the difficulties involved in translating the foreign policy attitude of the other into an adequate policy action.

India's Military Ineptitude
Closely related to the perceived failure of decision-making (as well as pragmatically speaking), India's defeat during the 1962 Sino-Indian war was explained in terms of the country's military weakness. Precipitating the conflict, India embarked on 'a militarily foolish strategy of establishing flag post [in contested territories] to justify its claims' (Mishra 1996, 173). Developed in response to the 1957 'discovery' of a Chinese road in the Aksai Chin area linking

Xinjiang and Tibet (Acharya 2000, 175; Mullik 1971, 120), this strategy was known as *'forward policy'*, after Nehru's 1960 directive that Indian troops 'are to patrol *as far forward as possible* [to] prevent the Chinese from advancing any further and also dominating from any posts which they may have already established on *our territory'* (cited in Prakash 1997, 176–177; emphasis added). It has been described as '*a strategy of compellence*—namely an effort to force an adversary to undo the consequence of a hostile act' (Ganguly 2004, 114; emphasis added; Palit 1991, 240–241).

Moreover, the total defeat of Indian troops confronted the country's leadership with the external affairs dilemma of militaristic vs. moralistic strategy in the context of a palpable existential threat (explained in Chapter 2). It presented poignantly the stark contrast between New Delhi's '"soaring idealism" incapable of defending the country's honor' and Beijing's assertive use of military capabilities to advance its foreign policy objectives (Jain 2008, 137). It has been suggested that the difference in foreign policy approaches reflects New Delhi's and Beijing's distinct (interpretation of their) historical experience—i.e. while India 'had primarily believed in using non-violent methods for winning its national liberation struggle', the 'Chinese Communists came to power through armed struggle' (Prakash 1997, 177). Thus, despite the 1947–1948 war with Pakistan, New Delhi did not perceive Islamabad as a 'substantial threat' to warrant a change in the 'moral and normative vision [of foreign policy that] would enhance India's ability to play a significant yet independent role in global affairs' (Ganguly 2004, 106).

This decision-making and military failure notwithstanding, the one persistent effect of the 1962 Sino-Indian war is the 'profound popular perception in India of a Chinese betrayal, which [would be] difficult to remove' (Mishra 1996, 172). This feeling of betrayal seems to have underscored New Delhi's relations with Beijing in subsequent years (Dixit 1996, 230; Mullik 1971). B.M. Jain (2008, 154) has even proffered that 'the old mindsets of 1962' still grip the policy-making process.

1962–1978: Sour Neighbors

The 1962 Sino-Indian conflict marked the nadir in bilateral relations. Yet, while the following two decades were characterized by 'chaotic uncertainty' (Jain 2008, 137), the conflict has 'dispelled any lingering illusions in the official Indian circles regarding Chinese inhibitions about employing force against India. It [also] brought into focus a grave threat in a quarter where geography had been regarded as an almost insurmountable barrier against serious attack by land' (Kavic 1967, 187). As has already been suggested, this realization forced India to undertake a re-evaluation of its nonalignment stance and ultimately to *tilt* its foreign relations closer to the Soviet Union (in the context of the Cold War confrontation). In this setting, the Sino-Indian relationship 'soured by an emotion-charged border dispute, embittered by a war and accelerated by conflicting political perspectives and foreign policy perceptions remained in a deep freeze all through 1968' (Prakash 1997, 179).

The re-launching of bilateral relationship was set in motion in May 1960 by Mao Zedong's 'unexpected warm greeting' with a 'smile' of an Indian diplomat at a reception in Beijing, during which he allegedly suggested that 'Sino-Indian relations should be repaired' (Ganguly 2004, 120). Indian commentators have sought to explain this unexpected outburst of bonhomie in the context of China's effort to 'befriend old enemies like the USA [and] neutralize others like India [after] the complete isolationism of the Cultural Revolution' (Prakash 1997, 180–181). Thus, (despite the suspicion) in the context of an Indian foreign policy driven by 'hard realism' as well as 'pragmatic recognition' of the need to diffuse tensions, New Delhi began to reestablish bilateral relations with Beijing (Jain 2008, 137). In April 1976 it formally restored full diplomatic relations with China and appointed an ambassador to Beijing (Ganguly 2004, 121). New Delhi's move was intended as a signal to China that 'India [seeks] a more *normal* pattern of relations' (Ranganathan 1997, 146). Consequently, 'in overall terms, the decade of 1965/1966 to 1975/1976 saw India-China relations gradually move from 'hostile coexistence', at worst, to diplomatic and cultural overtures, at best' (Acharya 2000, 177).

1979–1987: 'Congenial Atmosphere'

Shri Prakash (1997, 181–183) has pointed out that the 1979 visit by the then Foreign Minister Atal Behari Vajpayee to Beijing has introduced the facilitating conditions for promoting a 'congenial atmosphere' in Sino-Indian relations. Usually, Vajapyee's trip is discussed in the context of his earlier return to New Delhi owing to China's punitive military actions against Vietnam. As one commentator has observed, 'the acute discomfiture of the Indian guest was provoked by the Chinese declaration that they were "teaching Vietnam a lesson" just as they had taught India a similar one in 1962' (Ganguly 2004, 121). However, C.V. Ranganathan has indicated that 'carried away by China's engagement with Vietnam, political commentators [miss] the significance of this visit'. According to Ranganathan, by the time Beijing initiated its military operation in Vietnam, Mr. Vajpayee had already concluded the official part of his visit and had to cut short *only* his 'cultural tour' of China (Ranganathan 1997, 146). It was during this 1979 visit that India and China stumbled upon the formula which has underwritten their subsequent relations—'the boundary question should not prevent us from improving our relations in other fields, and [once] we have common ground, we can solve [the boundary question] through peaceful consultation' (Deng Xiaoping cited in Jain 2008, 138). Thus, by focusing on commonalities, 'the two countries have attempted gradually to construct a relationship which is far more realistic, mature, and without any "bhai-bhai" sentiments' (Dutta 1997, 156; Joshi 2005, 126).

The fledgling congeniality of this relationship tends to be confirmed by the June 1981 official visit to New Delhi by the Chinese Foreign Minister, Huang Hua, which marked the beginning of bilateral talks on the border issues (Acharya 2000, 181; Ganguly 1989, 1130). Following the parameters agreed during Vajpayee's 1979 visit to Beijing, these talks had two aspects: on the one hand, negotiations on issues directly related to border demarcation were to be based on 'a package deal' and, on the other hand, not-directly related fields [were to be discussed with] the border issue shelved' (Jain 2008, 138; Liu 1994, 138). In 1984, both countries granted each other the status of 'Most Favored Nation' (Srinivasan 2004). In the context of such a congeniality, in 1986 New Delhi upgraded the disputed territory of Arunachal Pradesh from a 'union territory' to the status of an Indian state (on the background of escalating tensions in the border regions), which had the effect of 'the most critical point in India-China relations since the 1962 war' (Acharya 2000, 183). However, the fact that the tensions did not escalate to a military conflict has led some to suggest the emergence of 'more hopeful and helpful overall environment' (Prakash 1997, 183). Thus, despite the seriousness of the situation, a 'full-scale war was averted thanks to the mutual restraint shown by both sides' (Jain 2008, 139). Such a 'congenial atmosphere' has been deepened in the following period.

1988–1998: 'Most Cordial Phase'

The 1988 visit to Beijing by the Indian Prime Minister Rajiv Gandhi—the first-ever meeting at this level since Nehru's 1954 trip to Beijing—has become a momentous event in Sino-Indian interactions. It marked the beginning of the 'most cordial phase' in bilateral relations (Acharya 2000, 184). The 'resumption of political dialogue at the highest level has been among the most important factors that [have] brought about this change in climate' (Dutta 1997, 156). Rajiv Gandhi's visit has been termed 'path-breaking', 'setting the tone for positive "atmospheric changes" in relations between India and China' (Jain 2008, 139) as well as 'the greatest breakthrough' facilitating 'the evolution of China-India rapprochement' (Singh 2003, 129). It has therefore been praised for 'providing a much needed shot in the arm to the border negotiations' (Acharya 2000, 184). Thus, the 1988 visit tends to be 'termed "historic" for [initiating] a new beginning in the process of improving Sino-Indian ties' (Jain 2008, 139), which has also 'marked a turning point in the normalization of their relations' (Ranganathan 1997, 147). At the same time it has been criticized for the Prime Minister's willingness [like his grandfather Nehru] to make unconditional concessions to Beijing—namely, (i) by agreeing that the settlement of the border dispute should not impede bilateral relations; (ii) by admitting that 'some members of the Tibetan émigré community might be engaging in "anti-Chinese" activities'; and (iii) by reiterating that 'Tibet was "an internal affair of China"' (Ganguly 2004, 122).

One of the significant outcomes of Rajiv Gandhi's visit has been the establishment of the Joint Working Group (JWG) on the border dispute (Prakash 1997, 184). A series of confidence and security building measures had also been set up in the context of the JWG, which 'have laid the basis for greater stability and predictability [between New Delhi and Beijing] and have also created a border security environment which [has been] far more relaxed than it was in nearly four decades' (Dutta 1997, 157). The momentum of 1988 has seemed accelerated by the end of the Cold War. In particular, the dissolution of the Soviet Union is often pointed out as a crucial ingredient of the rapprochement between the two countries. Thus, Indian commentators have signaled the 'reduction in tensions' as a result of the 'hallmarks of Sino-Indian relations' during this period: 'high level political contacts, a constant if cautious effort to resolve the border dispute, a greater understanding of each other's concerns in a spirit of accommodation, and growing economic cooperation' (Sen 2000, 256–259). Thus, both New Delhi and Beijing 'were consciously trying to build a working relationship insulated from the likely pressures generated by Chinese equations with India's neighbors' (Dixit 1998, 414).

Such an 'advanced stage of détente' was reflected in Beijing's increasingly more nuanced stance on Kashmir, which has been 'in stark contrast to China's pro-Pakistan posture [during] the Maoist phase' (Dutta 1997, 151–158). Some have even argued that during 'the last few years of the 1990s' Beijing had virtually come to 'endorse India's views on Kashmir' (Singh 2003, 128). This has indicated to observers that by 'concentrating on commonalities like economic relations, approaches to issues concerning the new world order, and human rights, while reserving the cases of disagreement, notably boundary-related matters for separate treatment [both] India and China have moved a long way on the road of normalization of relations, if not reconciliation and friendship' (Mishra 1996, 162–165). All this seemed undone by India's 1998 nuclear weapons tests, which mark the beginning of a new phase in Sino-Indian relations.

1998–Present: Searching for a Pragmatic Partnership
As one commentator has put it, 'the sunshine period in Sino-Indian relations disappeared behind a dark cloud following India's nuclear tests' (Jain 2008, 140). Although China's initial reaction seems to have been reserved, as soon as details of Prime Minister Vajpayee's letter to western heads of state became public (in which he justified the tests in terms of a potential Chinese threat), Beijing's reaction was extremely swift and sharp. It immediately pulled out of all scheduled JWG meetings and condemned India's 'hegemonic designs in Asia' (Sen 2000, 267). Thus, it was not the tests themselves, but their subsequent discursive contextualization by Indian state-elites that has turned 1998 into 'the second watershed [after 1962] in India-China relations' (Acharya 2000, 196). Attesting to the logic of India's foreign policy mythmaking, observers have claimed that the country's 'advances in missile technology and nuclear weapons, China may see the futility of using the Pakistan card [under] the strategic threat of [ballistic missiles] targeted on Chinese cities [which] for the first time has created *a positive incentive* for China to *talk peace* with India' (Mishra 1996, 175; emphasis added).

The argument here is that the 1998 nuclear tests have 'upset [Beijing's] security paradigms [and] calculations' and have forced China to 'see India as its major neighbor which can no longer be ignored' (Singh 2003, 157, 325).

Pragmatically speaking, however, a number of Indian commentators have acknowledged that New Delhi's recourse to a Chinese threat in its justification of the 1998 nuclear weapons tests was 'an unwarranted and provocative act on India's part, resulting in unnecessary tension with China' (Jain 2008, 141). Others have claimed that this foreign policy rhetoric signals the 'general ineptness of the Vajpayee government's diplomatic initiatives'; in particular, it has indicated the

> lack of foreign policy forethought, [which is] not surprising considering *the irrelevance of external considerations in motivating the decision to test*. To begin with, the Vajpayee government justified its actions by reference to the Pakistan and China threats. If New Delhi was surprised by the initially strong reaction of the US, it was also taken aback by the strength of the Chinese reaction. It did not take long for the realization to sink that a major diplomatic error has been made. Gratuitously blaming China, in a general context where Sino-Indian relations had been steadily improving made no security sense. Within a month of the tests, the very same government spokespersons who had waxed eloquent about the Chinese threat as the primary justification (along with the Pakistan threat) now officially declared that the Indian bomb was not 'country specific'. By late 1999, the official government position was that the Indian bomb was not even 'threat specific'. (Vanaik 2007, 385)

Despite the tension in bilateral relations, already in 1999 China had renewed its participation in the JWG (Sen 2000, 270; Mukherjee 1999). Also, 'in an attempt to mollify bruised Chinese sensibilities', the soon-to-be Foreign Minister, Jaswant Singh had gone to China, and 'although no substantive agreements were reached during his visit, the harsh rhetoric emanating from Beijing [has] subsided significantly' (Ganguly 2004, 104). Thus, although relations do not seem to have returned to pre-1998 levels of collaboration, observers have noted that bilateral relations have proceeded with a 'slow, but unmistakable trend [of] edging closely to one another, while still conscious of deep divides' (Clad 2004, 291).

Such perceptions seem to be confirmed in 2002, when the trespassing of Chinese troops into Indian territory in the state of Arunchal Pradesh was 'attributed to "differences in perception" between India and China' and, thus, was not allowed to undermine bilateral relations (Jain 2008, 142). This kind of 'political maturity' was also displayed in April 2005 during Wen Jiabao's visit to India when both countries agreed to upgrade their relations to a 'Strategic and Cooperative Partnership' (Jain 2008, 143). According to Indian commentators the pervasiveness of Beijing's pragmatism reveals that since its rise as 'the next global power, China's motivations vis-à-vis South Asia' have become 'less euphoric and emotional' and, instead, have increasingly exhibited a tendency to be 'interest-driven and therefore far more balanced and rational' (Singh 2003, 269).

In this setting, Indian commentators acknowledge that both New Delhi and Beijing are increasingly trying to settle their border conflict on the basis of a 'balanced' and 'rational' pragmatism. Such a perception is corroborated by the accord signed between China and India on opening trade through Sikkim which has virtually recognized India's sovereignty over this region, which was 'a significant concession on behalf of China' (Jain 2008, 149). India has reciprocated by departing from its traditional insistence on historic claims and legal precedents and recognizing 'the political nature of future negotiations [as well as] the necessity for "give and take"' (Mohan 2007, 12). Furthermore, in 2002, Prime Minister Vajpayee has declared that 'China did not pose a threat to India, nor does India believe that China regards India as a threat' (cited in Jain 2008, 141). A year later, he ascertained during a meeting with Hu Jintao that 'if our two countries will cooperate, it will result in the twenty-first century turning into an "Asian Century"' (cited in Kachru 2007, 302). Such proclamations of pragmatic partnership signal the current narrative interpretations of the interactions between New Delhi and Beijing. At the same time, other commentators insist that 'India's primary strategic concern should be to balance China' (Rajagopalan and Sahni 2008, 15). Such dissimilar emplotments of their bilateral relations provides the complex context of India's interactions with China in Central Asia. The following sections detail the dynamics of this encounter.

In the Eye of the Dragon: India's Encounter with China in Central Asia

The complicated history of bilateral relations has framed New Delhi's perceptions of China's Central Asian agency. Thus, the encounter of China in Central Asia has stirred up 'anxieties' that underpin New Delhi's 'big geostrategic questions': 'How will China's newly-found power influence the way in which it perceives and deals with the outside world? What are its motivations, ambitions, and goals? How will China use its growing power and how will this impact on the interstate system, and, particularly, on the region' (Bhattacharjea 2008, 2). At the same time, there is a pervasive awareness in the narratives of the 'Look North' policy that the multiplicity of contending dynamics of globalization has 'shifted the global strategic landscape' in Asia into a 'more complex strategic situation', whereby the 'rapid economic growth is changing strategic relationships among regional countries', while 'the uneven distribution of growth among regional countries may aggravate the political, economic, and cultural differences [between them] in ways which could create new sources of instability' (Kachru 2007, 97). The following sections outline Beijing's agency in Central Asia and the Indian interpretations of its effects on the 'Look North' policy.

Shanghaied into Cooperation: China's Agency in Central Asia

China's nascent centrality in Central Asia can be put down to several factors. On the one hand, reflecting the broader pattern of Russia's foreign policy inconsistencies during the tenure of President Boris Yeltsin, the Kremlin's preoccupation with the Caucasus (mainly the conflict in Chechnya) during the 1990s has led to the attenuation of Moscow's position in Central Asia. Some have even ascertained that in fact China's engagement in Central Asia is filling in the 'power vacuum in the East' (Lambridis and Koukoulis 2005, 479). On the other hand, Moscow and Beijing have been able to establish a pragmatic basis for their cooperation in the region, especially during the presidency of Vladimir Putin. In particular, the re-emergence of a hawkish Russian foreign policy seems to have brought closer Moscow's and Beijing's viewpoints. At the same time, shared threat perceptions have led China and Russia to view the other as its respective 'strategic rear' (Ovchinnikov 2000). In this respect, although they compete for Central Asia's energy resources, the coincidence of interests between Moscow and Beijing has facilitated the recognition of the benefits from their cooperation—i.e. they are 'positioning themselves to define the rules under which the USA, the EU, Iran and Turkey will be allowed to participate in the region' (Cohen 2001, 2). Some Indian commentators have even claimed that the amicability between China and Russia has become so entrenched that Beijing 'loaned $6 billion to Moscow' for the controversial 'nationalization' of the YUKOS oil company (Ghanta 2005).[11] A number of them also point out that 'the collapse of the Soviet Union [has] redefined the context' in which China's movement in the region is aided by its 'proximity, significant size, fast growing economy, and powerful military' as well as 'the mutual compatibility [between] the economies of the Central Asian republics and China' (Patnaik 2005, 211–216).

In this setting, the analysis of China's Central Asian policy acknowledges that Beijing's engagement in the region intends the introduction of a framework of predictability that allows it to make feasible calculations about future intentions. Traditionally, Beijing's foreign policy interests in the region are grouped in four dominant areas: (i) diversifying and ensuring China's access to energy resources; (ii) cutting any international links between Muslim Uyghur separatists in the province of Xinjiang and their ethnic and religious kin across Central Asia; (iii) encouraging economic and trade relations between China's western provinces and Central Asian states; (iv) indicating China's preparedness to become a global actor (Kavalski 2007b; Patnaik 2005, 215). From these four discourses, the stability of its volatile northwest seems to have been the central concern of Beijing—Xinjiang is home to 12 million Uyghurs (a Muslim Turkic group which constitutes almost 50 percent of the province's population), who have ethnic and religious affiliations to Central Asian populations; in addition nearly 300,000 Uyghurs live in Kazakhstan and Kyrgyzstan (Dillon 2004). Indian observers have recognized the importance of Xinjiang to China's Central Asian strategy (Mishra 2000, 333).[12] For instance, Beijing's ability during the 1990s to convince Central Asian states to sign treaties demarcating their joint border through different confidence and security building measures (including the unprecedented move to cede territory that it has claimed as part of the Chinese historical realm) has been specifically linked to the issue of Uyghur separatism. Thus, by 'affirming the territorial integrity of Central Asian states (Bhattacharjea 2008, 12), SCO has allowed China to 'block all possibilities of Muslim fundamentalists [infiltrating] Xinjiang from the [region]' (Singh 2003, 345).

Yet, Beijing's rapid movement from the difficult task of delineating and disarming its borders with Kazakhstan, Kyrgyzstan, Russia, and Tajikistan to promoting a multilateral organisation and establishing growing economic and security ties attest to more than just the conventional 'power politics' of national self-interest (Sun 2004). Although the proponents of the 'Look North' policy insist that China's relations with Central Asia are driven by a desire to mitigate 'the threats to its internal stability', maintain 'the peace along its Western periphery', and ensure 'its energy security' (Joshi 2007a, 152; Dutta 2003, 145; Patnaik 2005, 207), the creation of the 'Shanghai Five' in the mid-1990s promoted a climate that has not only begun to alleviate Central Asian (as well as Russian) suspicion about China's intentions, but also to lay the groundwork for a regional political community. Thus, the accession of Uzbekistan and the transformation of the 'Shanghai Five' into the Shanghai Cooperation Organization (SCO) in 2001 seem both to reveal Central Asian susceptibility to Beijing's power of attraction and indicate the ways in which Beijing intends to impacts Central Asian perceptions of itself. Indian observers have been quick to recognize the uniqueness of SCO. For instance, Sujit Dutta has declared that it is 'a huge departure for Chinese foreign policy. For the first time China has initiated a multilateral strategic partnership' (Dutta 2003, 159). SCO has thereby not only enhanced the visibility of 'China's economic and political interests in the region' (Gidadhubli 2007, 170), but it has also reaffirmed Beijing's 'new self-image'—i.e. it 'no longer sees itself as the plaything of international politics, but [as an] autonomous pole of power and purpose' (Bhattac-harjea 2008, 10). This independent agency has been greatly assisted by the recognition that 'for the first time in a century China has secure and normal relations with all Asian states' (Dutta 1997, 154). At the same time, it has been indicated that SCO facilitates the 'closer cooperation between countries secure in their "Asian identity"' (Varadarajan 2005).

SCO has, therefore, become the epitome of China's socializing propensity. Its diplomatic rhetoric and policy-practice of peace-building, development, and economic integration, Beijing signals its willingness to share with Central Asian states the opportunities associated with China's 'peaceful rise' within the context of compliance with promoted rules (Shambaugh 2005, 55). At the same time, Beijing has not been shy to utilize the financial windfall of its economic growth in 'persuading' Central Asian states. The narratives of the 'Look North' policy insist that Beijing is 'aware that [its expanding] economic ties would bolster its political relations with regional states'—that is, 'Chinese leaders are quite willing to consider ambitious and clearly uneconomical schemes [in order to] project China's geopolitical influence in Central Asia' (Dutta 2003, 155–156). Thus, on the one hand, Indian commentators recognize that SCO reflects a Chinese perception that in 'Central Asia, the internal security of states will be of under great stress in the years to come' (Bajpai 2000, 46). On the other, they are also aware that SCO intimates specific socializing discourses and practices through which Beijing engages in informational, procedural, and symbolic transference and diffusion of its norms. SCO has therefore become '*the principal basis for strategic interactions* between Central Asia and the big and medium powers that surround the region' (Varadarajan 2005; emphasis added).

India and China in Central Asia: Patterns of Relations
The encounter with China in Central Asia has produced diverse assessments within the narratives of the 'Look North' policy, all of which tend to reflect the difficulties in articulating a foreign policy strategy in a world marked by pervasive complexity (Kavalski 2007b). Thus, several commentators have insisted that coming to terms with Beijing's agency in Central Asia requires taking into account the 'fluid context' of 'bilateral, regional, and great power diplomacy, in which the players weave bewildering nets of connections and counter arrangements [which] appear contradictory' (Rana 2007, 213). At the same time, the establishment of SCO has brought about the realization that China is gradually becoming 'the hub of an increasingly wider [and] economically interdependent grouping in Asia with dense multi-level and multi-dimensional linkages' (Bhattacharjea 2008, 16). Its development encourages the establishment of 'multiform, multilayer, and multi-channel security dialogues' (Dutta 1997, 164); SCO is therefore 'critically important' as it 'has the potential to generate a greater cohesion among Asian countries' (Sharma 2005, 45). Some have even suggested that if Asia is to become a functioning region 'it would be due to the role

played by China [...] Thus, it would not be too much of an exaggeration to say that China defines Asia; there can be no Asia without China' (Sahni 2005, 84). In this setting, Indian perceptions of Beijing's agency in Central Asia can be put together in three broad groups: *partner, threat,* and *model.* Although not necessarily complementary, all three representations are elicited in the narratives of the 'Look North' policy.

China's Partnering in the 'Look North' Policy
The suggestion of a possible partnership between India and China reflects the presumptions of their post-1998 bilateral relations. In this respect, as both countries 'were becoming more confident of their identities and [foreign policy] independence [they] were [also] becoming far more balanced and forthcoming in appreciating each other's views and preferences' (Singh 2003, 325). Beijing's agency in Central Asia has thereby been interpreted as a *genuine attempt* 'to allay the natural fears of its neighbors and to respond to their concerns' (Bhattacharjea 2008, 16). At the same time, this attempt was not driven by a desire to 'control and influence' the region (Joshi 2003, 4). Consequently, Indian commentators have appreciated that the regionalization of Beijing's external relations follows 'from its broader strategy of resolving disputes along its territories [and] seeking out neighboring countries with whom it had some basic territorial difference and with whom it had to face a conflictual situation during the Cold War' (Sen 2000, 254–256).

Thus, while recognizing China's resource-driven agency in the region, the narratives of the 'Look North' policy nevertheless acknowledge the benefits for Central Asian states from joining 'the dynamic Asian heartland' and gaining access 'to the markets of the Asia-Pacific economic ring' (Patnaik 2005, 216). It is in this context that some Indian commentators see the possibility of a nascent partnership between New Delhi and Beijing. It is argued that the Chinese 'pipeline development fits very well as a viable energy supply route for Central Asian oil to India' through Xinjiang; thus, Beijing's assistance to the region also benefits New Delhi by enhancing not only 'the goodwill' between them, but also the 'trans-frontier interaction between the people on both sides would help in reviving the pre-1950s relations between the two countries' (Asopa 2007, 180; Bakshi 1999, 2282). Furthermore, the 'political closeness' between India and the Central Asian states 'should prompt China to seek greater Indian cooperation. India can provide China [with] a comforting cushion against encirclement by the West, or the Jihadi elements. The proximity of China to Central Asia and India, its infrastructure and economic profile could be of immense help to India, its infrastructure and economic profile could be of immense help to India. They can mutually benefit from [a joint] Central Asian engagement and should coordinate their efforts to acquire greater leverage in the region' (Patnaik 2005, 227–228).[13]

Another commonality between India and China emphasized by the discourses of the 'Look North' policy is their shared aversion to the narratives and practices of democracy-promotion advanced in Central Asia by various Western actors. Thus, although the two countries do not have 'identical views on human rights, [they] both agree that for developing countries, the most fundamental human rights remain the right to subsistence and the right to development. [New Delhi and Beijing] remain particularly opposed to the practice [of] using economic aid as an instrument for bringing pressure on certain countries' (Singh 2003, 161–162). In this respect, while India 'urges its neighbors to practice democracy, [it] also wants that the people of each country decide on the system that suits them [...] It is the prospect of aggressive peddling of democracy in various parts of the world that makes India uncomfortable' (Rana 2007, 163). Some have argued that such shared normative commitments between India and China reflect New Delhi's realization that it cannot 'get caught in a "balance of power" game' with China; thus, 'despite its commitment to democracy, [India] does not want to lose sight of its economic and security interests' (Kaul 2007, 244).[14]

Regardless of its rationale, this similarity of normative attitudes has urged a number of commentators to anticipate a pattern of partnership in the Central Asian interactions between India and China. In particular, the shared appreciation of and subscription to the inviolability of the national sovereignty of states has been expected to bring their foreign policy perspectives closer to one another. For instance, 'their attachment to traditional concepts of absolute sovereignty is strong, especially in matters pertaining to territory and security. Neither is amenable to external interference on military and arms-related matters; both oppose external inspections and interventions elsewhere, especially if undertaken without the benefit of UN validation. [Thus], the grip by national security elites on policymaking in each country makes any weakening of governmental attachment to sovereignty a long-term proposition at best' (Mansingh and Ranganathan 2001, 464–465). However, the very dynamism that underscores this perception of commonality between New Delhi and Beijing, also animates Indian threat-perceptions of China.

China as a Threat to the 'Look North' Policy

Despite proclamations of friendship and pragmatic strategic partnership, the context of Central Asia indicates the both India and China find it difficult to exorcise the ghosts of the past from their international interactions. The narratives of the 'Look North' policy suggest that the deeply-engrained 'apprehensions' between New Delhi and Beijing have made both of them very 'cautious of taking [joint] initiatives' (Reddy 2007, 212). India, in particular, remains wary of the '*uncertainty* [that hangs] over China's future political and military direction' and 'how [China's] growing power [in Asia] would be used, whether it will be responsive to the interests of others and value the principles of common security and the rule of universally accepted norms' (Dutta 1997, 155; emphasis added). Thus, despite its transformation and innovation, China's current policy in Central Asia is still merely an upgraded version of Beijing's long-standing policy of containing India through the provision of assistance to states in New Delhi's strategic neighborhood (Singh 2003, 331). Such attitudes reflect an entrenched mistrust of whether 'China's view of India has [really] changes since the late 1950s' (Rajagopalan 2005, 306).

Such perceptions of China's agency in Central Asia have suggested that 'Sino-Indian relations, despite fitful improvements, will remain competitive [because] the two states have divergent self-images and different political systems. They also each wish to emerge as major powers in Asia and beyond' (Ganguly 2004, 124).[15] Said otherwise, 'India's desire to play a role on its own or with others, in the strategic balance in Asia is in direct conflict with China's ambition of making Asia *its area of influence*' (Budania 2003, 89; emphasis added). In this context, Beijing's 'present posture [in Central Asia] cannot be viewed in benign terms—if China is being accommodating, it is only because the balance [of power] does not seem to be in its favor; once its capabilities grow, it may adopt more strident policies [in the region]' (Mattoo 2003, 64). For instance, despite the assertion that through SCO, China has launched 'a new type of multilateral institution that [is] likely to become the building block' of a new political and economic architecture in Asia' (Bhattacharjea 2005, 16), Indian commentators have remained doubtful of Beijing's 'true intentions' and 'great power ambitions' (largely because 'multilateralism is a new concept for China and it would take time before it finally digs in')—in other words, 'there has often been a discrepancy between China's [professed] international principles and its practice. China's active push for cross-border trade and investments [have been] in keeping with the [claim] that "peace and development" are interdependent and the major trend of the times. However, Beijing's first preference remains bilateral measures and if and when they fail, unilateral actions are there to attain its goals' (Dutta 1997, 164).

This strand of the 'Look North' policy interprets SCO as part of Beijing's 'assertive' foreign policy style aimed at 'the active use of persuasion and lobbying [for] the projection of [China's] core interests [and] national requirements' (Rana 2007, 32–36). This attitude reflects the context in which New Delhi was granted the status of observer country to SCO. It has been interpreted as a confirmation of India as 'China's junior partner' in the region—meaning that it 'dances' (or at least is expected to 'dance') to the tune of the 'senior partner' (Khanna 2008, 95). Sujit Dutta has argued that Beijing's claim of a peaceful rise to global power notwithstanding, its international agency should not be construed as an indication that China is 'a passive and disinterested actor'. Instead, its initiatives in Central Asia reveal that Beijing 'would like to shape [the] region's emerging security and economic architecture [in order] to serve its own geopolitical interests'. Dutta has therefore argued that 'in the long term, Beijing hopes to prevail as the most influential power in the region' (Dutta 2003, 145–163).

Thus, the realization that SCO has brought China and the countries of Central Asia 'closer politically and economically' (Gidadhubli 2007, 169) has contributed to New Delhi's growing suspicion of how genuine Beijing's proclamations in favor of multilateralism actually are (Singh 2003, 323). India has been particularly concerned by China's military assistance to Central Asian states (Bhattacharya 2005). This concern reflects Indian perceptions that 'the calculus of [regional] security hinges on capability, not words, nor current intent' (Rana 2007, 212). In other words, China's neighbors see [its international agency] both as a short and longer term opportunity for mutually beneficial cooperation and, at the same time, a potential future concern because of its raw power'—thus, the attitude of some observers is that in Central Asia 'China now calls the shots and tries to roughshod in the economy on its own terms' (Reddy 2007, 201).

Taking these 'misgivings' as a point of departure, Indian commentators have insisted that 'Central Asians would be more comfortable' if New Delhi were to engage in a more proactive 'balancing [of] China's increasing influence in the region' (Patnaik 2005, 215). It needs to be pointed out that the sensitivity of the 'Look North' policy to China's military buildup in the region corroborates the ideational precepts of India's post-1998 foreign policy (outlined in Chapter 3). In particular the intensity of such threat-perceptions underpins the assertive promotion of its national interests and strategic requirements in the discursive construction of its international relations.

China as a Model for the 'Look North' Policy
The sections above have outlined the modalities of the Indian perception of China as either a prospective partner or a looming threat to New Delhi's relations with Central Asian states. Such discursive formulations rest on the understanding that Beijing's regional agency is simultaneously 'need-based' and 'ambition-guided' (Singh 2003, 107). Reflecting on the shared ideational origins of these bifurcated foreign policy perspectives, the narratives of the 'Look North' policy illustrate that these images of China are not contending, but concurrent—that is, India's encounter of China in Central Asia suggests that their bilateral relationship would involve 'both competition and cooperation [as] real life is always more complex' (Khanna 2008, 83). In other words, 'China is not India's chief rival or enemy, nor is it a natural ally' (Singh 2006, 45). At the same time, however, these observations are highlight the perception that 'India lacks a long-term policy and diplomacy to suitably deal with the rising China in the altering balances of power' (Jain 2008, 228).

Thus, by acknowledging the complexity of Sino-Indian relations, a number of commentators have suggested that New Delhi's encounter with Beijing's agency in Central Asia has produced the image of *'China as a role model'* for India's international agency (Mattoo 2003, 20; emphasis added). The realization is that 'China came from far behind and overtook India [and] its success offers useful lessons' (Bhadrakumar 2008). Thus, despite the mythic narrative of national self-aggrandizement which postulates that 'India will be one of the heavyweights of the 21st century and perhaps even overtake China by the end of the century' (Kachru 2007, 311), owing to the experience of India's confrontation with the reality of China's engagement in Central Asia the narrative of the 'Look North' policy indicates that if India is to become the great power that it proclaims it needs to learn from (and perhaps even emulate) the model set-up by Beijing.[16] This foreign policy perception reflects the suggestion (already elaborated in Chapter 4) that India's relations with Central Asia facilitate the emergence of discourses which engage in parallel assessment of New Delhi's agency vis-à-vis other international actors. Thus, on an instrumental level the 'statistical record of economic development measured through the growth and structure of national income in China and India show that China in general has done much better than India. In the comparative perspective, some of the primary considerations on which China appears to have heavily relied during the course of its developments are worth noting for India to draw some lessons from' (Arora 1997, 243).

A number of these 'lessons' relate to the structure, process, and content of India's external relations. For instance, Kishan Rana notes that Beijing's relations with Central Asia reflect the 'strategic and tactical suppleness' of its foreign policy pragmatism, which does not waste time on identifying 'a threat or an opportunity' and instead unfold far-reaching 'strategic partnerships' (like SCO). The coherence and cohesiveness of these initiatives rests on a Chinese 'blend of soft power [which] is designed to produce an appealing image' for Beijing's agency and is, therefore, not only an accompaniment to its 'mainstream activities' (Rana 2007, 33–44). Thus, in contrast to India, China's initiatives in Central Asia indicate the development of a sophisticated 'holistic view' of foreign policy making, which 'embeds the state firmly within the interstate system as an organic and inseparable part, linking the fate even of the inside of the state to the fate or nature of its outside. In other words, no state is fully an autonomous unit, and in the real world, the norms of sovereignty and equality are seen to be moderated by the fact and possession of power' (Bhattacharjea 2008, 3–4).

The encounter with China's 'holistic' foreign policy in Central Asia has stimulated the emergence of a strand of the 'Look North' policy, which recognizes the need to emulate Beijing's ability to 'establish quickly an international reputation for being able to look after itself [and, thus] become a "great power", whereas India's potential remains unrealized' (Mansingh and Ranganathan 2001, 464–465). This image of China as model rests on: (i) 'China's ability to take hard internal decisions as well as to face up to pressure from the West that has been lionized by sections within virtually the whole spectrum of public opinion in India'; and (ii) 'China's emergence as an economic and military power of significance and manner in which it has been able to reform its economy without compromising on its security posture is also viewed with awe and admiration' (Mattoo 2000, 20–21). The understanding of *influence* implicit in these strands of the 'Look North' policy will be further discussed in Chapter 8.

Conclusion

This overview of New Delhi's encounter of China in Central Asia illustrates that Beijing continues to be 'a major influence' in determining India's external affairs not only with the region, but also in the broader framework of global politics. At the same time, this chapter reflects the perception that Sino-Indian relations still vacillate 'in the space between a security dilemma and cooperative security' (Mohan 2007, 396). The preceding discussion, however, reveals that more often than not, the common strategic goal of 'access to resources in Central Asia' (Sen 2000, 269) seem to reinforce the suspicion bred from the long history of mistrust between them. At the same time, the challenges for Sino-Indian relations in Central Asia derive from the 'uncertainty over China's future political and military direction' (Dutta 1997, 155).[17] In this respect, the chapter's discussion of Indian perceptions of China's Central Asian agency demonstrates the complex nature of security in Asia. It reveals that New Delhi's encounter with Beijing in the region is inflected both by the convoluted history of their bilateral relations and the dynamism of the 'new great game'. As illustrated, this context informs the construction of China simultaneously as a partner in, a threat to, and a model for the 'Look North' policy.

Finally, however, it should be pointed out that the analysis of the Sino-Indian interactions in Central Asia points to a unique problem faced by the external agency of both countries—the difficulty of bracketing their roles in global politics within the labels, language, and practices developed for the explanation and understanding of conventional Westphalian states.[18] The suggestion is that the 'nation-state' does not offer a 'sufficient framework' for understanding the actorness of New Delhi and Beijing in world affairs (Kachru 2007, xiv). Thus, owing to the idiosyncratic nexus of historical experience and current patterns of global interactions both find themselves donning the unfitting attire of statehood in their external relations. This problem has been best captured by Lucian Pye's poignant observation that the assessment of the international agency of actors like India and China instances the dilemmas of *civilizations pretending to be states* (Pye 1990, 58; Kavalski 2007b, 841). In South Asia in particular, the formation of polities around customs and ritual helps explain 'the absence of an Indian state' in the conventional sense of this term (Bal 2004, 27). The difficulty to factor in territoriality within the governance patterns of actors such as India and China forms a key aspect of the explanation and understanding of why there is 'no non-Western International Relations Theory' (Acharya and Buzan 2007; Ertürk 1999). In this respect, Shivshankar Menon, the Foreign Secretary of the Ministry of External Affairs acknowledges that

> sadly the language of strategic discourse in India is not yet developed enough to describe what we empirically know and face as reality around us. We need to develop our own strategic concepts and vocabulary. I am repeatedly struck by the use of concepts, ideas, and methods of analysis that come from other situations and interests (such as deterrence, parity, or reciprocity) and bear little relationship to our unique circumstance. That is something which needs serious examination on its own. (2007, 391)

While commenting on New Delhi's encounter of China in Central Asia, the narratives of the 'Look North' policy have also reflected upon the Euro-centric framework within which their interactions are traditionally positioned. For instance, Swaran Singh has very explicitly declared that

> Asian civilizations like China and India had never historically visualized themselves as territorial states. They had evolved their empires around a whole range of rituals and customs that bound the core to periphery of subdued vassal states.

This image of Self was extremely fluid and it kept expanding and shrinking given the power of Kings at the core. This meant that territorial boundaries were never clearly demarcated or even defined between China and India. This sense of territory was a European concept of [the] State and it was the negative interface of these Asia empires with colonial powers that compelled China and India to blend their vision of empires with this new concept of territorial nation-states. And here, the colonial subjugation was to make them obsessed with their sovereign independence—demonstrated in their control over certain territories—and their post-liberation elite was to find it unusually difficult to make any territorial concessions of any kind. Of course, their post-liberation animosities and border war were to further add to their complications, making any such accommodation virtually an impossible task for their leaders. (2003, 145–146)

This criticism of the Westphalian framing of India's interactions with Central Asia is only one aspect of New Delhi's perception of European and Euro-Atlantic agency in the region. According to Naunihal Singh, 'despite foreign policy failures and much debate over tactics, the Indian elite holds fast to *a vision of national greatness*'. Thus, the historical memory of great Indian civilizations has practical consequences. Indian officials believe they are representing not just a state but a civilization. Few state-civilizations are India's equal. Believing that India should be accorded deference and respect because of its intrinsic civilizational qualities, many Indian diplomats and strategists are wary of having to depend upon states that do not appreciate India's special and unique characteristics. Furthermore, Indians believe that India as *civilization* has something to offer to the rest of the world' (Singh 2006, 48–49; emphasis added). Taking the distinction between *civilizational* and *territorial* statehood as a point of departure, the following chapter draws the complex picture of India's encounter of Western agency in Central Asia.

7

THE PORCUPINE MEETS MARS AND VENUS: INDIA'S INTERACTIONS WITH THE WEST IN CENTRAL ASIA

Introduction

This chapter pulls together the disjointed literature on the relations between India and Western actors—mainly, the European Union (EU), the USA, and NATO—through the prism of the discursive construction of New Delhi's foreign policy towards Central Asia. Chapter 4 (in its discussion of Indian perceptions of a regional 'new great game') has already exposed that Central Asian states (i) have been 'drawn into the vortex of international politics' where several major powers struggle for 'control and influence' (Joshi 2007a, 151) and, at the same time, (ii) have been 'strategizing so shrewdly that they [i.e. regional states] may end up the only winners' (Mattoo 2003, 61). As has been suggested, this context has complicated New Delhi's policy options due to the proliferation of international agency in the region. Consequently, the two preceding chapters have detailed the construction of India's confrontation with Central Asian agency of Russia and China in the discourses of the 'Look North' policy. This chapter, therefore, focuses on the Central Asian interactions between India and Western actors.

Historically speaking, Western accounts of the social, political, and economic dynamics of South Asia have rarely been able to eschew the modalities of orientalism (Halbfass 1988), ornamentalism (Kaul 2003), and tropicalization (Arnold 2006). Capturing this tendency of the Western gaze, Indian commentators often declare:

Ask any American about India and chances are, he'll answer in one of three ways. He may describe a land crowded with the poor, sleeping on sidewalks, and begging from tourists, or give his mystic vision of elephants, tigers, and the Taj Mahal. Or he might tell the sad story of a friend or neighbor who was cast off by his company when his department was outsourced to India. (Rai and Simon 2007, xi)

At the same time, Indian narratives of the encounter with the West have also not been devoid of invention (Ballhatchet 1985; Fisher 2006; Khan 1998). As will be suggested shortly, such an emplotment of the agency of the EU, the USA, and NATO in Central Asia inflects their construction in the accounts of the 'Look North' policy through the shared image of 'the West'. That being so, an ungainly but important task is to distinguish between phantoms and substance in such narratives, particularly when grappling with the Central Asian agency of both Western actors and India.

Thus, some recent analyses have tended to befuddle (rather than assist) analytical imaginations. For instance Robert Kagan (2003) has (in)famously bifurcated Western agency by framing the international identity of the EU through the figure of *Venus* and that of the USA through *Mars*. Hence, in contrast to the perceived military might of the American Mars, the European Venus' alleged effete civilian power lacks the capabilities to deter non-compliance and to punish disobedience. Parallel to this mythmaking invention, India's foreign policy stance has been captured by Western commentators through the image of the *porcupine*—'vegetarian, slow-footed and prickly' (Mohan 2004, 260). This depiction hints at the perceived vulnerability of New Delhi's international agency, which 'uses its quills to deter aggressors and hides in a cave, especially when Pakistan is mentioned' (Leonard 2005, 10). The suggestion is that these illustrations are equally simplifying and misleading as well as fail to do justice to the complex strategic contexts within which the foreign policy engagements of both Western actors and India function.

India and Western Actors

Chapter 3 has explained that India's post-1998 foreign policy-making approach is underwritten by a 'natural tendency to politicize the developments on the diplomatic front' (Mohan 2007, 392). In this respect, the interpretation of Western agency within the articulations of the 'Look North' policy confirms the trends and impulses dictating the strategic trajectories of New Delhi. The required qualification is that this chapter does not impute the existence of a homogeneous and monolithic 'West'. Instead, the West is treated here as a singular actor owing to the fact that Indian commentators often do not seem to identify the distinctions between its main proponents—the EU, the USA, and NATO. For instance, some Indian commentators have pilloried the '*European desire* to extend *its* influence in [Central Asia] by means of *NATO-expansion* eastward and through the *Partnership for Peace* program' (Roy 2001; emphasis added). Similar confusion appears to inform the criticism of '*the US transnational project* called TRACECA [the Transport Corridor Europe-Caucasus-Asia] establishing a transport corridor (mainly for oil) between Europe and [the region]' (Muni 2003, 104; emphasis added), despite TRACECA's embeddedness within an EU-program for the post-Soviet countries (Kavalski 2007c). Furthermore, the attitudes expressed by Indian commentators in the discursive construction of the 'Look North' policy do not seem to distinguish particularly between the agency of the EU, the USA, or NATO in their expression of value judgments. It has to be recognized that the evaluation of American agency tends to evoke stronger passions and seems to polarize commentators more than the assessment of the EU or NATO (the latter is more often than not treated as a stylistic variation for American agency). As already indicated, there is a distinct awareness that 'the creation of the EU [can] be seen as [an expression of] the European states' desire to create a counterweight against US domination' (Nautiyal 2004, 153). Bearing in mind this qualification, Indian commentators ascertain that

> 'international norms' or 'world community' are phrases that are increasingly used to provide global legitimacy to actions [aimed] at preserving the interests and the dominant position of the USA and its allies. 'Globalization', 'liberalization', and 'interdependence' are [notions] used to describe the West's attempt [to] maintain its hegemony through treaties like the NPT and CTBT; technology control regimes like the London Club, MTCR, and [the] Wassenaar Regime; and international financial institutions like the IMF and the World Bank [which] are used as tools to impose on other nations, economic and other policies the West considers appropriate. (Udgaonkar 2001, 1773–1789)

Such a perception of a common ideational and institutional base of Western agency has led some analysts to observe the emergence of an 'unholy alliance of the North against the South' (Kaushik 1997, 56).

Indian perception of Western involvement in Central Asia appears to be inflected by the growing complexity of global politics after the fall of the Berlin Wall.[1] It is claimed that both Brussels and Washington had 'to readjust [their] equations' in the region 'on the basis of the uncertain political ties and economic realities of the post-Cold War era' (Mahapatra 2005, 156). Consequently, just like in the cases of Russia and China, the engagement of Western agency by the discourses of the 'Look North' policy has followed the changing patterns of international life. However, unlike the Central Asian policies of both Moscow and Beijing, Indian commentators note that the terrorist attacks of 11 September 2001 seem to have produced a qualitative change both in New Delhi's reading of the Central Asian agency of Western actors and in the Western involvement in Central Asia. Thus, the symbolism of these attacks has transformed '9/11' into an event, an idiom, and a moment that confronts scholars, policy-makers, and publics with the reality of complexity in global life (Kavalski 2007a, 445). In particular, it seems to have 'lent greater robustness to American policy' which now views the region as 'an area of considerable interest' (Mattoo 2003, 59). It has also been noticed that the increasing levels of 'Western military presence' in the region has altered the 'geopolitical scenario' of Central Asia and has 'accelerated' the 'new great game' (Joshi 2003, 68). A number of proponents of the 'Look North' policy have suggested that it was in the context of a nascent global 'war on terror' that forced Brussels and Washington both to recognize and to accept the validity of India's post-1998 foreign policy. At the same time, however, many have discerned that India's interactions with the West in Central Asia have evinced a limitation similar to the one undercutting New Delhi's relations with Beijing—to sum up, 'India needs the [West] much more that the [West] needs India' (Rajagopalan 2005, 303). As Chapter 8 will illustrate, this shortcoming hints at the *no influence* of the 'Look North' policy.

However, unlike Chapter 5 and Chapter 6, which contextualized India's confrontation with the Central Asian agency of Russia and China (respectively) within the narrative patterns of New Delhi's bilateral relations with Moscow and Beijing, the encounter with

Western agency in the region does not conform to this framework. As already suggested the emplotment of the West in the discourses of the 'Look North' policy reveals that it is a composite actor involving the EU, the USA, and NATO. This construction makes impossible the undertaking of a detailed narrative imbrication of New Delhi's interaction with each one of these actors within the limits of this chapter. Moreover, the suggestion is that such a detailed account is not necessarily required for the purposes of this investigation.

Consequently, the following sections outline Indian interpretations of the agency of the EU. Firstly, New Delhi's interactions with Brussels are probably the most understudied aspect of the Indian perceptions of Western agency. Secondly, understanding the context of the India-EU relationship would be impossible to extrapolate from the study of their diplomatic engagement in Central Asia. Thirdly, Indian understandings of the international actorness of the USA (and by extension of NATO) traditionally attract the bulk of scholarly and policy attention. In fact, the subsequent investigation of Indian narratives on Western agency in Central Asia demonstrates a similar preoccupation with Washington's involvement in the region. In this respect, the following sections engage in a much-needed discourse analysis of the India-EU bilateral relationship.

Overview of the Interactions between the European Union and India

In line with the narrative imbrication approach outlined in Chapter 1, the following analysis engages in a close reading of the declarations, documents and testimonies that mark the cornerstones of EU-India interactions. Such a narrative process-tracing is premised on the appraisal of the post-Cold War foreign policy developments in India and the EU. Firstly, this study teases out the emergence (and the nascent agency) of the external relations of Brussels. It then traces the transformations in the international actorness of New Delhi and its transpiring forward foreign policy. Thirdly, such an overview provides the context for the analysis of the composite genealogy, distinct grammars (of the *untimely, socialisation* and *parity*) and pervasive contradictions of India-EU relations. While such an assessment draws attention to the complexities of world politics, at the same time, it also offers a background for detailing the dominant themes underwriting Indian perceptions of the 'strategic partnership' between Brussels and New Delhi.

Genealogy, Grammars, and Contradictions of the EU-India Relationship

The relationship between the EU and India reflects the complex historical genealogy of the connections between Europe and South Asia, as well as the significance of the distinct grammars animating the social, political, and economic exchanges between these regions (Cameron et al. 2005, Jain 2007, Khosla 2004; Kirpalani and Seristo 1998). The engagement in textual process-tracing is intended as a sketch for a prolegomenon to the conceptual contexts of the EU-India relationship. In other words, the motivation here is not only to *discover* new and previously untouched perspectives on the complex relationship between Brussels and New Delhi, but also the *uncovery* (i.e. the *excavation*) of viewpoints from underneath layers of ossified or never-problematized knowledge (Bially-Mattern 2005, 5). By elaborating the contradictions of their foreign-policy-approaches, this investigation reveals that (as has been suggested in Chapter 3) the discursive interpretation of international relations can be read not only as the reproduction of policy-goals, but also as a representation of the mythmaking narratives that underpin external agency.

Genealogy of EU-India Interactions

Brussels routinely acknowledges that during the 1960s India was one of the first countries to set up relations with the emerging European Union (Cameron et al. 2005, 6). The relationship between India and the then European Community was formalized with the 1981 Agreement for Commercial and Economic Coope-ration. As the appellation of this document suggests, the gist of the interaction between Brussels and New Delhi was ensconced within the area of trade and commerce. This pattern of essentially economic relations was reiterated by the 1994 Cooperation Agreement on Partnership and Development. Despite its alleged broader scope, the preamble asserts that its main aim is 'to enhance commercial and economic contacts between India and the EU [by] creating favourable conditions for a substantial development and diversification of trade and industry within the framework of a more dynamic relationship which will further their development needs, investment flows, commercial and economic cooperation' (EC 1994b, 24). In fact the centrality of economic interests is intimated by Article 4, which spells out the three main areas of the EU-India interactions:

(i) 'improving the economic environment in India by facilitating access to Community know-how and technology'; (ii) 'facilitating contracts between economic operators and other measures designed to promote commercial exchanges and investments'; and (iii) 'reinforcing mutual understanding of their respective economic, social and cultural environment as a basis for effective cooperation' (EC 1994b, 26). Within these three areas, the 1994 Cooperation Agreement outlines a set of seventeen targets stretching from 'improvement in the economic environment and the business climate' to 'cooperation in the fields of information and culture' (EC 1994b, 26). In this respect, the EU and India agreed upon ten 'means' for achieving these objectives ranging from the 'exchange of information and ideas', 'provision of technical assistance and training programs' to the 'establishment of links between research and training centers, specialized agencies and business organizations' (EC 1994b, 27).

At the same time, the 1994 Cooperation Agreement made explicit the noncommittal nature of this relationship by acknowledging that Brussels and New Delhi 'will, within the limits of their available financial means and within the framework of their respective procedures and instruments, make available funds to facilitate the aims set out in this document especially as concerns economic cooperation'—therefore, it recommended that the EU and India 'hold friendly *ad hoc* consultations' (EC 1994b, 30; emphasis original). Yet, as the decade of the 1990s was coming to an end, there seemed to be a shared understanding in Brussels and in New Delhi that both of them were operating in a qualitatively new international environment. Thus, intent on increasing its visibility the EU unfolded a 'Strategic Partnership' with India. Such a strategic partnership between Brussels and New Delhi, thereby, has been translated as a 'new-found reciprocity and recognition of each other's potential and relevance', which occurred on the backdrop of transforming external contexts (Baroowa 2006, 3).

As suggested in Chapter 3, this discursive enhancement in the external relations of Brussels reflects the increasing awareness of its global propensity. For instance, the *European Security Strategy* (2003, 14) maintains that 'our [the EU's] history, geography and cultural ties give us links with every part of the world [...] These relationships are an important asset to build on. In particular, we should look to develop strategic partnerships with Japan, China,

Canada and India as well as with all those who share our goals and values, and are prepared to act in their support'. The strategic culture implicit in such assertions has been articulated in the context of the EU's increasing engagement in Asia. Brussels has acknowledged that 'the rise of Asia is dramatically changing the world [...] The establishment of a strong, coordinated presence in different regions of Asia will allow Europe at the beginning of the 21st century to ensure that its interests are taken fully into account there' (EC 1994a, 3). In this respect, the Strategic Partnership with India reflects the 'focus on strengthening the EU's political and economic presence across Asia, and rising this to a level commensurate with the global weight of an enlarged EU' (EC 2001, 15).

In this context, the EU-India relationship had already begun its discursive alteration within the context of regularized annual high-level meetings starting with the 2000 Lisbon Summit. Brussels declared that the summit was 'a turning point' as it provided the foundations for 'a coalition of interest in addressing global challenges' (EC 2001, 12). It furthered the 'enhanced partnership' (EC 1996) between India and the EU by providing a forum for the discussion and negotiation of differences. Chris Patten (2004), the then External Relations Commissioner of the EU, proclaimed that the regular summit-meetings opened 'a new chapter in the EU-India relationship' premised on the appreciation that 'just as we are changing fast, India herself is evolving'. Brussels has, thereby, reiterated its 'very direct interest not only in what happens on its own borders but also in the situation in South Asia' (EC 1996, 7).

Thus, the Strategic Partnership is promoted as 'the starting point of a collective reflection on upgrading EU-India relations' (EC 2004c, 11). At the same time, by acknowledging that 'the EU and India are increasingly seen as forces for global stability [and that] the focus of their relations has shifted from trade to wider political issues', Brussels intends 'a strategic alliance for the promotion of an effective multilateral approach' (EC 2004c, 3). These assertions recognize that 'the institutional architecture of EU-India relations defined by the 1994 Cooperation Agreement and the 2000 Lisbon Summit has created a complex structure of meetings at different levels in virtually all areas of interest and cooperation. It is now time to streamline and increase its effectiveness' (EC 2004c, 10). In this respect, the 2004 Strategic Partnership identifies five areas for the interactions between Brussels and New Delhi: (i) cooperation at international fora—on multilateralism, human trafficking and migration, conflict prevention and post-conflict reconstruction, non-proliferation of weapons of mass destructions, promotion of democracy and protection of human rights; (ii) economic cooperation—joint sectoral dialogues on regulatory and industrial policies; (iii) development cooperation; (iv) intellectual, scientific, and cultural cooperation; and (v) cooperation on the improvement of the institutional collaboration between India and the EU (EC 2004c, 3–10).

The implicit agenda of this 'streamlining' is 'to facilitate bridge-building' between Brussels and New Delhi by providing a framework for 'continuous dialogue... especially, on implementation of [their] international obligations and commitments, and the strengthening of global governance' (EC 2004c, 4). However, just like the 1994 Cooperation Agreement, the 2004 Strategic Partnership reiterates the noncommittal nature of Euro-Indian interactions. It plainly states that it is underwritten by the intention 'to produce *non-binding* guidelines for a further deepening of EU-India relations' (EC 2004c, 11; emphasis added). The replication of '*ad hoc*', '*non-binding*' discourses reflects the absence of strategic agreement—both on behalf of Brussels and of New Delhi—on a long term vision of their relations. This is made particularly conspicuous through a study of the *grammars* of their interactions.

Grammars of EU-India Relations

Traditionally, the public discourses of India and the EU accentuate the normative contiguity between the two polities. Thus, the intensification in the post-Cold War relationship between Brussels and New Delhi has been made possible by 'the excellent relations and traditional links of friendship' between them (EC 1994b, 24). Likewise, the premise of the 2004 Strategic Partnership is that India and the EU 'already enjoy a close relationship, based on shared values and mutual respect' (EC 2004c, 3). In its policy-response, the Indian government also recognized that the enhancement of bilateral interactions 'reveals a strong identity of views on the strategic priorities and issues of vital importance to both sides' (GoI 2004: 3). In this respect, the Indian Prime Minister Manmohan Singh declared at the 2006 Helsinki India-EU Summit that 'India and the EU are *natural partners* as we share common values of democracy, pluralism and the rule of law' (GoI 2006; emphasis added).

Thus, in their official articulations both Brussels and New Delhi tend to stress their normative similarity 'as the largest democracies in the world that share common values and beliefs' (GoI 2005). Despite the professed similarity of convictions, the narratives of EU-India interactions reflect (at least) three distinct grammars—one shared and two specific to Brussels and New Delhi respectively: (i) focus on the untimely; (ii) the EU's proclivity towards international socialization; and (iii) India's assertion of parity.

The emphasis on the *untimely* is probably the most conspicuous of the three grammars. Borrowing from a different context, the reference to the untimely here suggests that the EU-India relationship is 'exapted' not so much to present circumstances as to the future (Grosz 2004, 11). According to the 1994 Cooperation Agreement, Brussels and New Delhi '*will determine* together and to their mutual advantage the areas and priorities *to be covered* by concrete actions of economic cooperation' (EC 1994b, 27; emphasis added). The grammar of the untimely is also evident in the intention of 'stimulating a wide discussion in order to establish priority areas for action to look at future challenges' (EC 1996, 13). Likewise, the 2004 Strategic Partnership is infused with prescriptive proclamations that in their interactions India and the EU *'should seek to increase* cooperation', '*should devote* resources', '*should initiate* more concrete dialogue', and '*should work* together *to forge* an alliance' (EC 2004c, 5–10; emphasis added). Such a discursive reliance on rhetoric of the future rather than the promotion of measures and mechanisms for adapting to its contingencies is also evidenced by the declarations of India-EU Summits. For instance, after the 2005 New Delhi Summit, the two sides agreed that they '*will strengthen* collaboration', '*will encourage* contacts', '*will hold* dialogues', '*will continue to work* closely together', and '*will increase* cooperation' (GoI 2005; emphasis added). The suggestion here is that the grammar of the untimely is not only part and parcel of formal diplomatic discourse, but that it also intimates the particular attitudes that India and the EU hold about each other.

In this respect, the policy articulations of the EU suggest its educational vocation—in other words, its relations with India are targeted towards the *socialization* of the country into (what Brussels perceives to be) appropriate patterns of both domestic and international behavior under 'an agenda of "improved governance"' (EC 2002, 22). The intention of this grammar is the projection of specific standards aimed at 'building up its [India's] economic capabilities by way of provision of resources and technological assistance, in particular to improve the living conditions of the poorer sections of the population' (EC 1994b, 25). The focus on economic inequalities aims at '*imposing* an important human dimension' on Indian decision-makers (EC 1996, 15; emphasis added). Brussels also asserts that India's '"consumer class" [is] *not* on a par with Europe's middle class' (EC 1996, 4; emphasis added). Reflecting the patronizing tone of such a policy-attitude, the 1994 Cooperation Agreement has acknowledged that Brussels 'is prepared in the course of its endeavors to take into account the interests of India' (EC 1994b, 11). Likewise, the 2004 Strategic Partnership suggests that 'the EU must help India [to achieve] social and economic cohesion [because] poverty is still widespread, unemployment or underemployment is high and vast disparities persist' (EC 2004c, 9). The EU, therefore, has been intent on encouraging India 'to achieve greater convergence' with international standards (EC 2004c, 7). The socializing logic of Brussels' engagement is made apparent in its insistence on ensuring that 'Asian leaders *are committed to* addressing global issues of common concern' (EC 2004b, 12; emphasis added).

At the same time, New Delhi seems to interpret its interactions with Brussels as a relationship of *parity*, in which both parties can (and have to) learn from each other. This grammar of implicit mutual socialization reflects India's 'own vision of fairness' in contemporary world affairs based on both equity of outcomes and legitimacy of process—i.e. the claim is that 'equality of treatment is equitable only among equals' (Narlikar 2006, 63–65). For instance, the Indian government has made it explicit that 'just like India, [the EU] is one of the most important poles of a multi-polar world' (GoI 2004, 3). In this respect, New Delhi stresses that its own international significance derives from its 'rapidly growing consumer market, comprising over 250 million-strong middle class with increasing purchasing power' (GoI 2004, 4). Thus, from an Indian standpoint, the grammar of the interactions between Brussels and New Delhi reflects the dynamic parity between them. New Delhi insists that such a partnership of 'sovereign equality' (GoI 2004, 4) can actually assist the EU in achieving 'coherence among its expanding and increasingly diversifying population'; to that effect, India's experience 'with the second-largest Muslim community in the world is a paradigm of Asia's syncretic culture and of how Islam can flourish in a plural, democratic and open society' (GoI 2004, 10). The implication from such assertions is that New Delhi can also *educate* Brussels into certain standards of appropriateness. The grammar of parity, thereby, intimates India's desire 'to increase its ability to influence rule-making' (Lal 2006, 98). It has been suggested that the intention of this desire is 'to counter the agenda-setting capabilities of the EU' (Jain 2005, 11).

These three grammars tend to pervade the narratives of EU-India interactions and, as will be argued, are also implicit in the discursive emplotment of the 'Look North' policy. The simultaneity of complementarity and contradictions that underwrites their dynamics attests to the nascent complexity of world affairs encountered by the post-Cold War formulations of India's foreign policy described in Chapter 3. The claim here is that the interplay between these three grammars points to the discrepant perceptions that India and the EU hold both about themselves and each other. The following section details some of the contradictions reflected in the genealogy and grammars of EU-India interactions.

Contradictions of EU-India Relations
Just like in its bilateral relations with Russia and China, India's interactions with the EU are riddled by contradictory tendencies. Some of them stem from the distinct points of departure of their policy-approaches. Thus, while Brussels (and the capitals of other EU Member States) 'perceive India through the prism of British imperial lens' (Dixit 2000), the perceptions of New Delhi's policy-elites towards the EU 'continue to be essentially conditioned by the Anglo-Saxon media' (Jain 2005, 7). The starting premise of these viewpoints appears to prejudice the development of contextualized understanding of each other attuned to the complexities and nuances of policy making both in Brussels and in New Delhi.

Another set of contradictions emanate from the EU's sluggish recognition of India's potential and significance (Wagner 2006). Yet, even when Brussels made such an acknowledgement, it insisted that its cooperation with India falls 'within the framework of its programs in Asian and Latin American countries' (EC 1994b, 30). In this respect, despite India's impressive economic growth Brussels routinely circumscribes its achievements with the insistence that New Delhi still lags behind China 'with a more modest rate of growth' (EC 2001, 8). Such a stance reflects the EU's struggles in coming to terms with Indian sensibilities. For instance, although Brussels did not take any punitive measures after the 1998 nuclear tests, its verbal denunciation tended to confirm Indian perception of the EU's 'continued failure and reluctance to achieve a more pragmatic understanding of India's perspective' (Baroowa 2006, 8). Furthermore, the EU-India interactions are also dented by the seeming unwillingness of Brussels to discriminate between the positions of Pakistan and India through its 'search for balance between the two competing neighbors' (Jain 2005, 5; Ahmed 2002). At the same time, the EU has suggested that 'for India in particular, the strengthening of bilateral cooperation on political, economic and social cooperation' is conditional on 'enhanced partnership on global issues' (EC 2001, 21). It seems, therefore, that the intensifying rhetoric of the EU's security identity remains unconcerned that it 'impinges on India's interests' (Baroowa 2006, 9).

In this context, New Delhi interprets the 'normative power' of the EU (Manners 2002) as a disguise for its lack of effective military capabilities. Mohan (2004: 76) asserts that 'Europe's self-perception of its post-modern orientation is in essence a convenient escape from confronting emerging challenges'. Thus, while Europe sees itself as heralding a unique model of global (and security) governance, such a stance provokes 'disdain in India for the EU' (Jaffrelot 2006, 5). For instance, while Brussels 'associates the concept of effective multilateralism with a strengthening of the UN […] India tends to pursue a selective form of multilateralism in order to assert its national interest' (Wagner 2006). Such a discrepancy of visions underpins the contradictions in the international interactions between India and the EU. The narrative of assessment of their bilateral interactions intimates that what is often perceived as the very strength of the relationship between the two entities—i.e. that they 'broadly share a common vision of world affairs'—constrains the realization of prospective gains and the fulfillment of the promise of partnership (Cameron et al. 2005, 46). In this respect, some have declared that Indian discourses 'on multilateralism and the need for a multi-polar world are a smokescreen designed in particular for European consumption' (Jaffrelot 2006, 5). This attitude reflects the pragmatism of India's forward foreign policy, which informs New Delhi's 'jettisoning of *moralpolitik* in favor of realpolitik' (Jain 2005, 2; emphasis original). Such a departure from the European conceptualization of normative power underwrites the claims of Indian commentators that Brussels 'lacks consistency in its approach towards India' (Duran 2007).

Given such a 'mismatch of contexts, concerns and goals' most Indian commentators find it difficult to envisage a more substantial cooperation between the EU and India (Jain 2005, 6). The misconceptions that decision-makers both in New Delhi and in Brussels seem to hold about each other's policy-making are intimately intertwined with and reflected by the genealogy and grammars of their relationship. In this respect, it is not surprising that the EU 'hardly figures on the Indian "radar screen"' (Jaffrelot 2006, 2). Instead, some have argued that Beijing has become 'the measuring stick' for India's international agency (Cohen 2001, 266), while others aver that 'apart from Washington, the rest of the world is more or less unimportant for New Delhi' (Jain 2005, 5). The following section traces the dominant representations of the EU when it *does* figure on the 'radar screen' of India's policy-making.

Dominant Themes in India's Discourses on the EU

There are several dominant themes in India's representation of the EU evident in its public discourses: the economic significance of a single European market, Brussels management of dissimilar populations, and the baffling complexity of the EU's bureaucracy. The following brief outline is intended as a suggestive rather than an exhaustive exploration of the narrations of these themes. It also outlines the perceptual background against which the EU's international agency is being conceptualized within the narratives of the 'Look North' policy. In this respect, it is a sketch of the dominant Indian perceptions of the EU's external affairs.

The genealogy, grammars and contradictions of the EU-India relationship seems to confirm the suggestion that outsiders tend to perceive Brussels first and foremost as an economic actor. In this respect, although the EU is 'both a key part of the multilateral structures of world politics and a player of growing resonance and influence in its own right', the weight and presence of its agency 'seems to be consistently considered primarily in an economic context' (Chaban et al. 2006, 260). Thus, it is the commercial, trade, and aid capacities of the EU that underscore the perceptions of its global actorness. Likewise, India's reading of the EU gauges the agency of Brussels primarily from the script of its economic influence. In this respect, it is the economic imperatives that are 'of paramount importance and are bound to remain central to India's relations with the EU' (Baroowa 2006, 3). This perception is implicit in the appreciation and response both to the 1994 Cooperation Agreement and the 2004 Strategic Partnership as well as the initiation of regularized India-EU Summits. Jain (2005, 7) argues that it is the perception of the economic leverage of the European market that skews New Delhi's perception of 'the EU not as one entity but as a conglomerate of states'.

At the same time, however, Indian narratives of the EU reflect a significant degree of fascination with its ability to bring together states and peoples with diverse (often conflictual) histories and cultures. This perception dovetails with the interpretation of its own agency in the context of the 'Look North' policy (discussed in Chapter 4), where New Delhi is presented as a blueprint of a secular and democratic polity to be emulated by Central Asian states. As the Indian government has suggested, 'the EU has become one of the most politically influential and economically powerful regional entities in the world [because] of its ability to synthesize the divergent approaches/goals of the Member-States into a coherent whole' (GoI 2004, 4). In this respect, the EU's ability to unite a restive continent through shared institutional arrangements is a significant incentive for New Delhi's collaboration with Brussels. For instance, Mukhopadhyay (2006) asserts 'the distinctiveness of the EU lies in the flexibility to arrive at a decision mostly based on consensus. For [Indian] observers, it is understandably an experience to note the continuous compromise amongst 25-plus member nations on a daily basis in almost all aspects of European lives'.

The appeal of the EU as a symbol of 'unity in diversity', however, is somewhat occluded by the (alleged) baffling complexity of its institutional arrangements. In spite of Edward Luce's (2007) quip that India should be more understanding of European political structures (as the relationship between New Delhi and the various Indian states as well as 'policy coherence' (Sahni 2004, 259) within the government administration is not so dissimilar to that of the EU), a number of Indian commentators assert that 'the EU suffers from "a lack of consensus"', which prevents New Delhi from 'earning high points in Europe' because Brussels 'has no strategic vision' (Jain 2005, 67). As Singh (2004) argues, the bureaucratic structure of Brussels has turned the attempts 'to reach consensus [into] "a nightmare"'. Such a stance appears to validate the inference that the preoccupation of Brussels with internal processes prevents it from playing an effective global role. Thus, the perception of convoluted procedures impeding the process and practices of the EU tend to impact negatively on its 'diplomatic power' and impairs its regard as 'a cohesive force' (Chaban et al. 2006, 255). In this respect, Duran (2007) has criticized the 2004 Strategic Partnership as an 'empty rhetoric rather than a content driven strategy' owing to the 'obstacles imposed by the EU institutional architecture, and decision-making mechanisms'. In this context, a number of Indian commentators have noted that 'the [structural] fuzziness of the future of the union' has questioned 'whether the EU is indeed a power' (Mukhopadhyay 2006).

These themes seem to underwrite the contradictions emanating from the interplay between the genealogy and grammars of the EU-India relationship. Their dominant inkling is that the EU (although significant) is not central to the foreign policy aspirations of New Delhi. Capturing the popular and policy Indian mood of the interactions between Brussels and New Delhi, Jain (2005, 6) affirms that 'Europe is like "the dowdy old lady"', who does not only want to be 'liked', but also 'loved'; thus, 'Europe is disillusioned when it finds that India is not willing to reciprocate'. This understanding of the complexity of the EU-India interactions contributes to New Delhi's interpretation of Western agency in international life and its contextualization within the discursive articulations of the 'Look North' policy.

Indian Perceptions of Western Agency in Central Asia

The point of departure for the interpretation of the roles played by Western actors in Central Asia is the acknowledgement of their *legitimacy* (not merely their *presence*) in Asian affairs. Thus, the narratives of the 'Look North' policy suggest that for the EU this legitimacy derives from 'the density of its interests'; for the USA, its belonging to the Asia-Pacific 'gives [it] similar Asian legitimacy' (Rana 2007, 211); and for NATO—'as attested by its expansion'—the legitimacy derives from the 'new geopolitical and geostrategic boundaries' that it has created (Bhattacharjea 2008, 11). Nevertheless, as has already been indicated, it was '9/11' that 'changed the rules of the game as far as international relations [are] concerned' (Kachru 2007, 5) and 'radically metamorphosed the geopolitics of Central Asia' as far as Western agency is concerned (Patnaik 2005,

210). The realization of Western vulnerability to regional threats belies Brussels' and Washington's enhanced involvement and interest in Central Asia after '9/11'. As is conceded by proponents of the 'Look North' policy:

> Central Asia's political turbulence and its rich energy resources have [long] encouraged the US and European powers to have their share in the pie of political influence. This has been greatly facilitated by the events of 11 September [2001] that not only made Central Asia more vulnerable to the influx of refugees and activities of fundamentalist forces, but also provided a justification, not to be challenged on the face of it by even China and Russia, for the US and NATO interests to establish a military presence in the region to pursue the 'war on global terrorism' in Afghanistan and the adjoining region. (Muni 2003, 104)

In other words, the current ramifications of the 'new great game' reflect the social construction and mutual constitution of (simultaneously) regional politics and external agency: 'no one would feel unduly concerned if it were an obscure part of the world. But Central Asia is after all Central Asia because it is one of the most important regions of the world', especially after the initiation of the 'war on terror'—'the first war of the 21st century' (Sharma 2007, 128). Such an understanding notwithstanding, Indian commentators overwhelmingly admit that underwriting this prominence is the simultaneous treatment of the 'oil and gas of Central Asian states [as] objects of international politics' (Gidadhubli 2007, 170). At the same time, the discourses of the 'Look North' policy concede that the 'war on terror' has provided India with 'a rare chance to work with the US in changing Pakistan's national course towards political moderation, economic modernization, and regional harmony' (Budania 2003, 86).

It is in this context, that the discursive construction of '9/11' in the foreign policy making of Western actors 'has changed the terms of reference and the governing principles of inter-state relations' in Central Asia (Dixit 2004, 14). At the same time, the narratives of the 'Look North' policy reveal a pervasive view that Western actors have transformed themselves in response to the new threat-perceptions. For instance, the discussion of India's engagement in Central Asia often remarks that 'the changed paradigm' has forced NATO to 'reinvent itself' so that it can tackle its new 'adversary'—'instability' (Joshi 2007a, 151). Thus, the '"international community's" presence' in the region is explained through the desire for 'fighting [the] two security menaces'—'namely, terrorism and the proliferation of weapons of mass destruction' (Muni and Mohan 2005, 56). The contention, therefore, is that the 'Look North' policy indicates an attempt to convince both regional states and external actors that 'India is an opportunity not a threat' (Mohan 2007, 395). This understanding animates both Indian *support* and *opposition* to Western agency in Central Asia. Each of these trends is discussed individually in the following sections.

Supporting Western Agency in Central Asia

The perception of partnership between India and Western actors in Central Asia builds on the post-1998 transformation of New Delhi's foreign policy making as well as the altered significance of the region as a result of its socially constructed position in the 'war on terror'. Thus, the discourses of the 'Look North' policy declare that both Brussels and Washington are 'natural partners' to New Delhi (Mahapatra 2007, 173; Srichandan 2007, 458). Although such a partnership is of fairly recent provenance, its narrative explanations have seamlessly dovetailed with the self-aggrandizing logic of New Delhi's foreign policy making. For instance, Amit Gupta convincingly argues that 'from an American perspective', India is

> a significant partner for achieving strategic stability in Asia: it shares democratic values with the United States; it has a large military force that is professional and capable of fighting well; it has a burgeoning market for US goods and services; it can provide the type of intellectual labor that the United States requires to remain globally competitive; and it is one of the countries in Asia that can act as a counterbalance to China. (2008, 120)

In this respect, Shivshankar Menon, the Foreign Secretary of the Ministry of External Affairs, has indicated that the improved interaction with Western actors has been 'important to us, because of *the positive effect it has on our dealings with the rest of the world*, and on our access to markets, high technology, and resources crucial to our future economic growth and development' (Menon

2007, 390; emphasis added). Judging by their relations in Central Asia, there seem to be several reasons for the Indian support of Western agency.

- Firstly, many seem to appreciate the 'realist mode of thinking' (Mattoo 2003, 48) informing both Washington's and Brussels' policy in Central Asia. Such an approach seems to gel well with New Delhi's own realpolitik-driven external affairs in the region.
- Secondly, the proponents of the 'Look North' policy seem to concur that Western actors—and Washington in particular—cannot maintain their 'footprint' in Central Asia without India's 'active cooperation' (Sharma 2007, 138). Thus, the USA has been helping 'India [to] become a major power in the international system' (Gupta 2008, 120). As the then Minster of External Affairs, Yashwant Sinha proclaimed, 'the US interest in our [bilateral] relationship is like the interest of a friend. They are talking to us like how a friend talks' (cited in Nautiyal 2004, 150). Consequently, the July 2005 agreement between Prime Minister Manmohan Singh and President George W. Bush to initiate a civilian nuclear cooperation between the two countries appears to confirm these interpretations (Menon and Nigam 2007, 168; Mohan 2007, 396). Such a recognition of India's nuclear capabilities reveals that 'the rising power of India' has not provoked 'panic' among Western actors (Mahapatra 2005, 177), because it '*complements* [...] their diversified economic structures in terms of output, capital, stock, human resources, and trade in goods and services' (Srichandan 2007, 458; emphasis added). Corroborating the assertive logic of foreign policy making, other commentators have argued that the cooperation between India and Western actors in Central Asia was in fact made possible by the 1998 nuclear tests. The claim is that they (i) 'liberated' both New Delhi and Western governments from the constraints imposed by the uncertainty of India's nuclear capabilities (Kapur 2006, 3) and (ii) made Western actors concede to 'India's legitimate role in the regional and global strategic environment' (Budania 2003, 83).
- Thirdly, Indian commentators assert that Western agency would genuinely assist in strengthening the institutions and governance of statehood in Central Asia. Therefore, India needs to support (and affiliate) with Western efforts. For instance, commentators

have welcomed the unveiling of a three-pronged US-approach to Central Asian states which aims at 'security promotion, internal reform, and energy development' (Mattoo 2003, 51). Such an understanding dovetails with the mythmaking logic of New Delhi's post-1998 foreign policy making which depicts democracy as 'the idea of India' (Lak 2008, 293). Likewise, the expected 'spur in energy demand' as a result of EU-enlargement is projected to 'unleash economic growth in the region' (Mahalingam 2004, 132). The claim is that Western involvement in the energy markets of Central Asian states 'benefits all of them' as it leads to the development of alternative transport links (Joshi 2004, 204). Chapter 4 has indicated that the narratives of the 'Look North' policy interpret these developments as favorable not only to the strengthening of Central Asian states, but also to India's strategic interests.

- Fourthly, the narratives of the 'Look North' policy have positioned Western actors as leveraging India against China. As Chapter 6 explains, the relations between the two Asian countries have not been devoid of suspicion (especially, after the 1962 war between them). Thus, despite the current attempts to develop pragmatic relations, New Delhi still remains wary of Beijing's agency in Central Asia. In this setting, the convergence between Indian and Western interests with regards to the stability of Central Asia, reveals New Delhi's tacit endorsement for the West's attempt to 'put a collar on the Yellow Dragon' through an increased military presence in Central Asia (Muni 2003, 105; Kanwal 1999, 1614). This development is also interpreted as an indication that 'the more focused sections of the American establishment are *finally* waking up to the challenge unveiled by SCO under the leadership of China' (Mohan 2006; emphasis added). The support for Western agency in Central Asia exposes that 'India is keen to balance Chinese influence in the strategically vital region that abuts China, Iran, Russia, and Afghanistan' (Aneja 2002; Bhattacharya 2004, 360). The construction of this willingness to confront Beijing in the narratives of the 'Look North' policy is informed by the realization that 'China poses a threat to India's plans in Central Asia' (Dutta 2008). There seems to be a marked belief that 'the US strategic partnership with India can countervail the Chinese threat' (Budania 2003, 89).

- Fifthly, the discourses of the 'Look North' policy reveal that the development by Western actors of 'important stakes in Central Asia [due to] the campaign to fight terrorism and extremism globally' (Mattoo 2003, 49) would assist New Delhi's foreign policy objectives in the region. Said otherwise, 'the emergence of an international alliance against terrorism has brought positive results for India's regional security environment' (Budania 2003, 91). In particular, it seems to have allayed Indian anxiety that Central Asia 'could undergo a fundamental shift if the forces of religious extremism [are allowed to] sweep the existing regimes out of power' (Joshi 2007a, 146; Shams-ud-Din 1991). It is in this setting that '9/11' appears to have introduced a sense of convergence between Indian and Western security perceptions (Datta 2008, 6). The elimination of 'extremist elements from the Central Asian republics' (Dwivedi 2007, 239) has long been a feature of New Delhi's foreign policy objectives. Such a stance (as already indicated in Chapter 4) has been part of New Delhi's concern about 'the threats posed by Islamic forces active in Afghanistan' both to 'India's interests in the region and to the survival of Central Asian states' (Asopa 2007, 172; see also Rahul 1981; Sareen 1981). New Delhi's discursive formulations of '"zero tolerance" for terrorism' and the 'mercenary marauders from foreign countries [who] are recruited as foot-soldiers for Islam' as well as its pronouncements on the imminent threat from 'the strident march of virulent Islamist fundamentalism' and from 'Islamic narco-terrorism' (Kanwal 1999, 1611–1612) prevaricate much of the post-'9/11' rhetoric of President George W. Bush and his administration.

Thus, the 'war on terror' has been interpreted as an indication of Washington's conversion to New Delhi's point of view—namely, it offers 'a tentative connection between acts of terror committed against India and the United States' (Sidhu 2003, 216). Some analysts have even read Washington's foreign policy shift as 'a tacit acceptance of the long-term failure of American policy which used the "Islamic card" as an antidote to communist ideology and [to the] Soviet campaign in Afghanistan since 1979' (Raj and Mahapatra 2004, 292).[2] India has therefore emphasized its support for the anti-Taliban Northern Alliance (owing to the 'acute awareness of Al Qaeda-Taliban-[Pakistan's] ISI collaboration [and] its close nexus with the terrorist and jihadi forces in Jammu and Kashmir')—especially, after the 'humiliating deal' following the hijacking of an Indian Airlines plane to Afghanistan in December 1999 (Muni 2003, 107–115). Indian commentators have thereby been quite forthcoming in declaring the need 'to adopt a proactive strategy [which would] ensure that the Taliban do not continue to rule Afghanistan and [their] militia is disbanded' (Kanwal 1999, 1614). From India's point of view, Afghanistan has been at the heart of a 'complex web of security' which impinges on 'the security and stability of Central Asia' (Mohapatra 2007, 168; Roy 2001, 2275). The discourses of the 'Look North' policy have therefore tended to welcome the American-led overthrow of the Taliban regime. Analysts readily admit that 'New Delhi has regained its influence in the country post-9/11' (*Hindustan Times*, 30 April 2006). The consequent 'removal of the Taliban from the political scene in Afghanistan' has intensified India's 'Look North' and its attempt to 'woo the neighboring Central Asian nations [and] build a line of defence against extremism' (Aneja 2002).

Furthermore, it has been observed that as a result of '9/11', the West has begun to acknowledge that 'the "stans" have more in common with South Asia' (an argument Indian commentators have been making for quite some time)—a claim, which is then interpreted as both a recognition and an endorsement of '*India's sphere of influence* [in the region]' (Rajghatta 2005; emphasis added). Yashwant Sinha, the former Minster of External Affairs has reiterated that India's involvement in Afghanistan is part and parcel of a project to 'reduce the distance between India and Central Asia' (Sinha 2004, 6). Associated with this sentiment is the realization that Western actors—and the EU in particular—are eager to develop infrastructure projects that 'bypass Pakistan' (*India Express*, 21 March 2007). In New Delhi, this trend 'is being seen as a major opportunity to increase India's links with Central Asia' (*Hindustan Times*, 13 July 2008). At the same time, the perception is that Central Asian countries 'endorse India taking a more active interest in bringing back normalcy to Afghanistan in the post-Taliban period. India should be responsive to these orientations, because they meet India's interests also' (Dixit 2004, 19).[3] In this setting, some commentators have indicated that 'the Indian decision to set up an air-base in Tajikistan [which was discussed in Chapter 4] has been configured to give both the United States and Indian air forces the ability to conduct joint operations', not only against insurgents in Afghanistan, but also *'to project power in Central Asia'* (Gupta 2008, 124–125; emphasis added).

The five points above summarize the main themes behind India's support for Western agency in Central Asia. Their attitude indicates the discursive recognition of the 'Look North' policy that 'the issues of regional security and strategic order in Central Asia are a complex mix of domestic concerns and external anxieties' (Muni 2003, 122). At the same time, the rationale of these five areas of Indian discursive support for the Western involvement in Central Asian politics reiterates that the 'peace and stability in the Central Asian republics and Afghanistan seems to be *the most crucial factor* for India's security' (Roy 2001, 2273; emphasis added). Such a narrative tendency conforms to the discursive patterns of New Delhi's post-1998 foreign policy mythmaking.

Opposing Western Agency in Central Asia

Regardless of the existence of significant levels of support for the West, the narratives of the 'Look North' policy also evince substantial opposition towards its involvement in Central Asia. Rajesh Rajagopalan points out that despite (if not because of) their convergence of interests in the region, New Delhi's relations with the West 'cannot [be expected to] improve simply because they are "natural allies"—that would be a rare beast in international politics'. Therefore, the existence of cooperative interaction between India and Western actors in Central Asia should not be misunderstood as a 'consequence of any great confluence of interests. It reflects rather, *the lack of any major dissonance'* in their perspectives. Thus, India 'has little choice [and incentives] but to seek closer ties with the [West; and also] fighting others seeking a seat on the same bandwagon' (Rajagopalan 2005, 306; emphasis added).

From this point of view (and in line with the logic of India's post-1998 foreign policy making), the warming of relations between New Delhi and the West appears as nothing short of a strategic marriage of convenience. Bearing this in mind, India has rejected the 'repeated Russian attempts to call for a Russia-India-China strategic partnership' on the grounds of its perceived 'anti-American orientation' (Gupta 2008, 117; Kaushik 2007, 141). At the same time, however, the 'Look North' policy conveys that India has 'to temper the ramifications of assertive US policy orientations [in Central Asia] *despite the normative and moral framework within which these orientations [are] articulated'* (Dixit 2004, 14; emphasis added). Such statements reiterate India's suspicion of (as well as willingness to criticize) Western interventions in the affairs of (not only) Central Asian states which are framed in the language of human rights protection. For instance, Indian commentators have shown solidarity with the 'Central Asian political elites' and their 'resentment of the *intrusiveness of Western diplomacy'* in the wake of the Western-supported (if not sponsored) '"regime change" in Georgia' (Bhadrakumar 2004). As indicated in Chapter 6, such an attitude conforms to New Delhi's resistance to

> the manner in which human rights issues are used as an international affairs instrument. For one thing, [the] countries that profited enormously from colonialism and imperialism in the recent past, do not carry much credibility in the eyes of their former victims, who underwent gross human rights abuse of every kind. [Moreover] the application of [the] principles of human rights is highly selective; and those perceived as allies or special friends receive indulgent treatment. (Rana 2007, 164)

Thus, the beginning of such a divergence between New Delhi and Western actors can be traced to the legacy of anti-colonial sentiments. This perception demonstrates that Western strategies premised on the 'imposition of democracy' aggravate the 'real security issues of Asia' (Sharma 2004a, 264–267). Moreover, such practices indicate that 'the principle of sovereignty and the right of choosing one's own government are not significant in the new US strategy' (Nautiyal 2004, 138). Instead, 'the aggression against Yugoslavia [has] showed how illusory the security of any state is if it is not liked by the West' (Bhambhri 2005, 387). At the same time, such an opposition to Western involvement in Central Asia can be attributed to the well-established knee-jerk revulsion of 'alliance-type relationships' as 'a matter of national principle' (Mohan 2007, 396). Many observers have criticized the 'coalition of Western and pro-Western countries [whose] support for the "unipolar world order" and [the] "globalized world economy" seem set [to] acquire control over the natural resources of [Central Asia]. The Western countries are too eager to fill the "power vacuum" and take charge of the destinies and energy resources of the newly independent countries of [the region]' (Asopa 2007, 185). Attesting to the persistence of sentiments from the Cold War period, such foreign policy attitudes have been extremely critical of the ulterior motives underwriting both Washington's and Brussels' agency in Central Asia. These narratives have vilified the merely realpolitik objective to establish Western 'military hegemony' in the region 'under [the] cover of anti-terrorist rhetoric' so that 'NATO', the 'Europeans', and 'the United States' can control 'the "Great Silk Route"' (Kaushik 2007, 142).

It is noteworthy that a significant role for the opposition to Western agency in Central Asia derives not from 'ideological elements, on the left and [the] right' (Mohan 2007, 397), but from the very mythmaking logic of India's post-1998 foreign policy. The self-aggrandizing assertions of India's nuclear capabilities have indicated a growing concern about China's 'great power ambitions' and 'how that power would be used, whether it will be responsive to the interests of others and value the principles of common security and the rule of universally accepted norms' (Dutta 1997, 154–155). Thus, true to the tenets of realpolitik, India has continued to view China as 'a long-term security challenge' (Budania 2003, 89). The negative attitudes in this context relate to New Delhi's frustration that Western activities in Central Asia tend to enhance Beijing's international outreach (and not only in the region). For instance, the perception is that it is Western agency that has led Russia and China to put aside their differences and cooperate in the region. In fact, it is proffered that 'the US-led bombing of Yugoslavia' has urged 'Moscow and Beijing [to] demonstratively come together' (Bakshi 2002, 93). The claim has been that 'in view of the expanding NATO', 'Russia has forged strong cooperation with China' (Joshi 2007, 153; Dwivedi 2007, 239). Likewise, 'China's concern [over] NATO's eastward expansion towards its borders' has urged it to establish SCO as 'an attempt to block US influence and investment in oil-rich Central Asia' (Singh 2003, 349; Bhattacharjea 2008, 13). The creation of SCO has reinforced New Delhi's perception of cementing the collaboration between Moscow and Beijing and, at the same time, diminishing India's influence both to them and to the Central Asian states.

Furthermore, Indian commentators have appeared concerned that the warming relations between New Delhi and the West in Central Asia might re-energize the 'cooperation' between China and Pakistan (Jain 2008, 144). As discussed in Chapter 6, putting an end to Beijing's military support for Pakistan is central to the development of a pragmatic partnership between India and China (Mishra 1996, 175). In this respect, some analysts have queried 'how a US-India alliance that seeks to contain China could be operationalized without causing considerable disquiet in New Delhi [because] *from the Indian perspective it is not clear why the country should risk China's wrath'* (Gupta 2008, 121; emphasis added). Such a concern emanates from the perception that 'China is not likely to give up its strategic alliance with Pakistan' (Bhattacharya 2004, 359; Budania 2003, 88). Waheguru Pal Singh Sidhu spells out such anxieties:

[W]hile there is little possibility of a conventional war, let alone a nuclear war breaking out between India and China, such a possibility cannot be entirely ruled out if there is a nuclear exchange between India and Pakistan. For instance, if India were to absorb a first strike from Islamabad and launch a second strike against Pakistan, *could New Delhi be certain that it would not be struck by Pakistan's closest ally, China*, especially when India would have used most if not all of its second strike force? *Also, would China be relieved of its no-first-use pledge once India had struck Pakistan?* (2003, 225; emphasis added)

From the perspective of the 'Look North' policy, therefore, Western agency has introduced an additional level of complexity to the 'new great game' both by provoking a strategic alliance between Russia and China in Central Asia and by triggering a reinvigoration of China's relations with Pakistan. To complicate matters even further, the ongoing conflict in Afghanistan and its impact on neighboring Pakistan have been interpreted as yet another challenge to New Delhi's Central Asian agency. In this setting the issue of state collapse (which Chapter 4 discussed only in the context of the Central Asian republics) has become one of the key concerns for the narratives of the 'Look North' policy. Thus, the 'accelerated process of militarization of Asia' as a result of the 'war on terror' (Koshy 203, 165) has intensified 'the threats to security and stability' deriving from 'the "nature of things," i.e. from within [the state]' (Sharma 2004a, 263–264).

It is usual for Indian commentators to maintain therefore that 'the Afghan crisis holds the key to the stability of the Asian region' (Sharma 2002, 98). As explained, such an understanding informs New Delhi's narrative support for overthrow of the Taliban regime. The expectation however was that Western military action would at the very least diminish the threats to both India and Central Asia emanating from 'the hotbed of international terrorism, i.e. the states of Pakistan and Afghanistan' (Mann 2001, 2036). Thus, the resurgence of Taliban forces in both Afghanistan and the north-western frontier region of Pakistan and the increasingly palpable state failure of both countries has firmed up Indian criticism of Western agency because the 'violent turbulence in Afghanistan is affecting both India and the Central Asian republics negatively' (Roy 2001, 2277; Chandra 2008, 947; Sharma 2004a, 275). The West is thereby blamed for creating 'a government in Afghanistan which does not have any control outside the country's capital' (Raj and Mahapatra 2004, 298) and, at the same time, for deepening the 'state of turmoil' inside Pakistan (Kanwal 1999, 1612). NATO has been singled out not only as 'the newest actor in the Afghan conflict', but also as 'the most confused component in the American counter-terrorism mission. It seems to epitomize a military bloc [with] no clarity about its policy objectives' (Chandra 2008, 946; emphasis added). The suggestion then is that 'the longer the [West] remains engaged in Central Asia, the more pronounced the instability of the region would be' (*Indian Express*, 13 April 2004) and its 'security environment is likely to remain under a dark cloud' (Sharma 2004a, 275).

The proposition therefore is that for India the involvement of Western actors 'has a direct bearing on its vital interests [...] Today, Indian interests are substantial and are in the sphere of strategic, political, and economic security. Any competition among major powers for control and influence in India's extended neighborhood would have a bearing on its policy and diplomacy in the region. [So far] India is not forced to choose [but] if the competitive element in Central Asia becomes a dominant tendency, India would have to take hard decisions' (Joshi 2003, 8). The claim is that in the context of the 'new great game', 'India may be called upon to take positions and even obligations that may not be compatible with its own vital stakes in the region [and which] may also have *not too benign* socio-political and strategic spill-over for India' (Muni 2003, 99; emphasis added). Consequently, India's opposition to the involvement of Western actors in the region confirms the perception that more often than not New Delhi and Western capitals have had 'divergent worldviews' (Gupta 2008, 121). At the same time, it has also been asserted that the construction of such an opposition to Western agency indicates 'the first installment of an unfolding great national debate on the future direction of India's foreign policy' (Mohan 2007, 397).

Conclusion

This chapter has demonstrated the complex nature of New Delhi's encounter with the West in Central Asia. At the same time, it has indicated that the analytical context of the 'new great game' compounds even further Indian perceptions of the EU's, the USA's, and NATO's involvement in the region. The framework of such an emplotment animates the patterns of support for and opposition to Western actorness. The strategic oscillation evinced by the discursive formulations of the 'Look North' policy reveals the contradictory perspectives on the impact of the West on India's security environment and its agency in Central Asia.

Such a narrative engagement with the modalities of the 'new great game' illustrates the need for a contextual, yet continually evolving foreign policy making. This adaptive flexibility is required by the proliferation of extra-regional and intra-regional agency in Central Asia. In this respect, New Delhi's encounter with the regional agency of Western actors has reinforced the mythmaking logic of its assertive post-1998 foreign policy posturing. As this chapter illustrates the location of the West in the articulations of the 'Look North' policy reveals the tendency of foreign policy discourses to construct narratives that weave images of the past into the concerns of the present in order to validate a strategic vision of the future. The following Chapter 8 will engage with the implications from such mythmaking and their bearing on India's interactions both with Central Asia and the world.

8

CONCLUSION: THE NO INFLUENCE OF THE 'LOOK NORTH' POLICY

> *The year is 2040. At the United Nations, delegations are deeply divided over a troubling conflict. Two member states are fighting a border war over economic and immigration issues. The mass movement of people from poor to wealthy states continues to be one of the main challenges facing the world. The twenty-five permanent members of the UN Security Council are about to vote on whether to send UN troops and technicians to establish and keep the peace. Then one of the most powerful members of the Security Council tells the closed session that it is prepared to fund the UN force by itself, and to provide the technicians, in return for a guarantee that its soldiers will not be directly involved in the fighting. 'We have a proud tradition of not interfering in other country's affairs', says the ambassador from India, 'and we consider that sacrosanct, even if ordered to do otherwise by this august council'. That's right, India. The most powerful country in the world and a permanent member of the Security Council is taking a lead role in resolving yet another crisis with potential to destabilize the globe. Indian troops are already evacuating Indian citizens from the trouble spot, the ambassador says, taking holiday-makers and dual-nationals to safety aboard the navy's largest aircraft carrier, the Atal Bihari Vajpayee, and airlifting others in Indian-designed helicopters and aircraft [...] This is a scenario that may seem fanciful in the unipolar world of today, but it's not much of a stretch to predict that there will be some new superpowers on the block by 2040, if not well before then. One of them seems certain to be India.*
>
> Daniel Lak (2008, 261–262)

Far from 'fanciful', the epigraph above offers a good illustration of the mythmaking narrative of India's post-1998 foreign policy making. Within the space of a few sentences from 'one of the most powerful members of the Security Council' India becomes 'the most powerful country in the world' in the year 2040. In this account of New Delhi's agency in global politics, fantasy, wishful thinking, and make-believe provide the discursive devices that project an Indian desire for international prominence from the vision of a glorious future into the present. The symbolic significance of the 1998 nuclear weapons tests is conjured up in the fictitious 'aircraft carrier' named after the then Prime Minister Vajpayee. As Chapter 3 has suggested, the self-aggrandizing narrative of the country's external affairs is part of autochthonous 'invention of India' (Dutt 2006, 74) in the context of the social production of foreign policy. In this setting, the discourses of the 'Look North' policy intimate that 'India cannot wait until the rest of the world comes to its way of seeing things or at least acknowledges India's right to do things its own way'—the implication being that *in a more perfect world*, [New Delhi's] importance would be self-evident [because in] such a world each major power [would] act responsibly to keep order and promote justice in *its part of the world* (Singh 2006, 50–52; emphasis added). The narrative accounts of India's engagement in Central Asia are underwritten by such a vision of 'a more perfect world'.

The contention of this volume is that the 1998 nuclear detonations set off the myth of aggressive posturing, which spins the story of India's rise to global prominence in relation to its nuclear capabilities. The subsequent changes in the discourses of India's post-1998 foreign policy indicate not only a pragmatic operationalization of 'improved tactics', but a qualitatively different interpretation both of the country's role in global life and the character of the international system. These transformations reflect the growing tendency for the social production of foreign policy—i.e. foreign policy becomes a reflection and a projection of internal afflictions. External affairs, thereby, are deeply informed by abstract domestic desires that impact concrete international relations strategies and their discursive articulations. In the case of New Delhi, the proclamations of a resurgent Hindu nationalism have provided a narrative platform for the projection of the domestic discourses on national greatness onto the outlines of the post-1998 foreign policy. Said otherwise, the logic of nationalism has supplied powerful mythmaking narratives that help either to dispel or to make sense of both decision-making anxieties and societal insecurities.

As the analysis of the 'Look North' policy reveals, the social production of foreign policy has reasserted the mutual discursive sovereignty of a community in the form of a self-aggrandizing nation-state. Thus, despite the bifurcation between conflict and cooperation of New Delhi's encounter of other international actors in Central Asia, this should not be taken as an indication of the absence of nuances in the 'Look North' policy. Instead, such a simplifying analytical strategy is adopted for the purposes of presenting a generalizable model for rendering the external affairs of India more tractable. In practice, however—as India's interactions with Russia, China, and the West in Central Asia indicate—its foreign policy making is a composite process comprising elements (simultaneously) of convergence and divergence. This observation attests to the networked complexity of the 'new great game' in the region as well as the narrative multiplicity of the 'Look North' policy.

Furthermore, as Chapter 6 has illustrated, the formulation of India's external agency reveals the discursive difficulty of bracketing its roles in international politics within the labels, language, and practices developed for the explanation and understanding of Westphalian states. In this respect, the following section provides a brief overview of the arguments discussed in this volume and of the relevance of the methodological approaches employed for their uncovery. As has already been stated, the narrative process-tracing of the myths of India's diplomacy does not lend itself easily to the analytical modes proposed by the conventional research programs for the study of international politics. The chapter concludes with an assessment of India's foreign policy *influence* in light of the evidence derived from the narratives of its 'Look North' policy.

Overview of the Argument

The analysis of India's post-Cold War international relations in Central Asia in the preceding chapters has engaged in a discursive analysis of the formulation, practices, and patterns of its foreign policy formulation. Thus, the focus on the articulations of New Delhi's external affairs endeavors the 'uncovery' (Bially-Mattern 2005, 5) of the logics animating its 'Look North' policy. Assisting this investigation has been the narrative imbrication approach. Its creative splicing together of foreign policy statements (i) has offered a unique glimpse into the cacophony of voices involved not only in the interpretation, but also in the domestic legitimation of India's diplomacy; (ii) has presented it as a viable approach that allows Western-trained scholars to encounter (and engage with) non-Western accounts of global politics. The template provided by this volume's narrative imbrication illuminates the diverse and contested articulations of analysts, commentators, and policy-makers vying for the attention of the Indian public.

Thus, by demonstrating that foreign policy pronouncements offer a platform for the manifestations of national interests on the international arena, the narrative imbrication approach facilitates the emphasis on the import of mythmaking to India's external relations in providing access to a latent pool of malleable (and potent) symbols for the popular validation of its foreign policy agenda. Relying on the discursive study of foreign policy, this study has identified the logics informing the transformations of New Delhi's international relations, by tracing the contextual circumstances within which its Central Asian policy is enmeshed.

As the overview of the 'Look North' policy demonstrates, the end of the Cold War (with the associated loss of old certainties) has befuddled the formulation and exercise of India's foreign policy. The unwillingness to accept complexity as a characteristic feature of global life has produced a need for securitized foreign policy subjectivity. In particular, Chapter 3 has explained that the logic of mythmaking underpinning India's post-1998 external affairs reflects 'the belief in "verification" of history' which makes 'increasingly clear that we must understand the need for securitized subjectivity as existing in the nexus of structural and psychological processes—that is, security is a thick signifier. Globalization is a pertinent issue in this respect as it displays all possible features of causing emotional traumas of alienation, loss of self-esteem, and images of lost objects such as territory. As individuals experience increased levels of ontological insecurity and existential anxiety in relation to global forces, the search for securitized subjectivity is likely to increase' (Kinnvall 2006, 60; Nayar 2006, 15). Said otherwise, the logic of such foreign policy mythmaking comes to indicate that India is experiencing an especially turbulent period of ontological insecurity and existential anxiety. With the benefit of hindsight, some of the interlocutors of India's post-1998 foreign policy mythmaking have claimed that 'by the 1990s, India's isolation in the subcontinent as well as the international strategic sphere had increased, and its diplomatic as well as military options were in danger of shrinking to the point that it would have become a *paper tiger*' (Kapur 2006, 10; emphasis added).

Thus, in the wake of the Cold War the foreign-policy-elites in New Delhi found themselves in a situation where they had to declare the bankruptcy of the key notions underpinning India's international agency—that is, they were forced to break with

Nehru's legacy and, at the same time, they had to piece together a coherent external agency in the absence of the country's erstwhile strategic partner. The preceding chapters have illustrated the profound sense of incredulity in New Delhi as a result of the collapse of 'the bipolar old world order in 1989', which 'turned the whole logic of the previous would system upside down' (Sharma 2004a, 266). This dislocation has affected India's relations with Central Asia. New Delhi seemed 'so preoccupied with the loss of a dependable ally in international politics that it could not welcome the arrival of new independent entities on the political scene of Central Asia' (Asopa 2003, 185). As will be explained shortly, the initial uncertainty of India's relations with the region has hampered its subsequent attempts to overcome the limitations from New Delhi's belated agency in Central Asia.

The trauma from this loss of foreign policy bearings has become a crucial ingredient in the development of an assertive stance to New Delhi's post-1998 international interactions. Such an outlook reflects the perception that 'diplomacy' after the Cold War is *'globalized'*:

> States have intensified their engagement abroad, first, through strategizing their foreign policy to align it closely to their national interests; and, second, through intensive efforts to reach a wider circle of countries, while also deepening relations with existing partners. It is clear that the acceleration of globalization-driven interdependence has intensified external relation-building activities. World affairs are more fluid than before and therefore demand greater attention. (Rana 2007, 2)

In identifying the mythmaking qualities underpinning New Delhi's post-1998 foreign policy this book has focused on its relations with Central Asia. In this context, this study has engaged in an innovative assessment of Indian interpretation of the dominant participants in the regional 'new great game'. It is apparent that all three case studies—of India's encounter of Russia, China, and the West in Central Asia—demonstrate the tension between convergence and divergence, cooperation and conflict, support and opposition in New Delhi's international relations outlook. This oscillation is simultaneously confounding and timely. It is confounding because of the enthusiasm and conviction with which opposing standpoints are propounded (very often by the same individuals). At the same time, it is timely because it reveals a range of options for Indian state-elites to address both the complexity of the 'new great game' and the 'extreme turbulence' of global life. The discussion of the preceding chapters thereby suggests that India's post-1998 external relations as well as its 'Look North' policy are underwritten by the desire to increase the country's 'strategic autonomy', which would allow New Delhi to have 'greater flexibility to pursue its national interests' (Budania 2003, 84).

The preceding chapters have therefore revealed that the modalities of the 'Look North' policy have indicated a proclivity towards a narrative projection of India as a blueprint for the future development of Central Asia. In particular, the construction of the region as the testing ground for the grappling international agency of actors vying for global outreach has provided a dramatic geopolitical backdrop for these articulations. Such a discursive assertiveness is in compliance with New Delhi's post-1998 foreign policy stance. However, this study contends that the discursive proclamations of India's external agency in Central Asia have not been matched by comparable transformations in the ideational and institutional makeup of New Delhi's foreign policy formulation. Thus, despite the proliferation of discourses on India's nascent global grandeur, the absence of a readily available Indian vision of global politics—a *Pax Indica*, if you will—prevents New Delhi from living up to the expectations generated by such narratives. The following sections elaborate this proposition in greater detail.

No Influence: An Assessment of India's International Agency
The claim here is that India's international agency lacks the power to influence others—that is, power in international life refers to an actor's *ability* to influence other actors through the capacity to make some policy-choices more attractive than others (but without recourse to force or the threat of force). In other words, influence refers to the voluntary change of behavior and beliefs in order to suit the model/example set by someone else. At the same time, influence can have effects 'even if unintentionally' (i.e. it has the ability to produce results) because it is 'an attribute that an actor possesses [...] and works through social relations' (Barnett and Duvall 2005, 45). In this respect, a critical element of the discourses of the 'Look North' policy is the confidence in India's becoming

'*a kind of a model* for other countries' (Dutt 2006, 205; emphasis added). In particular, 'comments [made] by Central Asian scholars have revealed that the political and economic experience of India—including handling dissent in a secular, democratic setup—appears to be of considerable benefit to the region' (Dwivedi 2003, 624). This certainty derives from the assertive posturing of the post-1998 articulations of its external affairs, which convinces commentators to proclaim that 'India has many things to offer to the new [Central Asian] republics' (Asopa 2007, 183). The development of nuclear capabilities has reinforced the conviction in India's growing regional and international status by signaling that New Delhi 'has moved from being totally moralistic to a being a little more realistic' and, at the same time, reinforce the mythical narrative that 'nuclear weapons are an international currency of force and power' (Singh 1998, 47). The claim therefore is that 'as India's power status is increasing, it is inevitable that it would like to use the influence of its military capabilities to further other political objectives in its foreign and security policy' (Budania 2003, 90). The nuclear assertiveness of New Delhi's international strategy has urged the proponents of the 'Look North' policy to proclaim that 'now, the Central Asian republics are looking towards India to help them combat the menace of terrorism' (Mann 2001, 2049–2050). In other words, although 'nuclear weapons cannot be seen as a solution to India's myriad external or internal security problems, as *a country of unique status and civilizational influence*, India cannot do without them' (Singh 2006, 45–46; emphasis added). Already in the second half of the 1980s, Achin Vanaik has indicated that such an argument is 'both true in a superficial sense and untrue in a deeper sense'. Indeed, nuclear weapons are instruments of power, but the mere possession of such assets rarely translates into international prestige. As he puts it, the

> irony is not only are they [the proponents of nuclearizing foreign policy] totally wrong in this respect, they are also guilty of giving too great a weight to nuclear might as a component of political power. The USA and USSR have never been globally more powerful in nuclear terms. The have also never been globally less powerful in political terms, i.e. in their capacity to impose their will on countries and peoples—this capacity has steadily shrunk, albeit in an uneven manner.

Indian acquisition of nuclear weapons will enhance in one sense international and regional 'prestige' and 'status'. But translating this 'status' into the power to *influence* neighboring countries or others is an altogether different thing [...] Thus political 'gains' are nebulous. (1987, 75; emphasis added)

More recently, other commentators have noted that the 'projection of hard military power is no longer the only requirement for a country that wants a global political role that matches its size and economic heft' (Lak 2008, 269). Thus, the logic expressed in the self-aggrandizing narratives of New Delhi's post-1998 foreign policy infers that 'the reality [of] rapid economic growth is steadily increasing India's relative economic power. This in turn has positioned India to emerge as one of the dominant political players in the international system' (Mohan 2007, 392). This observation has been underpinned by the understanding that the 'process of globalization has given a new dimension to the meaning of security, which now includes non-military threats that states and the international society face due to the complex pattern of interdependence' (Kaul 2007, 240). The following sections therefore address the notion, practice, and implications of *influence* in world politics, the pervasive failure of New Delhi to establish itself as a model for appropriate behavior in international life, and the power of attraction missing from the discourses of the 'Look North' policy. The assertion is that India's international interaction in Central Asia evince that its international agency still has *no influence* in global affairs.

Influence: Understanding the Power of Attraction

Despite the narrative construction of the post-1998 foreign policy, the possession of nuclear weapons and the concomitant assertive foreign policy posturing have not been able to enhance India's *influence*. The notion of influence reflects the *power of attraction* of an international actor. For instance, and actor A has a power of attraction over actor B, because actor B *wants to follow the example of, emulate*, and, thereby, *be socialized by* actor A. This is done *not by force*, but *by attraction*—actor B *likes* actor A's behavior, norms, and values as expressed both on the international and the domestic stage and wants to be associated with it. The hackneyed example is the EU, whose power of attraction became a magnet for

East European states. As a result they were charmed enough to demand membership. Arguably, it was this non-military influence of the EU, which pulled the former communist states to willingly initiate a transformation of their institutions of governance through closely monitored stages of accession-driven socialization. Other instances of this power of attraction include the US-sponsored project of transatlantic security community building in after World War II and, more recently, China through the dynamics of its seemingly conditionality-free 'charm offensive' (Kurlantzik 2007).

The issue of influence suggests an actor's ability to establish itself as a *model* in global politics. As already suggested it is closely related to the notion of power, which (in itself) is one of the central and, yet, most elusive concepts in the study of the relations between states. The focus on influence here uncovers the more traditional meaning of power which centered 'on the idea of ability' (Carroll 1972, 589).[1] In a similar fashion, Stefano Guzzini (2004, 538) has argued that power in international life is 'fundamentally a psychological relation influencing the other's mind'. The notion of influence, thereby, re-defines power as 'socializing power'—'the power of shaping the habits and attitudes of the individuals and small groups of which any society is composed, and upon whose habits and attitudes its governing power depends' (Carroll 1972, 588–611). Thence, *power as ability* indicates the *socializing power* of external actors (such as India) to shape the policy-preferences of the state-elites of target countries (such as the Central Asian states).

This understanding of influence is informed by the growing skepticism about the definition of power solely in terms of its intended effects. D. White (1971, 150) has argued that the elucidation of power 'in terms of intended effects is misconceived'; hence, it is not intention that matters but the *ability* to cause change of policy-behavior. Therefore, Klaus Knorr has suggested that the 'power of influence' does not necessarily rest with traditional resorts to coercive behavior', but is an effect of what he refers to as *'nonpower influence'*. He argues that 'nonpower influence can be generated… when B admires and follows A's example of comportment or of creativity in solving domestic problems' (Knorr 1977, 106-108; emphasis added). In this respect, Adler and Barnett (1998, 39–40) conclude that 'power can be a magnet; a community formed around a group of strong powers creates the expectation that weaker states that join the community will be able to enjoy the security and potentially other benefits that are associated with that community'.

One of the fullest accounts of influence is provided by Rudolph Rummel during his elaboration of the notion of power as the *ability* and *capacity* to produce effects. He defines the effects of power through its intended and unintended results. Thus, while the former indicate primarily the material capabilities to exert outcomes, the latter reflect the 'quality of being' of those exercising it. The unintended consequences of power reveal influence as an effect of the 'power to draw attention'—i.e. the willingness to identify through association/partnership rather than confrontation—which has the 'capacities-to-produce-effects'. In international life, the desire to identify through association with other states or membership of particular international organizations can be for various reasons, but it provides the ones aspired to with the 'capability to alter the perception and opportunities' of the aspirants (Rummel 1976, 163–168).[2]

The issue of influence suggests an actor's ability to establish itself as a *model* in global politics. Currently, it is the EU, the USA, and China that seem to be able to shape the strategic visions of others. Although distinct and contending, their models share the attribute of 'nonpower influence'. Thus, paraphrasing Kautilya's propositions on governance, influence in international life can be interpreted as 'the power to control not only outward behavior, but also the thoughts of one's subjects and enemies' (Boesche 2002, 32). This ability derives not from military power, but from the power of attraction—the perception of an actor as a model engenders a desire in others to become like it by adopting the most important elements of its international identity.

Not a Model: The Lack of Vision in the 'Look North' Policy

The discussion of the narratives of the 'Look North' policy in the preceding chapters is rife with examples of Indian aspirations to be seen as a model by Central Asian states. At the same time, the confrontation with the reality of Central Asian politics and the involvement of other international actors has made Indian commentators aware that New Delhi has little (if any) influence in the region. More conspicuously, the absence of power of attraction (and so far, at least, the seeming lack of willingness to develop one) has plagued India's international engagement not only with Central Asia, but also other global regions. In other words, the perception of India as a *model*—'the outside world's ideas about a particular country' (Gupta 2008, 110)—cannot be maintained, nor flourish without influence. As has already been indicated in Chapter 4 (and illustrated by India's encounter with Russia, China, and the West in Central Asia), New Delhi's 'policy towards its immediate and extended neighborhood is indistinct and incoherent' (Jain 2008, 228; Bhadrakumar 2008) because of its underlying *'lack of vision'* (Alexander 2004, 357; emphasis added). New Delhi's failure both to articulate and to project a coherent strategy for its involvement in Central Asia underpin the inability to 'intertwine India's geopolitical interests with the interest of [regional] countries' as well as 'India's noticeable absence' from regional politics (Bhadrakumar 2008). The realization therefore is that

> if India is poised to play an altogether new and a major role in the twenty-first century world order, then it must be able to evolve for itself a distinct notion quite convincing to the world also, as to what kind of role can India assume in the new millennium – a role, totally different from the one, presumably perceived in the present-day geopolitics [...] In the new millennium, there are new probabilities for the rising countries in the world arena, to spell out new prospects for world peace and stability and contribute positively by working out their own roles in geopolitics. Such a nation can emerge as a real leader of the region/world'. (Reddy 2007, 213–221)

In other words, the claim here is that India has a number of influential individuals and businesses, but it, itself—as an international actor—does not have an *influential* foreign policy strategy that could establish it as an alternative to existing ones. Such an assertion should not be misinterpreted as an allegation that India does not have a respected and significant historical and cultural heritage. However, the international recognition of this legacy (just like the recognition of its nuclear capabilities) does not amount to *influence*, which would be able to arouse a desire for emulation among other actors. In the language of some of the proponents of the 'Look North' policy, the lack of influence reflects the failings of India's 'public diplomacy'—a notion capturing 'the development, maintenance, and promotion of a country's soft power' (Rana 2007, 7). New Delhi's influence in this context becomes a product of the complex interaction between dynamics internal to India and their projection and interpretation abroad. Commentators indicate that when discussing 'the issue of India's image abroad, we should not be too much concerned about it. First, we have to make the image inside the country because it is this image that gets carried. Image is but a reflection of the existing realities' (Rai 2003, 34). Also (as will be detailed shortly), the self-aggrandizing logic of its post-1998 international agency projects an expectation that 'India would like its *brand name* to be that of a hi-tech state'; however, 'the international reality is somewhat different since both poverty and insurgent challenges to the state exist [...] India's biggest security challenge, therefore, will be to provide economic hope to *its* new generation' (Gupta 2008, 110–114; emphasis added). In this setting, a senior official of the Ministry of External Affairs has acknowledged that 'despite the excellent underpinnings we possess based on our historical and cultural affinities. [...] I do not think we have been able to achieve the kind of momentum to the shared concerns about common problems and economic and trade opportunities' (cited in Muni 2003, 112). As the discussion of Central Asia indicates, the narrative construction of India's current external affairs does not project a specific (if any) vision of world order that would distinguish if from the other participants in the 'new great game'.[3] Thus, New Delhi's engagement in Central Asia questions *'whether India has an ambition for creating an area of influence'* (Budania 2003, 90; emphasis added). Consequently, the international identity of New Delhi has no distinct attributes that regional actors might want to emulate.

Why No Influence: Where Has the Power of Attraction Gone?

The discursive construction of India's post-1998 assertive foreign policy plays a significant role in the failure to establish India as a model. In particular, the symbolic value from the possession of nuclear weapons has not been able to translate into any meaningful form of influence. On the one hand, the demands (as well as the challenges) of 'maintaining a psychological advantage of military superiority over Pakistan' (Budania 2003, 85) appear to drain a substantial part of India's symbolic and material resources. As the preceding chapters have demonstrated, New Delhi's preoccupation with the actual and imagined strategies of Islamabad has befuddled its reception as a model—i.e. as an actor able to project an alternative and independent vision of regional and/or global order. Instead, the perception of self-centeredness deriving from the mythmaking logic of its foreign policy making undercuts India's (potential) power of attraction. It has been commented by external observers that the patterns of New Delhi's international interactions demonstrate that

> India wants to go on playing Cold War games in the times of post-Cold War global politics. It has convinced itself that it is a 'great power' just like the USA and the USSR used to be before 1989. In this respect, it has donned in its foreign policy that Cold-War-like tactics can secure its interests in international life. Thus, although it has managed to shift its approach to foreign policy making in 1998, New Delhi still has not shifted the paradigm of its external affairs outlook. This underpins its continued lack of influence—its perception by others as a model—despite the more assertive and aggressive foreign policy stance and macroeconomic success. In this respect, India has still not clarified for itself in what capacity it is to be counted as a great power, hot to act in order to be perceived as such, and with whom to ally itself in order to be regarded as so. (Jonson 2004, 14)

On the other hand, commentators have claimed that the 'euphoria [about the nuclear explosions] is limited to a small urban group in a country where 73 per cent of voters are rural and have never heard of NPT and CTBT. Public memory in India is notoriously short, and today's big news gets overtaken by new events quickly [...] If India *wants to be respected* it has to become economically strong and that requires *much more than a nuclear muscle*' (*The Times of India*, 17 May 1998; emphasis added). Kishan Rana maintains that for all its posturing, the suggested inability to 'articulate its international strategic objectives in a clear and precise manner' indicates that 'hubris is now the potential danger'. In particular, the desire to formulate foreign policy through '*nationally* accepted' aspirations reveals that 'diplomacy is used mainly as a sophisticated control device and a safety valve [for domestic public opinion]. In some situations, the orchestrated expression of home opinion on foreign affairs issues is used as a pressure point on foreign countries. This sword is two-sided: while it mobilizes publics in support of government positions, it has the potential of limiting options or forcing the government's hand where *nationalist passions are aroused and becomes hard to control'* (Rana 2007, 45–75; emphasis added).

The reliance on 'nationalist passions' in foreign policy making underwrites the propensity to assertive (and often militaristic) geopolitical strategizing. These self-aggrandizing proclamations wax enthusiastically that India did emerge as 'a more powerful country when it conducted a series of nuclear tests and declared itself as a nuclear weapons power' (Mahapatra 2005, 170). Consequently, the mythic foreign policy narrative contends that 'India has a special role to play in the world. That role is primarily "to be Indian"' (Singh 2006, 250). This national assertiveness persuades that its manner of international agency is the only viable one for ensuring that 'the charm and graciousness of the Indian way of life will continue' (Kachru 2007, 297). As Chapter 3 demonstrates, it is frequently asserted that the pre-1998 'Indian passivity and inability to think outside the Nehruvian box was instrumental in producing a pattern of stalemated relationships. By failing to militarily and economically engage the powers and to build opportunities that facilitated negotiated restraints in military issues, Nehru-style Indian practitioners facilitated the great powers' intervention in Indian strategic affairs' (Kapur 2006, 15). Thus, while the (soft) power of attraction is a crucial facet in the construction and wielding of influence on the international, its association with Nehruvian principles and practices has undercut the projection of India as a model on the international stage. In this context (and despite the euphoria about the country's anticipated rise to global prominence), the exercise of New Delhi's external affairs (especially in Central Asia) still appears to confirm Alastair Buchanan assertion that 'though India is Asia's second largest state, she *possesses little external influence* [...] she is a static power in diplomatic terms at present, and the evolution of local relationships elsewhere in Asia is unlikely to be greatly affected by her conceptions or initiatives [...] *India is no longer seen as a great alternative society* whose success and therefore whose magnetism for other Asian societies must be encouraged' (Buchanan 1974, 294; emphasis added).[4]

Another set of issues explaining India's lack of influence relate to the narrative framing of the 'Look North' policy. Chapter 4 has illustrated that the engagement of Central Asia involved the construction of New Delhi as an example of secular and democratic politics. Thus, reaffirming the logic of its post-1998 foreign policy, 'India's democracy is bearing a greater impact on many of its neighbors. For the smaller states of the region, India is something of a model for the peaceful management of a multi-ethnic, multi-religious, and multi-lingual state' (Singh 2006, 193). The assertion is that the interaction between the 'macro-climate of the world and the micro-climate [at home]' (Bhattacharjea 2008, 8) informs both foreign policy making and the external perception of an actor regarding its status and appeal as a model. In this context, international stature is 'adjudged by the ability to develop the cultural and moral resources of the democratic forms of social organization that make possible the humane and rational use of a country's material wealth and power. This potential can only be unleashed if the nation's leaders, people, and its institutions make an unflinching commitment to good governance, economic freedom, and investment in people. Without these inputs, *even a people as capable and aspiring as us Indians cannot succeed*' (Kachru 2007, xxii; emphasis added).

India's lack of influence in international life confirms this proposition. As many commentators have noted 'India is more than qualified to be a global power [...] However, India's global power profile will be judged on whether the growth process is "socially inclusive" and whether the benefits of economic liberalization and economic reform have trickled down to the grassroots' (Jain 2008, 223). Thus, more often than not, the proponents of the 'Look North' policy indicate that India's international stature is perceived not so much by the levels of its economic growth, but by the shortcomings of its social inclusion. For instance, 'India's greatest weaknesses are its poor quality of universal modern education outside the sciences and its shortcomings in infrastructure and governance' (Rai and Simon 2007, 245). In particular, 'as a result of the information revolution' there is a growing awareness that India cannot meet the 'heightened economic expectations [of its citizens]' and that 'the resulting tensions disrupts the law and order situation and the internal stability of the state' (Dixit 2004, 24). Thus, 'what is holding India back' are the 'problems stemming from [the] bureaucratic traditions, political developments, and the social history of the country'; in turn, the 'corruption' feeding on this nexus 'has impacted the social infrastructure, the quality of life of the deprived and the destitute, and the social services provided by the state' (Kachru 2007, 188–198). Such 'weaknesses' and 'problems' prevent India from becoming a magnetic model and attract others to its sphere of influence and 'way of life'.

In this setting, the assertion that India is 'viewed as a new Asian power on the rise' (Mahapatra 2005, 170) reflects the complex mythmaking narrative underpinning of the 'Look North' policy. For instance, Chapter 6 has indicated that Indian commentators are aware that the social fragility of China has not prevented Beijing from positioning itself as a model and a pole of attraction for Central Asian states. In fact, Indian observers themselves have pointed out that China can (and should) be a model for New Delhi's international agency, if India is to enhance the influence of its foreign policy and achieve the objectives of its external affairs. Therefore, there is a strong perception that Beijing has managed to 'successfully overcome its weakness and change the power relations between itself and the outside world' (Bhattacharjea 2008, 8).

Perhaps paradoxically, such a context has once again provided an environment for reinforcing the assertive mythmaking of India's post-1998 foreign policy making. The narrative of the 'Look North' policy invariably reiterates that 'there is no denying the fact that Asia has become the principal theater where contemporary international struggles are playing themselves out' (Muni and Mohan 2005, 56). In such a setting, it is 'the nature of the international system [that] shapes the strategic choices of states'—that is,

> common interests should not be the starting point in determining the quality of [India's] relations with the major Asian powers. Rather, common interests are themselves determined by the structure of power in the international system. The correct question to ask of India's relations with the major Asian powers is not 'how to build common interests with a major Asian power', but rather 'what are our common interests given a particular configuration of power in Asia'. Trying to build common interests in a manner that ignores the imperatives of the existing configuration of power would be at the least futile and in the extremes, potentially dangerous. (Rajagopalan 2005, 296–300)

Having no intention to disregard the significance of these narratives, the claim here is that the question emerging from the discussion of New Delhi's agency in Central Asia is whether India can 'offer an alternative vision of a new world order' (Bhattacharjea 2008, 10) just like the USA, the EU, and China have done. In other words, the analysis of India's external affairs still does not seem to offer a convincing response to the query whether India '*can change enough*' to become a pole of attraction in an international environment marked by 'extreme turbulence' (Kachru 2007, 14; emphasis added). The current setting seems to suggest that India would retain its relative position of *no influence* for some time to come.

NOTES

Chapter One

1 For a discussion of other instances of India's regional foreign policy see Dhar (1991), Murdian (1994), and Sharma (2003).
2 For an example of non-Western analyses of Central Asia see Ertürk (1999), while Alatas (2006) offers a good overview of what he calls the 'alternative discourses' of Asian social science.

Chapter Two

1 Chapter 3 offers a detailed interpretation of the impact of the 1998 nuclear tests on the discourses of India's foreign policy.
2 In fact, during the launch of India's nuclear program, the then Prime Minister, Lal Bahadur Shastri announced that the development of 'peaceful nuclear explosives [is] for purposes such as tunneling through mountains' (quoted in Datta 2008, 52).
3 Ahmed (1993, 226–235) gives an interesting interpretation of Nehru's notion and practice of 'peaceful coexistence' as an 'innovative' combination between Kautilyan and Ashokan traditions, which tend to follow the geopolitical and normative (i.e. idealistic) models of Indian foreign policy making discussed later on in this chapter. It needs to be mentioned that the overwhelming majority of Indian commentators neither articulate, nor seem to recognize the very distinct normative undercurrents of geopolitics.
4 This issue is addressed at greater length in the section on 'the social production of foreign policy' in Chapter 3 and is crucial to understanding the mythmaking narratives of India's post-1998 international agency.
5 Other commentators distinguish between 'internal; and 'international' dimensions of 'national security': 'One cannot lose sight of the internal dimensions of national security: poverty, lack of education and health care for a very large fraction of the population, an unjust social order which is responsible for these, and for the growing disparities of income; large scale unemployment, large-scale corruption, nexus between politicians and criminals, a soft state, etc. Among the interna-

tional dimensions one has international debts; dependence on so-called aid and on imported technology which make the country vulnerable to foreign pressures and sanctions; adverse terms of trade; ecological threats; depletion of non-renewable resources; forces of "globalization," "liberalization," and neo-colonialism; international, etc. These are being listed to illustrate the large number of factors that affect national security' (Udgaonkar 2001, 1773).

6   This observation also offers insight into understanding India's 'no influence' in Central Asia, which is discussed in Chapter 8.
7   Indo-Soviet/Russian relations are explored in greater detail in Chapter 5.
8   For the historical context of this development see Brass (1990) and Kohli (1988).
9   See also the discussion of nonalignment by Appadorai (1981).
10 See Chapter 8 for a further discussion of the notion of *influence*.
11 According to Rajendra Jain (2002, 131) this dilemma could be reformulated as a choice between 'joining the *Pax Americana* and the charting of an Independent Nehruvian course'.
12 It could be argued that this ambivalence is a legacy of Nehru's own ambiguity, under whose supervision 'India's foreign and security policy and strategy… has been based more in terms of power and interest, with a veneer of both idealism and globalism' (Das 1970, 451–452).
13 The distinction between state and civilization in Indian perceptions of its international identity are addressed at greater length in the conclusion to Chapter 6.
14 It needs to be reminded that in practical terms, the 1998 nuclear tests ended New Delhi's policy of 'nuclear ambiguity', which involved 'both affirming and denying' that the country had nuclear weapons capability (Bidwai and Vanaik 1999, 69; Datta 2008, 52; Menon and Nigam 2007, 50)
15 Chapter 6 details China's reaction to these proclamations.
16 Chapter 6 explains that the origins of such foreign policy reticence are usually traced to the 1962 war with China, where the misinterpretation of each other's objectives and in particular of New Delhi's 'forward' drive brought about probably the most devastating blow both to India's international identity and to its own perception of its role(s) in world affairs.
17 As Pratap Bhanu Mehta (2006, 18–19) reminds us, it should not be forgotten that the nuclear weapons tests 'would not have been technically feasible unless previous governments had laid the groundwork'.
18 As Chapter 6 explains, it was the perception that 'New Delhi [was] still pursuing a grand British vision' of a forward foreign policy that led China to instigate the 1962 war, thus 'putting a premature end to any hope of friendly ties' between the two countries (Singh 2003, 124).
19 In fact, the historian Percival Spear (1970, 110–111) has maintained that historically there 'was never an Indian concept of the balance-of-power of stable states within the orbit of Indian culture. Instead there was a continuing tradition of empire and overlordship… The political constituents of India had no idea of forming a "concert of India"…

There was no thought of unity and no thought of stability... The Indian tradition of imperial unification and the absence of national feeling explain the lack of any lack of shame on the part of Indian rulers either to seek foreign help in defeating a local rival or to accept foreign overlordship when it was seen to be capable of enforcing it'.

20 B.M. Jain (2008, 21) offers a more reserved criticism of Nehru's foreign policy: 'It is a fatuous estimate about Nehru that he lacked strategic vision. Nor is it fair to pass judgment that he lacked security or strategic concepts to deal with adversaries or neighboring states. As a profound student of world history and keen observer of international political developments, Nehru fashioned and articulated the strategic doctrine, albeit not systematically defined, based on his own worldview. As a statesman, he was deeply concerned about India's future as a great power in the world. His long-term strategic perspective, however, did not find favor with his colleagues and the Opposition. No doubt, he was a foreign policy master. No one had a political courage to question his lies. Nehru's ideological élan, coupled with intellectual and moral commitments, at time overshadowed his own judgments about the hard-boiled realities of international politics impinging upon India's security concerns'. Likewise L. Raman Pillai (1969, 200) has observed that Nehru found it increasingly difficult and frustrating 'to defend and explain his foreign policy moves instead of just announcing them or, at times in the past, saying nothing about them'. In this respect, Imtiaz Ahmed (1993, 217) has altogether questioned Nehru's commitment to democratic principles 'given his predominant, almost "Caesarist" position in post-independence India'. Others have suggested that the 'hegemonizing' of foreign policy making by Nehru is simply an effect of media representations: 'Under the circumstances [of the post-Independence period], it should be no surprise that coverage of Indian foreign policy and diplomatic initiatives by Indian newspapers and journals through the first decade of independence had turned into a long affair with Nehru' (Inder Malhotra cited in Rai 2003, 28–29).

21 In contrast, other commentators have suggested that this reading of 'Nehru's defence policies' demonstrates that 'Nehru may remain *ununderstood*' (Subrahmanyam 2008[1972], 1179; emphasis added). Thus, despite pervasive criticisms of their moralistic approach to foreign policy, both Nehru and Gandhi have been evoked in justifying India's recourse to the nuclear option: 'In discussions of India's exercise of the nuclear option, one frequently reads mention of the legacy of Mahatma Gandhi and Jawaharlal Nehru, which it is claimed, India has given up. It is hazardous to transfer great personalities like Nehru and Gandhi to a period several decades after their death, and guess what they would have done if they were alive today. However, two things appear to me to be central to their thought and action. Firstly, both Gandhi and Nehru were against racialism and colonialism, and against dominance/hegemony. [...] Secondly, while they advocated peace, they were not mere pacifists, but said on several occasions that *durable peace demanded a just and equitable international order*.

Therefore, it seems to me that today they would have fought against neo-colonialism in all its forms and would not have submitted to the attempts of the nuclear weapons states to maintain their hegemony through treaties like the NPT, CTBT [and] technology control regimes' (Udgaonkar 2001, 1790–1791; emphasis original).

22 Corroborating this proposition, Vinan Roy and William Simon (2007, 131) asserted (perhaps somewhat over-optimistically and over-prematurely as the ongoing debates surrounding the US-Indian nuclear agreement seem to have indicated) that 'Marxism is dead except in isolated pockets, and commercial interests rule foreign policy decisions'.

Chapter Three

1 On 'logrolling' see Tavares (2007).
2 This inference draws on the discussion in Deshpande (2003, 44).
3 It has to be pointed that, at the time, the former Indian President R. Venkataraman evoked the myth of India's economic strength to suggest that 'no doubt the imposition of sanctions will hurt India in the short run. But India has the resilience to take it on. If we decide to "*Be Indian and Buy Indian*" it would hurt those imposing sanctions as such. No Country can ever afford to ignore the present and potential Indian market. We will not die if deprived Kentucky Chicken, colas, etc. [But] *no country wants to be left behind when India's economy grows!* Nobody can ignore the Indian middle class consumers of 250 million people. Sanctions will turn out to be King Canute's command to the waves. India with its commitment to world peace should not join the nuclear club and become a party to the enforcement of the very NPT she had fought against. Its goal is the elimination of nuclear weapons and not gaining a coveted place' (*The Economic Times*, 23 June 1998; emphasis added)
4 A process also referred to as 'the Christianization of Hinduism' (Nandy 1983, 25; Alatas 2006, 16). See Alates (2006, 16) for a discussion of the problem of approaching Hinduism with a 'Western' understanding of the notions 'myth' and 'religion'.
5 See the conclusion to Chapter 6 for a discussion of the significance of the distinction between *state* and *civilization* in India's foreign policy formulation.
6 See Mohanty (2006).
7 For additional perspectives on Indian engagements with the topic of globalization see Babu (1998) and Melkote (2001).
8 For some commentators this development is indicative of a 'South Asian paradox' in India's and Pakistan's post-Independence development: 'In the first place, while Pakistan was created in the name of religious nationalism, it still operates within the orbit of secular governance. Conversely, India, which established itself as a secular state with a secular constitution has launched a significant attempt to reorient itself along distinct Hindu lines. Secondly, whereas in "Islamic" Pakistan religious groups have to date not been able to attract more than 5 per cent of the popular vote, "secular" India has voted into gov-

9 This aspect was briefly introduced in the section on 'engaging with/in foreign policy making' in Chapter 2.
10 N. Manohoran (2003, 332–333) has illustrated that with the end of the Cold War, there has been a marked increase in India of political formations 'based on manufactured/special identities'.
11 Then, what transpires is a perception of a nuclear apartheid demonstrating that 'the security of some states (including the most powerful one)' is dependent on nuclear weapons 'while other states would be denied such security. Why should a country forgo its nuclear option *now*, not knowing how the world is going to develop, *all the more so since various recent developments amount to abandonment by nuclear weapons states of the goal of nuclear disarmament*' (Udgaonkar 2001, 1789–1790; emphasis original).
12 For Kishan Rana, the tension between the inside and the outside of the state, which are implicit in the formulation of its external affairs, reveals that foreign policy 'both takes the home abroad and brings the abroad home. And when things go wrong in foreign affairs, someone at home will surely say that the foreign ministry has been too busy looking after the interests of foreigners' (Rana 2007, 2).
13 Many have illustrated that not only Hindu nationalist who saw the necessity of developing nuclear capabilities in the wake of the 1962 war with China (Dixit 1998, 421; Mahapatra 2008, 179).
14 Although additional critical remarks regarding the logic of India's post-1998 foreign policy making would be elaborated in Chapter 6, it has to be noted that the use of external affairs for the settlement of domestic conflicts indicates that the 'notion that India's "patience" finally ran out and it was "driven" to test is simply a self-serving hypocrisy. The real reason has to do with changing elite self-perceptions! And these have been decisively altered over the last decade by a host of domestic factors, most notably the ruthless drive of the Sangh combine to reshape the whole discourse of Indian nationalism in a Hindu essentialist, belligerent, aggressive, intolerant, and anti-democratic direction. The Sangh has substantially succeeded precisely because it has operated in a milieu of uncertain and tension-filled nationalism characterized by growing elite frustration and insecurity about the country and its own role. Though our "strategic experts" typically separate "national security" matters from internal politics, this is a great mistake and prevents them from recognizing the indissoluble connection between this nuclearization and the general political agenda of the Sangh' (*The Economic Times*, 23 June 1998).
15 Likewise, Upendra Kachru (2007, xiii) has warned that the belief in India's 'becoming an economic superpower in the near future [...] is fraught with danger'. According to him, this conviction seems to overlook the 'accelerated rate of change and structural reconfiguration that is taking place continuously' and which is 'causing unprecedented upheavals in society'. See also the assessment of Roy-Chaudhury (2008).

Chapter Four

1 Many commentators have corroborated that the alleged homogeneity of Central Asia is '*fairly deceptive*. The Central Asians articulate their identities in a variety of particularistic terms. The multidimensional national identity in Central Asia has several layers [which] unfold a complex kaleidoscope of identity-formation and its manifold impact on the socio-political environment. [Such] multidimensional has over the years become internally heterogeneous. This obviously leads to a political scenario which is basically friction-oriented and hence fragile and unstable' (Sharma 2004b, 428; emphasis added).

2 Additionally, the very authors advocating the diversification of India's foreign policy to Central Asia tend to slide into explanations and policy-prescriptions that reinforce the perception of regional homogeneity.

3 Similar objectives have been proffered by Aneja (2002), Mohan (2004, 221–224), Muni and Mohan (2005, 68), Patnaik (2005, 228), and Roy (2001, 2286).

4 Commentators ascertain that consecutive Indian governments have consistently conjured up visions of all Muslim states under the leadership of Pakistan 'acting as one single bloc to the detriment of India' (Murdian 1994, 38).

5 In this setting, from an Indian point of view, 'Central Asia constitutes an important part of post-Cold War Asia, which India could ill afford to neglect while finding new moorings for its foreign policy. This was so not only because a new Central Asia had emerged on the scene with tremendous economic and strategic potential to play a role in Asian and international affairs, but also because the victory of the Mujahideen in Afghanistan against the Soviet forces with Pakistan playing a frontline role through its military's ISI wing, had emboldened Pakistan as a major regional factor in India's northwest' (Muni 2003, 107; Dixit 1996b).

6 See Chapter 6 for a detailed analysis of the 'Pakistan effect' on India's encounter of China in Central Asia.

7 As the following chapters will explain, the conviction that India can act as a 'balancing' factor in the interactions of Central Asian states with other external actors dominates the narratives of the 'Look North' policy. This motif underpins New Delhi's encounter of Russia, China, and the West (the USA, the EU, and NATO) in the region.

8 See Chapter 6 for some of the nuances of India's perception of the democratization of Central Asia in the context of the constructed partnership between New Delhi and Beijing in the discursive articulations of the 'Look North' policy.

9 It has to be pointed out that there is a marked tension among Indian commentators regarding the *naturalness* of the nation-state in Central Asia. Chapter 6 discusses this point with regard to the conflict between *state* and *civilization* in India's own international identity. With regards to Central Asian states, it has been pointed out that a 'popular misconception deliberately created about Central Asia relates to political unity and statehood. It is asserted that political unity has been a rare histor-

ical commodity in the history of Central Asia. Political unity or rise of nation-states in world history is a modern phenomenon which has given birth to national chauvinism, and interethnic and inter-religious conflicts. Whether it is the unfolding of a divine idea or a divine curse on earth, only the future historian will be competent to judge. For some countries, which have managed to contain national, ethnic, and regional aspirations democratically, it has been a boon and a source of stability. For others, it has been a curse. During the Soviet period also, Central Asia went through the experience of nation-state formation, and has inherited all the merits and demerits which are associated with contemporary plural societies. [Thus] although their boundaries were artificially drawn without taking into account such crucial factors as consent of the concerned Republics, their demographic composition and historical claims, *over the years these borders have acquired legitimacy*' (Shams-ud-Din 1997, 331; emphasis added).
10 This aspect has already been discussed in the section on India's pre-1998 foreign policy engagement with Central Asia during which time such a concern emerged (and has been closely related to India's confrontation with Pakistan).
11 It is noteworthy (as well as peculiar) that in their suggestions for rectifying this trend towards 'tyrannical democracy' in Central Asia, some Indian commentators have proposed the development of a (simultaneously) paternalistic and patronizing form of polities in the region: 'The final and the best option is [for Central Asian leaders] to go to the people, beg for their forgiveness, appeal to them to forget the trauma of transition, convince them about the emerging political polyphony in a civil society, explain to them the vast difference between politics and economics of the socialist era, and *seek a fresh ballot of legitimacy*, of course with a change. After all it is they [the people] who are supreme in a democracy and the presidents are their servants: *to serve them and to lord over them.* [This] is the only way out for Central Asian presidents, *for their safe and immune exit from politics* to retirement. Meanwhile, they can take steps to groom political successors' (Dash 2007, 207. Emphasis added). Such proclamations seem to confuse the kind of example that India is expected to project through the narratives of the 'Look North' policy and also raise questions with whose plight are such discourses ultimately concerned. At the same time, they also uncover the 'dark side' of Indian politics—its mentality of subordination to hierarchical authority. Quoting the former Prime Minister P.V. Narisimha Rai, Panjak Mishra reveals that 'Indian politics are essentially feudal. "Neither the democratic nor the federal principle had taken root to supplant the feudal ethos [...] Democracy in action consisted at best of the question: Who should reign"' (Mishra 2000, 240).
12 Despite their calls for regional unity and strong regional cooperation, some of the proponents of the 'Look North' policy concede that Central Asian states 'do not appear to have much say in their own future' and that they are 'unable to recover without [external] assistance'. In this respect, the perception is that the policy alternatives for

the region 'narrow down to a choice between [the] West and/or the USA, religious fundamentalism, Chinese domination, or the [acceptance of] a working relationship with Russia' (Bal 2004, 320). It is noteworthy that such assessment does not envision a distinct role for India in Central Asia's future, apart from moderating between those external agencies. Chapter 8 will make explicit that such failure to articulate a distinct alternative vision of world politics underpins the assertion that India's international agency both in the region and in global affairs has *no influence*.

13 Echoing such sentiments, some analysts have indicated a marked sense that 'there are enormous prospects for evolving a framework for Central Asian regional cooperation on the lines of other regional alliances, without giving it a monolithic character such as religion or ethnicity, thereby, avoiding friction between national identities. Regional approaches are important for Central Asia in creating peace and stability in that region' (Roy 2001, 2286).

14 This is not least because of the dynamism of *new regionalisms*, which would be elaborated shortly in the context of the 'new great game' in Central Asia.

15 For a good overview of Indian perceptions of regionalism see Bajpai and Mallavarapu (2005).

16 At the same time, the perceived 'visibility of high goodwill towards India' in the region is portrayed as simply '*heart-warming*' (Dwivedi 2003, 624; emphasis added).

17 In direct confirmation of the mythmaking logic informing the narratives of New Delhi's post-1998 foreign policy formulation, Bal goes as far as to argue that if India had followed the precepts of *Realpolitik* it 'would have [already] gained *direct* access to Central Asian resources, which are now denied to it [because of the lack of shared territorial connection]' (Bal 2004, 22; emphasis added).

18 R.R. Sharma (2003, 72) adds to these explanations of external origins of the civil war in Tajikistan, the centrifugal forces of 'ethnic nationalism', which '*appear spontaneously* when an institutional vacuum occurs. Therefore, ethnic nationalism predominates when institutions collapse, when existing institutions are not fulfilling people's basic needs, and when satisfactory alternative structures are not readily available'.

19 For other (although mostly similar) definitions of the patterns of Central Asian politics intuited by the notion of the 'new great game' see Bal (2004, xiv), Dixit (2004, 16), Gidadhubli (2003, 166), Joshi (2007a, 151), Mahalingam (2004, 124), Mattoo (2003, 48), Menon (2003), Patnaik (2005, 207), Shams-ud-Din (1997, 339), Sharma (2005, 67).

Chapter Five

1 Indian commentators appear to maintain a keen interest on the topic of Soviet collapse. The central argument of quite a number of analyses us that even if the Soviet Union has dissolved, something akin to a 'Soviet spirit' stays alive and permeates Russian decision-making. For instance, Bal (2004, 301–301) has intimated that 'the circumstances

leading to the dissolution of the USSR would continue to be the subject of deliberation. However, it must be acknowledged that the demise of an ideology, which is in reality a decision arising from a collective state of mind among the ruling elite at a given point in time, does not necessarily alter ground realities in respect of security, cultural, economic, and other aspects'.

2 At the same time, from India's point of view 'close relations with the Soviet Union were a *sine qua non* for combating a possible nuclear threat from China' (Jetly 1986, 66; emphasis original).

3 In this setting some commentators have conceded that 'the initial years of the Yeltsin period were marked by uncertainty, especially aggravated by transitional problems. During most of 1992, Russian foreign policy was *blurred* by the profound economic, social, political and ethnic crises in the country' (Mahapatra 2004, 133; emphasis added).

4 For a detailed overview of India's military purchases from Russia see Jain (2008, 114–118).

5 Such conviction reiterates an Indian foreign policy perception established already during the Cold War that 'the Soviet people appreciate and [furthermore] are in solidarity with India's peace-loving foreign policy' (Banarjee 1977, 172).

6 Relying on Russian sources, some Indian commentators have queried not only the relevance of Moscow's international agency, but also its capacity to hold the country together—i.e. 'today the question is not whether the Russian Federation will exist as an independent state or not; the problem is when and how contemporary Russia will disappear from the political map of the world and what part of the former great country will have the same name' (Bhambhri 2005, 387).

7 It should be acknowledged that Indian commentators invariably qualify such statements with the observation that 'Russia can be considered a sleeping lion' (Reddy 2007, 221)—that is, one can always expected the unexpected from Moscow.

8 See Chapter 6 on the warming up of relations between India and China in the post-Cold War period.

9 Similarly to the Soviet proposal for an Asian collective security arrangement, Moscow's proposal for the creation of a 'strategic triangle' between Russia, India, and China has received 'a cool reception' in New Delhi (Banarjee 1977, 173).

10 The poignancy of the close bilateral relationship between Russia and China to New Delhi is exposed by statements which demonstrate that 'in contrast to India, which was visited by President Yeltsin only once, Russia's summit meetings with China became an annual feature. The two countries forged what can be termed as a strategic partnership in Central Asia through the grouping of the Shanghai Five—now the Shanghai Cooperation Organization. [Also] the meetings at the level of Prime Ministers, foreign, defence and other ministers, and the two-way exchange of delegations between Russia and China have been much more numerous in the past decade in comparison with India-Russia exchanges' (Bakshi 2002, 83).

11 Some Indian commentators indicate that China's amicability towards Russia is little else but a strategy for 'buying time' to strengthen its own relations in and with Central Asia (Asopa 2007, 175). See Chapter 6 for a discussion of the threat-perceptions and images accompanying India's encounter of China in the region.

Chapter Six

1 See the conclusion of this chapter for an analysis of the difficulty of positioning this border conflict and the broader pattern of Sino-Indian relations within the context of Westphalian notions of territorial statehood.
2 On this point see also Krishna (1984).
3 The 1962 Sino-India war is discussed later on in this chapter.
4 See Chapter 3 for a discussion of the discursive study of foreign policy making.
5 For Pakistan's perspectives see Rais (1977) and Syed (1964).
6 See Mansingh (1998), Sandhu (1988), and Raghavan (1998).
7 Such statement reflects the later justification by the Indian Prime Minister Vajpayee that the 1998 nuclear weapons tests were provoked by a 'Chinese threat'. This issue addressed later on in this chapter.
8 Swaran Singh explains that it was 'China's colonial experience and especially its interface with British India that made its Tibet vision so security-centric [which, in turn, made] Beijing paranoid about Tibet's internal resistance'. As Singh argues, it was 'this mindset that [determined] China's misreading of India's intentions and becoming skeptical of India's initiatives which were largely based on India's high-principled foreign policy' (Singh 2003, 51).
9 The following outline rests mostly on the periodisation of Sino-Indian relations suggested by Prakash (1997).
10 The conviction underscoring this slogan was reflected in a 1955 statement by the Indian President Radhakrishnan: 'One of the most remarkable things in the world's history is the relationship between our two countries of peaceful cooperation across the centuries. We bear traces of the influences that we have exerted on each other in the literature and art of our two peoples. Our cultures have interwoven, our trade has flourished, mutual appreciation has grown and *there has not been a single instance of military conflict.* Something precious and unique has been built up over a long past. Though intercourse between our two peoples was interrupted for some centuries, it has now been revived. We have passed through trial and tribulations and have achieved the power to shape our future and are facing similar problems' (cited in Mattoo 2000, 17–18. Emphasis added).
11 See Chapter 5 for a further elaboration of the suspicions raised by Indian commentators regarding the close relationship between Russia and China in Central Asia.
12 Some Indian commentators have nevertheless contested the legitimacy of China's claims to Xinjiang, in terms very similar to the ones outlining the skepticism of the validity of Beijing's sovereignty over Tibet.

For instance, Sujit Dutta claims that the 'ethnic mix and the fact that *the region was historically outside China's cultural sphere* have made Xinjiang's integration into China problematic. Local ethnic groups did not have to confront central Chinese imperial power on a daily basis even after the Manchu Qing Dynasty annexed the region in 1759. Local identities were therefore largely intact until 1949' (Dutta 2003, 147).

13 Some commentators have insisted that 'in response to Islamic extremism, some modest level of intelligence sharing had already occurred between India and China with regard to the "spillover" of radical Islamist politics into Kashmir and Xinjiang—areas sensitive to each country's national security concerns' (Clad 2004, 270). Ashley Tellis has therefore proposed that the pattern of 'Sino-Indian relations in Asia will thus be driven, first, by the growth of Chinese and Indian economic and military capabilities, and, second, by the interaction of their interests with those of [other external actors]. The third and final variable defining the complexity of these relations will be the critical role played by other Asian states… Irrespective of the strategies chosen, all the Asian states actively participating in the Sino-Indian relationship will seek to play off the two major regional powers against one another so as to secure some benefit for themselves, even if in the process they turn out to be more valuable to the principals than the principals are to them' (Tellis 2004, 136–137).

14 See Chapter 4 for discussion of the dominant interpretation of India's secular and democratic state-building project within the narrative framework of the 'Look North' policy.

15 For others, the rivalry between India and China in Central Asia is likely to arise from the intersection of their security concerns with their economic interests: 'Although China and India thus have mostly parallel security goals in Central Asia, the potential for conflict could arise, mainly from any Chinese efforts to transform cooperation with the local states into a larger system of influence dominated by Beijing… The possibility of Sino-Indian rivalry in Central Asia, curiously, is more likely to arise in the realm of economics than of security, and this rivalry will be conditioned primarily by the strategies adopted by China with respect to the region's natural resources' (Tellis 2004, 155–157)

16 See Chapter 8 for a further discussion of the issue in the section on the 'No Influence' of India's foreign policy.

17 Chapter 7 demonstrates this point further in the context of New Delhi's opposition to Western agency in Central Asia, because of its perceived contribution to Beijing's international outreach both in the region and in global affairs.

18 This issue is briefly mentioned in Chapter 2 at the beginning of the section '1998 and After: Nuclear Assertiveness'.

Chapter Seven

1 The Indian perception of intensifying global complexity has been outlined in Chapter 2.

2 Christopher S. Raj and Chintamani Mahapatra also explain the histori-

cal origins of this foreign policy stance of the USA. They argue that 'during much of the Cold War the biggest US fear in West Asia was secular Arab nationalism which remained defiant to the West and friendly towards the Soviet Union. Therefore, Islamic movements were promoted by America. Even Israel supported the rise of Islamic forces within the Palestinian movement which were competing with the PLO, only to discover later that these very forces gave birth to the militant Hamas' (Raj and Mahapatra 2004, 296).

3 Such a perception derives from the conviction that 'Afghanistan and Pakistan continue to be the key actors creating destabilization in the Central Asian republics as well as in India' (Roy 2001, 2276).

Chapter Eight

1 Carroll (1972, 589) points out that a mere comparison of the definition of power in the Oxford and Webster's dictionaries from the 1930s to 1970s illustrates such alteration in the meaning of the concept. Therefore, Carroll argues that in some sense the original meaning of *power as ability* can be retrieved through negation – i.e. that power indicates a framework of '*noncontrol*' or a situation of 'deliberate suspension of control' (Carroll 1972, 601–602; emphasis added).

2 Moreover, Rummel treats the meaning of influence as a product of inter-subjective interaction centered on a symbolic perception of binding expectations: 'power like money is itself "worthless", but is accepted in the *expectation* that it can later be "cashed in", this time in the activation of binding obligations' (Rummel 1976, 187; emphasis original). In a similar fashion, but not so perceptively, Barnett and Duvall (2005, 55–57) advance the concept of 'productive power' which concerns 'the social process and the systems of knowledge through which meaning is produced'.

3 In this respect, S.D. Muni asserts that 'critically, the most important aspect of India's role in Central Asia is its own strength and resilience. There is need for India to make full use of its cultural identities (not simply in terms of films and music) and historical links with the region. There is still greater need for India to deploy adequate economic resources to back its diplomacy. *Whatever has been done so far in terms of assistance, trade, and investments is not very impressive.* It is true that India suffers from the connectivity hurdle in harnessing the full potential of Ondo-Central Asian Corperation, but there is also much scope for India to improve the economic management of its diplomacy. It is incumbent upon Indian diplomacy to think all possible options in overcoming the economic constraints and connectivity hurdles' (Muni, 2003, 127–128; emphasis added).

4 Note that Kapur (2006, 20) uses this statement by Alastair Buchanan as a corroborating evidence for the necessity of a militarized foreign policy.

BIBLIOGRAPHY

Abraham, I. (1999) *The Making of the Indian Atomic Bomb* (New Delhi: Orient Longman).
Acharya, A. (2000) 'India-China Relations: An Overview' in Bajpai, K. and Mattoo, A. (eds) *The Peacock and the Dragon: India-China relations in the Twenty-First Century* (New Delhi: Har-Anand Publications): 168–198.
Acharya, A. and Buzan, B (2007) 'Why Is There No Non-Western International Relations Theory', *International Relations of the Asia-Pacific* 7(3): 287–312.
Addy, P. (1984) *Tibet on the Imperial Chessboard* (New Delhi: Academic Publishers).
Adler, E. and Barnett, M. (1998) 'A Framework for the Study of Security Communities' in Adler, E. and Barnett, M. (eds) *Security Communities* (Cambridge: Cambridge University Press) 29–66.
Ahmed, I. (1993) *State and Foreign Policy: India's Role in South Asia* (New Delhi: Vikas Publishing).
Ahmed, R. (2002) 'EU Asks India to Ditch Narrow View of Pakistan', *The Times of India*, 10 October.
Alatas, S. (2006) *Alternative Discourses in Asian Social Science* (New Delhi: Sage).
Alexander, P.C. (2004) *Through the Corridors of Power: An Insider's Story* (New Delhi: HarperCollins).
Allison, T. (2001) 'Myanmar Shows India the Road to Southeast Asia', *Asia Times*, 21 February.
Ambekar, G.V. and Divekar, V.D. (eds) (1964) *Documents on China's Relations with South and Southeast Asia, 1949–1962* (New Delhi: Oxford University Press).
Aneja, A. (2002) 'India, Iran Wooing Central Asia', *The Hindu*, 21 October.
———. (2007) 'The Great Game Along the Silk Route', *The Hindu*, 20 April.
Appadorai, A. (1981) 'Nonalignment: Some Important Issues', *International Studies* 20(1): 3–11.
Appadorai, A. and Rajan, M.S. (1985) *India's Foreign Policy and Relations* (New Delhi: South Asian Publishers).

Arnold, D. (2006) *The Tropics and the Travelling Gaze: India, Landscape, and Science* (Seattle, WA: University of Washington Press).
Arora, G.K. (1997) 'Economic Development in China: Some Lessons for India' in M. Rasgotra and V.D. Chopra (eds) *India's Relations with Russia and China: A New Phase* (New Delhi: Gyan Publishing): 235–246.
Asopa, S. K. (2003) 'Regional Interests in Tajikistan' in Singh, M. (ed) *India and Tajikistan: Revitalizing a Traditional Relationship* (New Delhi: Anamika Publishers): 155–196.
———. (2006) *Struggle for Spheres of Interest in Trans-Caucasia-Central Asia and India's Stakes: An Appraisal of India's Central Asia Policy* (New Delhi: Manak Publications).
———. (2007) 'India and Post-Soviet Asia: An Appraisal of India's Central Asian Policy' in Roy, J.N. and Kumar, B.B. (eds) *India and Central Asia: Classical to Contemporary Periods* (New Delhi: Concept Publishing): 172–189.
Babu, B.R. (ed) (1998) *Globalization and the South Asian State* (New Delhi: South Asian Publishers, 1998).
Bagchi, I. (2007) 'As Big Powers Play in Asia, Where Does India Stand?', *The Times of India*, 7 September.
Bajeli, D.S. (2005) 'History's Reflections', *The Hindu*, 26 August.
Bajpai, K.P. (1999) 'The Fallacy of an Indian Deterrent' in Mattoo, A. (ed) *Pokhran II and Beyond: India's Nuclear Deterrent* (New Delhi: Har-Anand Publications): 150–185.
———. (2000) 'India, China, and Asian Security' in Bajpai, K. and Mattoo, A. (eds) *The Peacock and the Dragon: India-China relations in the Twenty-First Century* (New Delhi: Har-Anand Publications): 26–49.
———. (2002) *Roots of Terrorism* (New Delhi: Penguin).
Bajpai, K.P and Mallavarapu, S. (eds) (2005) *International Relations in India: Theorizing the Region and Nation* (New Delhi: Orient Longman).
Bakshi, J. (1999) *Russia and India: From Ideology to Geopolitics* (New Delhi: Dev Publications).
———. (2002a) 'Post-Cold War Sino-Russian Relations: Indian Perspective', *Strategic Analysis* 26(1): 80–117.
———. (2002b) 'The Shanghai Cooperation Organization before and After September 11', *Strategic Analysis* 26(2): 265–276.
———. (2005) 'India and Central Asia: Policy Review and a Projection into the Future' in Sisoda, N.S. and Bhaskar, C.U. (eds) *Emerging India: Security and Foreign Policy Perspectives* (New Delhi: Promilla & Co.): 230–246.
———. (2006) 'India-Russia Defence Cooperation', *Strategic Analysis* 30 (2): 449–466.
Bal, S.N. (2004) *Central Asia: A Strategy for India's Look-North Policy* (New Delhi: Lancer Publishers).
Ballhatchet, K. (1985) 'Indian Perceptions of the West', *Comparative Civilizations Review*, 13/14(2): 160–170.
Banerjee, D. (1997) *Myanmar and Northeast India* (New Delhi: Delhi Policy Group).

Banerjee, D. and Kueck, G.W. (eds) (1999) *South Asia and the War on Terrorism: Analyzing the Implications of 11 September* (New Delhi: India Research Press).
Banerjee, I. (ed) (2004) *India and Central Asia* (Middlesex: Brunel Academic Publishers).
Banarjee, J. (1977) *India in Soviet Global Strategy: A Conceptual Study* (Calcutta: Minerva Associates).
Bandyopadhyaya, J. (1991) *The Making of India's Foreign Policy* (New Delhi: Allied Publishers).
———. (2002) *World Government for International Democracy* (Howrah: Manuscript).
———. (2003) *The Making of India's Foreign Policy* (New Delhi: Allied Publishers).
Baral, J.K. and Mahanty, J.N. (2002) 'The US War against Terrorism: Implications for South Asia', *Strategic Analysis* 26(4): 508–518.
Barnett, M and Duvall, R. (2005) 'Power in International Politics', *International Organization* 59(1): 39–75.
Baroowa, S. (2006) 'The Emerging Strategic Partnership Between India and the European Union: A Critical Appraisal' in *Europe, India and China: Strategic Partners in a Changing World* (Aix-en-Provence: Université Paul Cézanne Press): 2–20.
Baruah, A. (2004) 'Multilateralism—the Best Solution', *The Hindu*, 11 October.
Basu, R. (2007) *Globalization and Indian Foreign Policy* (Jaipur: Vital Publications).
Bedi, R. (2002) 'India and Central Asia: India's Growing Presence and Role in the Resource-Rich and Strategically Significant Central Asian Region Has Important Implications' *Frontline* 19(19), 14–27 September.
Behera, N.C. (2003) 'Forging New Solidarities: Nonofficial Dialogues' in Mekenkam, M., van Tongeren, P. and van de Veen, H. (eds) *Searching for Peace in Central and South Asia: An Overview of Conflict Prevention and Peacebuilding Activities* (Boulder, CO: Lynne Rienner): 210–236.
Bell, D. (2002) 'Language, Legitimacy, and the Project of Critique', *Alternatives* 27(2): 327–350.
Bhadrakumar, M.K. (2004) 'New Regionalism in Central Asia', *The Hindu*, 14 July.
———. (2008) 'India Must Return to Eurasian Energy Game', *The Hindu*, 18 February.
Bhagat, G. (1990) 'Kautilya Revisited and Re-visioned' *Indian Journal of Political Science* 51(2): 186–212.
Bhambhri, C.P. (2005) 'Plea for an Alternative Eurasian Vision', *International Studies* 42(3/4): 386–388.
Bhatt, C. (2001) *Hindu Nationalism: Origins, Ideologies, and Modern Myths* (Oxford: Berg).
Bhattacharjea, M.S. (2008) 'Does China have a Grand Strategy?' in Vohra, P. and Ghosh, P.K. (eds) *China and the Indian Ocean Region* (New Delhi: National Maritime Foundation): 1–19.
Bhattacharya, A. (2004) 'The Fallacy in the Russia-India-China Triangle', *Strategic Analysis* 28(2): 358–361.

———. (2005) 'Revisiting China's "Peaceful Rise": Implications for India', *East Asia* 22(4): 59–80.
Bhattacharyya, S. (2004) 'Lure of the Silk Route', *Hindustan Times*, 19 August.
Bhonsle, R.K. (2008) *South Asia: Political, Security, and Terrorism Trends* (New Delhi: Vij Books).
Bially-Mattern, J. (2005) *Ordering International Politics* (London: Routledge).
Bidwai, P. and Vanaik, A. (1999) *South Asia on a Short Fuse: Nuclear Politics and the Future of Global Disarmament* (New Delhi: Oxford University Press).
Black, P.L. (2004) *Vladimir Putin and the New World Order: Looking East, Looking West?* (Lanham, MD: Rowman & Littlefield).
Boesche, R. (2002) *The First Great Political Realist: Kautilya and His and Arthashasra* (Boulder, CO: Lexington Books).
Booth, K. and Wheeler, N.J. (2008) *The Security Dilemma: Fear, Cooperation, and Trust in World Politics* (Basingstoke: Palgrave).
Brass, P.R. (1990) *The Politics of India since Independence* (Cambridge: Cambridge University Press).
Brasted, H. and Khan, A. (2007) 'Pakistan, the BJP, and the Politics of Identity' in J. McGuire and I. Copland (eds) *Hindu Nationalism and Governance* (New Delhi: Oxford University Press): 430–448.
Brennan, T. (1990) 'The National Longing for Form' in Bhabha, H.K. (ed) *Nation and Narration* (London: Routledge): 44–70.
Buchanan, A. (1974) *The End of the Postwar Era: A New Balance of World Power* (London: Weidenfeld & Nicolson).
Budania, R. (2003) 'The Emerging International Security System: Threats, Challenges, and Opportunities for India', *Strategic Analysis* 27(1): 79–93.
Business Line (1998a) 'Announcing the Bomb', 12 May.
———. (1998b) 'The BJP and the Bomb', 12 May.
Butalia, U. (2000) *The Other Side of Silence: Voices from the Partition of India* (Durham, NC: Duke University Press).
Cameron, F., Berkofsky, A., Bhandari, M. and Halley, D. (2005) *The EU-India Relations* (Brussels: European Policy Centre).
Campbell, D. (1998) *Writing Security* (Minneapolis, MN: University of Minneapolis Press).
Carr, E.H. (1989[1939]) *The Twenty Years' Crisis: 1919–1939* (London: Macmillan).
Carroll, B. (1972) 'Peace Research: The Cult of Power', *Journal of Conflict Resolution* 16(4): 585–616.
Cassirer, E. (1963[1945]) *The Myth of the State* (New Haven, NJ: Yale University Press).
Chaban, N., Elgström, O. and Holland, M. (2006) 'The European Union as Others See It', *European Foreign Affairs Review* 11(2): 245–62.
Chakravarti, P.C. (1962) *India's China Policy* (Bloomington, IN: Indiana University Press).
Chandi, A.J. (2000a) 'China's Naval Power' in Bajpai, K. and Mattoo, A. (eds) *The Peacock and the Dragon: India-China relations in the Twenty-First Century* (New Delhi: Har-Anand Publications): 77–102.

———. (2000b) 'India, China, and Pakistan' in Bajpai, K. and Mattoo, A. (eds) *The Peacock and the Dragon: India-China relations in the Twenty-First Century* (New Delhi: Har-Anand Publications): 298–332.

Chandra, V. (2008) 'Taking Stock of Seven Years of War on Terror in Afghanistan', *Strategic Analysis* 32(6): 943–948.

Chatterjee, S. (2006) *Mind and Vision: Perceptions of Reform in Kazakhstan and Kyrgyzstan* (New Delhi: Bookwell Publishers).

Chaudhuri, P.P. (2002) 'Why the Indo-Russian Relationship is Going Nowhere in a Hurry', *Hindustan Times*, 16 December.

Chaulia, S. (2002) 'BJP, India's Foreign Policy, and the "Realist Alternative" to the Nehruvian Tradition', *International Politics* 39(2): 215–234.

Chengappa, R. (1998) 'The Bomb Makers', *India Today*, 22 June.

———. (2000) *Weapons of Peace* (New Delhi: Harper Collins).

Chenoy, A.M. (2008) 'India and Russia: Allies in the International Political System', *South Asian Survey* 15(1): 49–62.

Chiriyankandath, J. (2004) 'Realigning India: Indian Foreign Policy after the Cold War', *The Round Table* 93(374): 199–211.

Chopra, V.D. (1997a) 'India-Russia-China: Changing Equations' in Rasgotra, M. and Chopra, V.D. (eds) *India's Relations with Russia and China: A New Phase* (New Delhi: Gyan Publishing): 15–36.

———. (1997b) 'Indo-Russian Relations: Historical Background' in Rasgotra, M. and Chopra, V.D (eds) *India's Relations with Russia and China: A New Phase* (New Delhi: Gyan Publishing): 123–143.

Choudhari, N. (1989) *Sino-Indian Quest for Rapprochement: Implications for South Asia* (Dhaka: BIISS).

Clad, J. (2004) 'Convergent Chinese and Indian Perspectives on the Global Order' in Frankel, F.R. and Harding, H. (eds) *The India-China Relationship: What the United States Needs to Know* (New York: Columbia University Press): 267–294.

Cohen, S. (2001) *India: Emerging Power* (Washington, DC: Brookings Institution Press).

Crossette, B. (1993) *India: Facing the Twenty-First Century* (Bloomington, IN: Indiana University Press).

Damodaran, A.K. (1981) 'India and Nonalignment', *International Studies*, 20(2): 203–214.

Das, D. (1970) *India: From Curzon to Nehru and After* (New York: John Day Company).

Das, G. (2000) *India Unbound* (New Delhi: Viking).

Dash, P.L. (2007a) 'Central Asia: Tulips Have Different Hews' in Roy, J.N. and Kumar, B.B. (eds) *India and Central Asia: Classical to Contemporary Periods* (New Delhi: Concept Publishing): 190–210.

———. (2007b) 'Sixty Years of Indo-Russian Synergy', *World Focus* 28(335/366): 473–477.

Datta, R. (2008) *Beyond Realism: Human Security in India and Pakistan in the Twenty-First Century* (Boulder, CO: Lexington Books).

Dhar, P. (1991) *India, Her Neighbors, and Foreign Policy* (New Delhi: Deep and Deep Publications).

Deodhar, V., Michaelowa, A. and Krey, M. (2003) 'Capacity Building Options for EU-India Collaboration', *HWWA Discussion Paper* 247.
Desai, R. (1999) 'Culturalism and Contemporary Right: Indian Bourgeoisie and Political Hindutva', *Economic and Political Weekly*: 695–712.
Deshpande, G.P. (1985) 'Not So Friendly Friends: India and China', *Link* 28(8): 73–76.
Deshpande, S. (2003) *Contemporary India: A Sociological View* (New Delhi: Viking).
Devare, S. (2006) *India and Southeast Asia: Towards Security Convergence* (Singapore: ISEAS).
Dhanapala, J. (1985) *China and the Third World* (New Delhi: Vikas Publishing House).
Dietl, G. (1997) 'Quest for Influence in Central Asia: India and Pakistan', *International Studies* 34(2): 111–143.
Diez, T. (1999) 'Speaking "Europe": The Politics of Integration Discourse', *Journal of European Public Policy*, 6(4): 598–613.
———. (2005) 'Constructing the Self and Changing Others: Reconsidering Normative Power Europe', *Millennium* 33(3): 613–36.
Dillon, M. (2004) *Xinjiang* (London: Routledge).
Dixit, A. (1998) 'The Civil War in Afghanistan: No Signs of Respite' *South Asian Survey* 5(1): 99–112.
Dixit, J.N. (1996a) *My South Block Years: Memoirs of a Foreign Secretary* (New Delhi: USB Publishing).
———. (1996b) 'Ties with Central Asia: Time to Move Forward', *Indian Express*, 16 July.
———. (1998) *Across Borders: Fifty Years of Indian Foreign Policy* (New Delhi: Picus Books).
———. (2000) 'Cooperation with Europe', *Indian Express*, July 10.
———(2001) *India's Foreign Policy and Its Neighbors* (New Delhi: Gyan Publishing).
———. (2004) 'Emerging International Security Environment: Indian Perceptions with Focus on South Asian and Central Asian Predicaments' in Santhanam, K. and Dwivedi, R. (eds) *India and Central Asia: Advancing the Common Interest* (New Delhi: Anamaya Publishers): 13–25.
Dubey, M. (1993) 'India's Foreign Policy in the Evolving Global Order', *International Studies* 30(2): 117–129.
Duke, S. (1994) *The New European Security Disorder* (London: Macmillan).
Duran, D. (2007) 'The EU-India Strategic Partnership: What's New?' *IPCS Article* 2222, 27 February.
Dutt, S. (2006) *India in a Globalized World* (Manchester: Manchester University Press).
Dutt, V.P. (2000) *India's Foreign Policy in a Changing World* (New Delhi: Vikas Publishing House).
Dutta, S. (1995) 'India's Evolving Relations with China', *Strategic Analysis* 17(4): 477–502.
———. (1997) 'India-China Relations: The Post-Cold War Phase' in Rasgotra, M. and Chopra, V.D. (eds) *India's Relations with Russia and China: A New Phase* (New Delhi: Gyan Publishing): 151–166.

———. (2003) 'China's Emerging Ties with Central Asia' in Joshi, N. (ed) *Central Asia—The Great Game Replayed: An Indian Perspective* (New Delhi: New Century Publications): 142–165.

———. (2008) 'Raising the Bar: China Poses Threats to India's Central Asian Gas Plan', *The Times of India*, 26 June.

Dwivedi, R. (2003) 'Third India-Central Asia Regional Conference', *Strategic Analysis* 27(4): 621–625.

———. (2007) 'Religious Extremism in Central Asia: A Case Study of Uzbekistan' in Roy, J.N. and Kumar, B.B. (eds) *India and Central Asia: Classical to Contemporary Periods* (New Delhi: Concept Publishing): 226–246.

Eckstein, H. (1992) *Regarding Politics: Essays on Political Theory, Stability and Change* (Berkeley, CA: University of California Press).

Ertürk, K.A. (ed) (1999) *Rethinking Central Asia: Non-Eurocentric Studies in History, Social Structure, and Identity* (London: Ithaca Press).

European Commission (1994a. 'Towards a New Asia Strategy', Brussels: COM(94)314final.

———. (1994b) 'Cooperation Agreement Between the European Community and the Republic of India', *Official Journal of the European Communities* L223(27.8.94): 24–34.

———. (1996) 'EU-India Enhanced Partnership', Brussels: COM(96)275final.

———. (2001) 'Europe and Asia: A Strategic Framework for Enhanced Partnerships'. Brussels: COM(2001)469final.

———. (2002) 'India: Country Strategy Paper', Brussels, 10 September.

———. (2003) 'Wider Europe: A New Framework for Relations with Our Eastern and Southern Neighbours', Brussels: COM(2003)104final.

———. (2004a) 'European Neighbourhood Policy: Strategy Paper', Brussels: COM(2004)373final.

———. (2004b) 'The Social Dimension of Globalisation: The EU's Policy Contribution on Extending the Benefits to All', Brussels: COM(2004) 383final.

———. (2004c) 'An EU-India Strategic Partnership', Brussels: COM(2004) 430final.

European Security Strategy (2003) 'A Secure Europe in a Better World' (Brussels: EUISS and European Commission).

Fisher, M. (2006) *Counterflows to Colonialism: Indian Travellers and Settlers in Britain, 1600–1857* (Hyderabad: Orient Longman).

Foucault, M. (1977) 'Nietzsche, Genealogy, History' in Bouchard. D. (ed), *Language, Counter-Memory, Practice: Selected Essays and Interviews of Michel Foucault* (Ithaca, NY: Cornell University Press): 139–64.

Gandhi, R. (1996) 'From Armenia to Almaty: Detachment Policy Bad for Business', *The Times of India*, 26 November.

———. (2003) 'Understanding Religious Conflicts' in Mekenkam, M., van Tongeren, P. and van de Veen, H. (eds) *Searching for Peace in Central and South Asia: An Overview of Conflict Prevention and Peacebuilding Activities* (Boulder, CO: Lynne Rienner): 291–303.

Ganguly, S. (1989) 'The Sino-Indian Border Talks, 1981–1989: A View from New Delhi', *Asian Survey* 29(12): 1123–1135.

———. (2002) 'India's Alliances 2020' in Chambers, M.R. (ed) *South Asia in 2020: Future, Strategic Balances, and Alliances* (Carlisle, PA: Strategic Studies Institute): 363–384.
———. (2003/2004) 'India's Foreign Policy Grows Up', *World Policy Journal* 20(4): 41–47.
———. (2004) 'India and China: Border Issues, Domestic Integration, and International Security' in Frankel, F.R. and Harding, H. (eds) *The India-China Relationship: What the United States Needs to Know* (New York: Columbia University Press): 33–75.
———. (2006) 'Introduction' in Ganguly, S. (ed) *South Asia* (New York: New York University Press): 1–14.
Ganguly, S., Shoup, B. and Scobell, A. (eds) (2006) *US-Indian Strategic Cooperation: Into the 21st Century* (London: Routledge).
Geary, P. (2002) *The Myth of Nations* (Princeton, NJ: Princeton University Press).
Ghanta, B. (2005) 'Russia and China Announce Strategic Partnership', *India Daily*, 3 February.
Ghosh, P.S. (1998) 'Bomb, Science, and the State', *The Hindu*, 9 June.
Ghosh, S. (1996) *China-Bangladesh-India Tangle Today: Towards a Solution* (New Delhi: Sterling Publishers).
Ghoshal, B. (1994) 'Trends in China-Burma Relations', *China Report* 30(2): 187–202.
Gidadhubli, R.G. (2003) 'The Politics of Energy Resources in Central Asia' in Joshi, N. (ed) *Central Asia—The Great Game Replayed: An Indian Perspective* (New Delhi: New Century Publications): 166–197.
———. (2007a) 'Russia's Renewed Interest in Southeast Asia' in Reddy, Y.Y. (ed) *Emerging India in Asia-Pacific* (New Delhi: New Century Publications): 197–206.
———. (2007b) 'Politics of Oil and Natural Gas in Central Asia: Conflicts and Cooperations' in Roy, J.N. and Kumar, B.B. (eds) *India and Central Asia: Classical to Contemporary Periods* (New Delhi: Concept Publishing): 156–171.
Giles, B. (1996) 'Evolution of India's Perceptions on Central Asia in the Twentieth Century', *Strategic Analysis* 19(5): 748–779.
Goonewardena, K. (2004) 'Postcolonialism and Diaspora: A Contribution to the Critique of Nationalist Ideology and Historiography in the Age of Globalization and Neoliberalism', *University of Toronto Quarterly* 73 (2): 657–690.
Gopal, R. (1964) *India-China-Tibet Triangle* (Lucknow: Pustak Kendra).
Government of India (2004) 'India's Response to EU Communication Titled "An EU-India Strategic Partnership"' (New Delhi: Government of India).
———. (2005) 'Political Declaration on the India-EU Strategic Partnership', New Delhi, 7 September.
———. (2006) 'Prime Minister's Statement at the Press Conference at the 7th India-EU Summit', Helsinki, 13 October.
Grosz, E. (2004) *The Nick of Time: Politics, Evolution, and the Untimely* (Durham, NC: Duke University Press).
Gujral, I.K. (2004) *Viewpoint: Civilization, Democracy and Foreign Policy* (New Delhi: Allied Publishers).

Gupta, A. (2008) 'The Reformist State: The Indian Security Dilemma' in Gupta, A. (ed) *Strategic Stability in Asia* (Aldershot: Ashgate): 105–126.
Gupta, B.S. (1983) 'The Indira Doctrine', *India Today*, 13 August.
Gupta, K. (1987) *Sino-Indian Relations 1948–1952: Role of K.M. Panikkar* (Calcutta: Minerva Associates).
Gupta, R. (ed) (1989) *India's Security Problems in the Nineties* (New Delhi: Patriot Publishers).
———. (2003) *States in India, Pakistan, Central Asia and Russia* (New Delhi: Kalpaz Publications).
Guzzini, S. (2004) 'The Enduring Dilemmas of Realism in International Relations', *European Journal of International Relations* 10(4): 533–568.
Hagerty, D.T. and Hagerty, H.G. (2005) 'India's Foreign Relations' in Hagerty, D.T. (ed) *South Asia in World Politics* (Lanham, MD: Rowman & Littlefield): 11–48.
Haidar, M. (2003) 'India and Central Asia: Linkages and Interactions' in Joshi, N. (ed) *Central Asia—The Great Game Replayed: An Indian Perspective* (New Delhi: New Century Publications): 257–294.
———. (2004) *Indo-Central Asian Relations* (New Delhi: Manohar Publishers).
Halbfass, W. (1988) *India and Europe: An Essay in Understanding* (Albany, NY: SUNY Press).
Hall, S. (1996) 'The Question of Cultural Identity' in Hall, S., Held, D., Hubert, D., and Thompson, K. (eds) *Modernity* (Cambridge: Polity Press): 595–634.
Hansen, T. and Jaffrelot, C. (eds) (2001) *The BJP and the Compulsions of Politics in India* (New Delhi: Oxford University Press).
Hardgrave, R. and Kochanek, S. (1993) *India: Government and Politics in a Developing Nation* (New York: Harcourt Brace Jovanovich College Publishers).
Harshe, R. and Seethi, K.M. (eds) (2005) *Engaging with the World: Critical Reflections on India's Foreign Policy* (Hyderabad: Orient Longman).
Hasan, M. (ed) (2007)*Nehru's India: Selected Speeches* (New Delhi: Oxford University Press).
Hasan, M. and Nakazato, N. (eds) (2001) *The Unfinished Agenda: Nation Building in South Asia* (New Delhi: Manohar).
Hill, C. (1993) 'The Capability-Expectations Gap, or Conceptualising Europe's International Role', *Journal of Common Market Studies* 31(3): 305–28.
Hindustan Times (1998a) 'Sign of Self-Confidence, Say Experts', 12 May.
———. (1998b) 'BJP Shows It Can Stick to Stand', 12 May.
———. (2003) 'India's N-Command in Place', 5 January.
———. (2003) 'Striking a Parallel with Iraq', 8 April.
———. (2003) 'Indian Army to Raise US-Type Special Forces', 20 April.
———. (2006) 'Pakistan Blocking Access to Central Asia', 15 April.
———. (2006) 'India to Station MiG-29 Fighter-Bombers at Tajikistan Base', 20 April.
———. (2006) 'India and Uzbekistan to Fight Terror and Promote Regional Stability', 26 April.
———. (2006) 'Why Afghanistan Matters to India', 30 April.

———. (2008) 'India's Afghan Road To Be Ready', 13 July.
Hoffman, S.A. (2004) 'Perception and China Policy in India' in Frankel, F.R. and Harding, H. (eds) *The India-China Relationship: What the United States Needs to Know* (New York: Columbia University Press): 33–75.
Husain, A. (1993) 'Opinion', *India Today*, 15 March.
Indian Express (2004) 'Out of the New Great Game', 13 April.
———. (2002) 'VP Malik Politely Tells Kalam: You're Wrong on N-deterrence', 20 June.
———. (2006) 'Shaken by Shanghai', 18 June.
———. (2007) 'India Looks at Central Asia: Europe Links Bypassing Pakistan', 21 March.
———. (2007) 'Central Asian Games', 14 August.
———. (2008) 'Using Economics to Unload History's Baggage', 26 September.
Indian Ministry of Defence (2001) *Annual Report, 2000–2001* (New Delhi: Government of India).
Jaffrelot, C. (2006) 'India and the European Union: The Charade of a Strategic Partnership', *CERI-Focus*, 6 March.
Jahanbegloo, R. (ed) (2008), *India Revisited: Conversations on Contemporary India* (New Delhi: Oxford University Press).
Jain, B.M. (2008) *Global Power: India's Foreign Policy, 1947–2006* (Lanham, MD: Lexington Books).
Jain, J.P. (1974) *China, Pakistan, and Bangladesh* (New Delhi: Radiant Press).
Jain, R. (2002) 'Indian Foreign Policy on the Threshold of the Twenty-First Century' in Snyder, F. (ed) *Regional and Global Regulation of International Trade* (Oxford: Hart Publishing): 131–164.
———. (2005) 'India, the European Union and Asian Regionalism' paper presented at the EUSA-AP conference, Tokyo, December 8–10.
———. (ed) (2007) *India and the European Union: Building a Strategic Partnership* (New Delhi: Radiant Publishers).
Jawahar, K. (2002) 'India and Kazakhstan: Significant Changes', *SAPRA India*, 24 February.
Jayapalan, N. (2001) *Foreign Policy of India* (New Delhi: Atlantic Publishers).
Jayaramu, P.S. (2007) 'India's Foreign Relations', *International Studies* 44(2): 175–179.
Jayasuriya, K. (2004) *Asian Regional Governance* (London: Routledge).
Jayawardena, A. (1993) 'Changes in Soviet Foreign Policy since Gorbachev and Their Impact on South Asia' in Kodikara, S.U. (ed) *External Compulsions of South Asian Politics* (New Delhi: Sage):107–124.
Jetly, N. (1986) 'Sino-Indian Relations: A Quest for Normalization', *Indian Quarterly* 42(1): 56–68.
Jha, S.K. (1997) 'Indo-Russian Relations: In the Light of New Realities' in Rasgotra, M. and Chopra, V.D. (eds) *India's Relations with Russia and China: A New Phase* (New Delhi: Gyan Publishing): 75–96.
Jog, K.P. (ed) (2005) *Perceptions on Kautilya's Arthashastra* (Mumbai: Popu-lar Prakashan).
Jonson, L. (2004) *Vladimir Putin and Central Asia: The Shaping of Russian Foreign Policy* (London: I.B.Tauris).

Joshi, M. (2005) 'India and the Future of Asia: Arranging a Soft Landing for Pakistan' in Sharma, R.R. (ed) *India and Emerging Asia* (New Delhi: Sage): 103–129.
Joshi, N. (2002) 'The Putin Visit', *The Hindu*, 11 December.
———. (2003) 'Issues in Central Asian Stability' in Joshi, N. (ed) *Central Asia—The Great Game Replayed: An Indian Perspective* (New Delhi: New Century Publications): 67–96.
———. (2004) 'Regional Economic Cooperation and Transport Links with Central Asia: An Indian Perspective' in Santhanam, K. and Dwivedi, R. (eds) *India and Central Asia: Advancing the Common Interest* (New Delhi: Anamaya Publishers): 203–213.
———. (2007a) 'Geopolitical Perspectives on Central Asia: An Indian View' in Roy, J.N. and Kumar, B.B. (eds) *India and Central Asia: Classical to Contemporary Periods* (New Delhi: Concept Publishing): 143–155.
———. (2007b) 'India's Policy Toward Central Asia', *World Focus* 28(335/336): 440–446.
Kachru, U. (2007) *Extreme Turbulence: India at the Crossroads* (New Delhi: HarperCollins).
Kagan, R. (2003) *Of Paradise and Power: America and Europe in the New World Order* (New York, NY: Knopf).
Kale, S.S. (2009) 'Inside Out: India's Global Reorientation', *India Review* 8(1): 43–62.
Kampani, G. (2000) 'Comprehensive Test Ban Treaty Endgame in South Asia', *James Martin Center for Nonproliferation Studies Paper*.
Kangle, R.P. (1963) *The Kautilya Arthsastra* (Bombay: University of Bombay Publishers).
Kanwal, G. (1999) 'India's External Security Environment: A Review', *Strategic Analysis* 23(9): 1611–1615.
Kapur, A. (1976) *India's Nuclear Option: Atomic Diplomacy and Decision-Making* (New York: Praeger).
———. (2006) *India—From Regional to World Power* (London: Routledge).
Kapur, H. (1997) *India's Foreign Policy, 1947–1992* (New Delhi: Sage).
Katzenstein, P. (2005) *A World of Regions* (Ithaca, NY: Cornell University Press).
Kaul, C. (2003) *Reporting the Raj: The British Press and India* (Manchester: Manchester University Press).
Kaul, M.M. (2007) 'India's Look East Policy: Posture and Reality' in Reddy, Y.Y. (ed) *Emerging India in Asia-Pacific* (New Delhi: New Century Publications): 240–259.
Kaul, T.N. (1992) *The Future of the Commonwealth of Independent States: Will It Survive* (New Delhi: Vikas Publishing House).
———. (1997) 'India's Relations with Russia and China: In the Post-Cold War Period' in Rasgotra, M. and Chopra, V.D (eds) *India's Relations with Russia and China: A New Phase* (New Delhi: Gyan Publishing): 39–44.
Kaushik, D. (1996) 'India and Central Asia: Past and Present Relations and Future Hopes', *Contemporary Central Asia* 1(1): 226–239.
———. (1997) 'India's Relations with Russia and China: An Overview' in Rasgotra, M. and Chopra, V.D (eds) *India's Relations with Russia and China: A New Phase* (New Delhi: Gyan Publishing): 45–58.

———. (1998) 'India and Central Asia: Renewing a Traditional Relationship' *South Asian Survey* 5(3): 231–244.
———. (2000) 'Regional Cooperation: The Central Asian Experience', *Contemporary Central Asia* 4(1/2): 32–42.
———. (2003a) 'Russia and Central Asia: Emerging Pattern of Relationship' in Joshi, N. (ed) *Central Asia—The Great Game Replayed: An Indian Perspective* (New Delhi: New Century Publications): 9–46.
———. (2003b) 'A Decade of Independent Tajikistan: Some Reflections' in Singh, M. (ed) *India and Tajikistan: Revitalizing a Traditional Relationship* (New Delhi: Anamika Publishers): 29–46.
———. (2007a) 'Central Asia: Changing Geopolitical Alignment in the Aftermath of 11 September' in Roy, J.N. and Kumar, B.B. (eds) *India and Central Asia: Classical to Contemporary Periods* (New Delhi: Concept Publishing): 134–142.
———. (2007b) 'India and Central Asia', *International Studies* 44(3): 280–282.
Kavalski, E. (2006) 'From the Western Balkans to the Greater Balkans Area: The External Conditioning of "Awkward" and "Integrated" States', *Mediterranean Quarterly* 17(3): 86–100.
———. (2007a) 'The Fifth Debate and the Emergence of Complex International Relations Theory', *Cambridge Review of International Affairs* 20(3): 435–54.
———. (2007b) 'Partnership or Rivalry between the EU, India and China in Central Asia', *European Law Journal* 13(6): 839–56.
———. (2007c) 'Whom to Follow? Central Asia between the EU and China', *China Report* 43(1): 43–55.
———. (2008) *Extending the European Security Community: Constructing Peace in the Balkans* (London: I.B.Tauris).
Kavalski, E. and Zolkos, M. (2007) 'The Hoax of War: The Foreign Policy Discourses of Poland and Bulgaria on Iraq', *Journal of Contemporary European Studies* 15(3): 377–393.
———. (eds) (2008) *Defunct Federalisms: Critical Perspectives on Federal Failure* (Aldershot: Ashgate).
Kavic, L.J. (1967) *India's Quest for Security: Defence Policies, 1947–1965* (Berkeley, CA: University of California Press).
Keohane, R. (1986) *Neorealism and Its Critics* (New York: Columbia University Press).
Khan, G. (1998) *Indian Muslim Perceptions of the West during the Eighteenth Century* (Karachi: Oxford University Press).
Khanna, V.C. (2003) 'Relationship of China, India, and Russia: Retrospect and Prospect', *China Report* 39(3): 350–356.
———. (2008) 'Implications for India: Competition or Cooperation?' in Vohra, P. and Ghosh, P.K. (eds) *China and the Indian Ocean Region* (New Delhi: National Maritime Foundation): 83–96.
Khilani, S. (1999) *The Idea of India* (New York: Farrar Straus Giroux).
Khosla, I.P. (ed) (2004) *India and the New Europe* (New Delhi: Konark).
Kinnvall, C. (2006) *Globalization and Religious Nationalism in India: The Search for Ontological Security* (London: Routledge).

Kirchner, E. (2006) 'The Challenge of European Union Security Governance', *Journal of Common Market Studies* 44(5): 947–968.
Kirpalani, V. and Seristo, H. (1998) 'The European Union and India: Potential for More Trade and Investment', *World Affairs* 2(1): 88–98.
Knorr, K. (1977) 'Is International Coercion Waning or Rising?' *International Security* 1(4): 92–110.
Kohli, A. (1988) *Democracy and Discontent: India's Growing Crisis of Governability* (Princeton, NJ: Princeton University Press).
Kohli, R. (1995) *Kautilya's Political Theory: Yogakshewa—The Concept of Welfare State* (New Delhi: Deep and Deep Publications).
Kondapalli, S. (2007) 'Eleventh Round of Border Talks: India-China Border Dispute', *World Focus* 28(335/336): 414–417.
Koshy, N. (2003) *The War on Terror: Reordering the World* (New Delhi: Left Books).
Krishna, G. (1984) 'India and International Order: Retreat from Idealism' in Bull, H. and Watson, A. (eds) *The Expansion of International Society* (Oxford: Clarendon Press): 269–280.
Kumar, A. (2000) 'China and Export Controls' in Bajpai, K. and Mattoo, A. (eds) *The Peacock and the Dragon: India-China relations in the Twenty-First Century* (New Delhi: Har-Anand Publications): 146–154.
Kumar, B.B. (2007) 'India and Central Asia: Links and Interactions' in Roy, J.N. and Kumar, B.B. (eds) *India and Central Asia: Classical to Contemporary Periods* (New Delhi: Concept Publishing): 3–33.
Kumar, R. (2005) *South Asian Union: Problems, Possibilities, and Prospects* (Delhi: Manas Publications).
Kumar, N.S and Rao, U.S. (1996) 'Guidelines for Values-Based Management in Kautilya's Arthsastra', *Journal of Business Ethics* 15(4): 415–423.
Kumaraswamy, P.R. and Subrahmanyam, K. (eds) (2004) *Security Beyond Survival* (New Delhi: Sage).
Kuppuswamy, A. (2006) 'Indo-Myanmar Relations: A Review', *SAAG Paper* 2043.
Laffan, B., O'Donnell, R. and Smith, M. (2000) *Europe's Experimental Union: Rethinking Integration* (London: Routledge).
Lak, D. (2005) *Mantras of Change: Reporting India in a Time of Flux* (New Delhi: Penguin Viking).
———. (2008) *The Future of a New Superpower* (New York: Viking).
Lake, D. and P. Morgan (eds) (1997) *Regional Orders* (University Park, PA: Penn State University Press).
Lal, R. (2006) *Understanding China and India* (Westport, CT: Praeger).
Lall, J. (1988) 'The Sino-Indian Border Problem as a Leftover of History' in Mansingh, S. (ed) *Indian and Chinese Foreign Policy in Comparative Perspective* (New Delhi: Radiant Publishers): 442–456.
Lambah, S.K. (2004) 'The Current Situation in Afghanistan: An Indian Perspective' in Santhanam, K. and Dwivedi, R. (eds) *India and Central Asia: Advancing the Common Interest* (New Delhi: Anamaya Publishers): 295–306.
Lambridis, P. and Koukoulis, T. (2005) 'The Awakening of the Red Dragon', *Asia Europe Journal* 3(4): 479–499.

Larsen, H. (2002) 'The EU: A Global Military Actor', *Cooperation and Conflict* 37(3): 283–302.
Latham, A. (1998) 'Constructing National Security: Culture and Identity in Indian Arms Control and Disarmament Practice', *Contemporary Security Policy* 19(1): 129–158.
Leonard, M. (2005) 'India Joins the West', *Prospect*, 15 November.
Liu Xuecheng (1994) *The Sino-Indian Border Dispute and Sino-Indian Relations* (Lanham, MD: University Press of America).
Luce, E. (2007) 'In Spite of the Gods: The Strange Rise of Modern India', speech at the Carnegie Council for Ethics in International Relations, New York, 1 February.
Mahalingam, S. (2004) 'India-Central Asia Energy Cooperation' in Santhanam, K. and Dwivedi, R. (eds) *India and Central Asia: Advancing the Common Interest* (New Delhi: Anamaya Publishers): 111–143.
Mahapatra, C. (1999) *Indo-US Relations into the 21st Century* (New Delhi: IDSA).
———. (2005) 'The United States and the Asian Powers' in Sharma, R.R. (ed) *India and Emerging Asia* (New Delhi: Sage): 156–180.
Mahapatra, D. A. (2004) 'Russia's Policy towards the Kashmir Issue in the Changing World Order', *International Studies* 41(1): 129–143.
———. (2006) *India-Russia Partnership: Kashmir, Chechnya, and Issues of Convergence* (New Delhi: New Century Publications).
Malkani, K. R. (1994) 'Understanding the BJP', *Seminar* 417.
Manchanda, R. (2007) 'Militarized Hindu Nationalism and the Mass Media: Shaping Hindutva Public Discourse' in McGuire, J. and Copland, I. (eds) *Hindu Nationalism and Governance* (New Delhi: Oxford University Press): 356–379.
Mann, P. (2001) 'Fighting Terrorism: India and Central Asia', *Strategic Analysis* 24(11): 2035–2054.
Manners, I. (2002) 'Normative Power Europe: A Contradiction in Terms?', *Journal of Common Market Studies* 40(2): 235–258.
Manohoran, N. (2003) 'Multiculuturalism in India: Diverse Dots in a Multiple Mosaic' in Mekenkam, M., van Tongeren, P. and van de Veen, H. (eds) *Searching for Peace in Central and South Asia: An Overview of Conflict Prevention and Peacebuilding Activities* (Boulder, CO: Lynne Rienner): 326–335.
Mansingh, S. (1994) 'India-China Relations in the Post-Cold War Era', *Asian Survey* 24(3): 278–292.
———. (ed) (1998) *Indian and Chinese Foreign Policy in Comparative Perspective* (New Delhi: Radiant Publishers).
———. (2000) 'Why China Matters' in Bajpai, K. and Mattoo, A. (eds) *The Peacock and the Dragon: India-China relations in the Twenty-First Century* (New Delhi: Har-Anand Publications): 155–167.
Mansingh, S. and Ranganathan, C.V. (2001) 'Approaches to State Sovereignty' in Deshpande, G.P. and Acharya, A. (eds) *Crossing a Bridge of Dreams: Fifty Years of India and China* (New Delhi: Tulika): 446–465.
Mattoo, A. (2000) 'Imagining China' in Bajpai, K. and Mattoo, A. (eds) *The Peacock and the Dragon: India-China relations in the Twenty-First Century* (New Delhi: Har-Anand Publications): 13–25.

———. (2003) 'United States of America and Central Asia: Beginning of the Great Game' in Joshi, N. (ed) *Central Asia—The Great Game Replayed: An Indian Perspective* (New Delhi: New Century Publications): 47–66.
McGuire, J. and Copland, I. (eds) (2007) *Hindu Nationalism and Governance* (New Delhi: Oxford University Press).
Mehrotra, O.N. (1997) 'Indo-Russian Relations after the Disintegration of the USSR' in Rasgotra, M. and Chopra, V.D. (eds) *India's Relations with Russia and China: A New Phase* (New Delhi: Gyan Publishing): 97–112.
Mehta, P.B. (2006) 'India: The New Clear Politics of Self-Esteem' in Ganguly, S. (ed) *South Asia* (New York: New York University Press): 17–24.
Mehta, V.R. (1992) *Foundations of Indian Political Thought* (New Delhi: Manohar).
Melkote, R.S. (ed) (2001) *Meanings of Globalization: Indian and French Perspectives* (New Delhi: Sterling).
Menon, K. (1991) 'Pak. Ties with Russia on the Upswing', *The Hindu*, 23 December.
Menon, N. and Nigam, A. (2007) *Power and Contestation: India since 1989* (London: Zed Books).
Menon, R. (2003) 'The New Great Game in Central Asia', *Survival* 45(2): 187–204.
Menon, S. (2007) 'The Challenges Ahead for India's Foreign Policy', *World Focus* 28(335/336): 389–391.
Mishra, M. (2000) 'China's Xinjiang Conundrum' in Bajpai, K. and Mattoo, A. (eds) *The Peacock and the Dragon: India-China Relations in the Twenty-First Century* (New Delhi: Har-Anand Publications): 333–348.
Mishra, P. (2000) 'A New, Nuclear India?' in Silvers, R.B. and Epstein, B. (eds) *India: A Mosaic* (New York: NYREV Inc.): 227–273.
Mishra, R. (1996) *India and International Relations* (New Delhi: Kanishka Publishers).
Misra, K.P. (1981) 'Towards Understanding Nonalignment', *International Studies* 20(1): 23–37.
Mistry, D. (2009) 'Tempering Optimism About Nuclear Deterrence in South Asia', *Security Studies* 18(1): 148–182.
Mistry, P.S. (2003) 'Rethinking India's International Economic Diplomacy', *Economic and Political Weekly* 38(28): 2943–2950.
Modelski, G. (1964) 'Kautilya: Foreign Policy and the International System in the Ancient Hindu World', *American Political Science Review* 53(3): 549–560.
Mohapatra, N.K. (2007) 'Political and Security Challenges in Central Asia: The Drug Trafficking Dimension', *International Studies* 44(2): 157–174.
Mohan, C. R. (2004) *Crossing the Rubicon: The Shaping of India's New Foreign Policy* (London: Palgrave).
———. (2006) 'Shaken by Shanghai', *Indian Express*, 18 June.
———. (2007a) 'Soft Borders and Cooperative Frontiers: India's Changing Territorial Diplomacy towards Pakistan and China', *Strategic Analysis* 31(1): 1–23.
———. (2007b) 'Indian Foreign Policy', *World Focus* 28(335/336): 392–397.

Mohanty, J.K. (2006) *Terrorism and Militancy in Central Asia* (New Delhi: Kalpaz Publications).
Mohanty, M. (2006) 'Social Inequality, Labor Market Dynamics, and Reservation', *Economic and Political Weekly* 41(35): 3777–3789.
Mohite, D.H. and Dholakia, A. (2001) *India and the Emerging World Order: Foreign Policy and Security Perspectives* (New Delhi: Kalinga Publications).
Morgenthau, H. (1973[1948]) *Politics among Nations* (New York: Alfred A. Knopf).
Morin, E. (2006) 'Realism and Utopia', *Diogenes* 39(209): 135–144.
Mukherjee, A. (1999) 'Turnaround in Chinese Attitude toward India', *Hindustan Times*, 16 February.
Mukherjee, B. (1996) *India in Early Central Asia* (New Delhi: Herman).
Mukhopadhyay, A. (2006) 'The EU-India Helsinki Summit', *IDSA Strategic Comment*, 10 October.
Mullik, B.N. (1971) *My Years with Nehru: The Chinese Betrayal* (Bombay: Allied Publishers).
Mullojanov, P. (2008) 'International Intervention in Central Asia: The Triumph of Geopolitics?' in Coicaud, J. and Wheeler, N.J. (eds) *National Interest and International Solidarity* (Tokyo: United Nations University Press): 120–150.
Muni, S.D. (1996) 'Regionalism Beyond the Regions: South Asia Outside of SAARC', *South Asian Survey* 3(1): 327–338.
———. (1997) 'The Cold War in Asia: India's Options', *Strategic Analysis* 19(12): 1599–1612.
———. (2003) 'India and Central Asia: Towards a Cooperative Future' in Joshi, N. (ed) *Central Asia—The Great Game Replayed: An Indian Perspective* (New Delhi: New Century Publications): 97–141.
Muni, S.D. and Mohan, C.R. (2005) 'India's Options in a Changing Asia' in Sharma, R.R. (ed) *India and Emerging Asia* (New Delhi: Sage): 52–79.
Murdian, P.R. (1994) *India and the Middle East* (London: I.B.Tauris).
Naik, J.A. (1995) *Russia's Policy towards India: From Stalin to Yeltsin* (New Delhi: MD Publications).
Nandy, A. (1983) *The Intimate Enemy: Loss and Recovery of Self under Colonialism* (New Delhi: Oxford University Press).
———. (1990) 'The Politics of Secularism and the Recovery of Religious Tolerance' in Walker, R.B.J. and Mendlovitz, S.H. (eds) *Contending Sovereignties: Redefining Political Community* (Boulder, CO: Lynne Rienner): 125–144.
Narayanan, R. (2007) 'The Chinese Discourse on the "Rise of China"', *Strategic Analysis* 31(4): 645–663.
Narlikar, A. (2006) 'Peculiar Chauvinism or Strategic Calculation? Explaining the Negotiating Strategy of a Rising India', *International Affairs* 82(1): 59–76.
Nautiyal, A. (2004) 'US Policies in the Post-Cold War Era: An Indian Perspective', *Strategic Analysis* 28(1): 138–156.
Nayar, B.R. (2006) *India's Globalization* (Washington, DC: East West Center).

Nayar, B.R. and Paul, T.V. (2003) *India in the World Order: Searching for Major Power Status* (Cambridge: Cambridge University Press).
Noorani, A.G. (2003) *Sarvakar and Hindutva* (New Delhi: Manohar).
Norbu, D. (2000) 'India, China, and Tibet' in Bajpai, K. and Mattoo, A. (eds) *The Peacock and the Dragon: India-China relations in the Twenty-First Century* (New Delhi: Har-Anand Publications): 275–297.
Nehru, J. (1961) *Selected Speeches: September 1946—April 1961* (New Delhi: Government of India Publications Division).
Ollapally, D.M. (2005) 'Foreign Policy and Identity Politics' in Bajpai, K.P and Mallavarapu, S. (eds) *International Relations in India: Theorizing the Region and Nation* (New Delhi: Orient Longman): 117–141.
Olson, M . (1990) 'The Logic of Collective Action in Soviet-type Societies', *Journal of Soviet Nationalities* 1(2): 8–33.
Ortega, M. (ed) (2004) *Global Views on the European Union* (Paris: EU Institute for Security Studies).
Ovchinnikov, V. (2000) 'No Need to Fear the Russian Tiger', *Rossiyskaya Gazeta*, 19 September.
Palat, M.K. (1994) 'Central Asia and South Asia: Structuring of a New Relationship', *South Asian Survey* 1(1): 49–57.
———. (1999) 'The "Romance" of the Silk Road', *The Hindu*, 9 January.
Palit, D.K. (1991) *War in High Himalaya: The Indian Army in Crisis* (London: Hurst).
Pandey, G. (2001) *Remembering Partition: Violence, Nationalism, and History in India* (Cambridge: Cambridge University Press).
Pandey, S.K. (2007) 'Asia in the Debate on Russian Identity', *International Studies* 44(4): 317–337.
Pandit, R. (2007) 'Indian Forces Get Foothold in Central Asia', *The Times of India*, 18 July.
———. (2008) 'Outpost at Tajikistan Still on India's Radar', *The Times of India*, 21 January.
Panikkar, K.M. (1955) *Geographical Factors in Indian History* (Bombay: Bharatiya Vidya Bhavan).
Pannikkar, K.N. (1995) *Culture, Ideology, Hegemony: Intellectuals and Social Consciousness in Colonial India* (New Delhi: Tulika).
Pant, G. (2005) 'Reform and Resurgence: The Trajectory of Change in West Asia' in Sharma, R.R. (ed) *India and Emerging Asia* (New Delhi: Sage): 181–205.
Pattanaik, S.S. (2004) *Elite Perceptions in Foreign Policy: Role of Print Media in Influencing Indo–Pak Relations, 1989–1999* (New Delhi: Manohar).
———. (2008) 'War on Terror and Its Impact on Pakistan's Kashmir Policy', *Strategic Analysis* 32(3): 389–412.
Patnaik, A. (2002) 'Central Asia and the CIS Integration', *Contemporary Central Asia* 6(3): 1–13.
———. (2003) *Nations, Minorities, and States in Central Asia* (New Delhi: Anamika Publishers).
———. (2004) 'Mongolia–Russia Relations', *International Studies* 41(1): 152–154.

———. (2005) 'Central Asia's Security: The Asian Dimension' in Sharma, R.R. (ed) *India and Emerging Asia* (New Delhi: Sage): 206–231.
Patten, C. (2004) 'The EU and India', *The Hindu*, 17 February.
Patwardan, A. (1998) 'How We Learned to Love the Bomb', *The Hindu*, 7 June.
Perkovich, G. (2000) *India's Nuclear Bomb* (Berkeley, CA: University of California Press).
Phadnis, U. and Patnaik, S. (1981) 'Nonalignment as a Foreign Policy Strategy', *International Studies* 20(2): 223–238.
Pillai, K.R. (1969) *India's Foreign Policy: Basic Issues and Political Attitudes* (Meerut: Meenakshi Prakashan).
Pillai, S.K. (2003) 'Border Conflicts and Regional Disputes' in Mekenkam, M., van Tongeren, P. and van de Veen, H. (eds) *Searching for Peace in Central and South Asia: An Overview of Conflict Prevention and Peacebuilding Activities* (Boulder, CO: Lynne Rienner): 249–266.
Prakash, S. (1997) 'India-China Relations: Past to Present' in Rasgotra, M. and Chopra, V.D (eds) *India's Relations with Russia and China: A New Phase* (New Delhi: Gyan Publishing): 167–188.
Prasad, B. (1963) 'Studies of India's Foreign Policy and Relations: Survey of Recent Research', *International Studies* 5(3): 435–323.
Pugh, M. and Sidhu, W.P.S. (2003) *The United Nations and Regional Security* (Boulder, CO: Lynne Rienner).
Pye, L. (1990) 'China: Erratic State, Frustrated Society', *Foreign Affairs* 69 (4): 56–74.
Qurashi, H. (2006) 'The Century of Asia', *The Hindu*, 14 January.
Raghavan, V.R. (1998) *India-China Relations: A Military Perspective* (New Delhi: Gyan Publishing House).
Rahul, R. (1981) 'Central Asian States', *International Studies* 21(1): 625–642.
Rai, A.K. (2003) 'Diplomacy and the News Media: A Comment on the Indian Experience', *Strategic Analysis* 27(1): 21–40.
Rai, V. and Simon, W. (2007) *Think India* (New York: Dutton).
Rais, R.B. (1977) *China and Pakistan: A Political Analysis of Mutual Relations* (Lahore: Progressive Publishers).
Raj, C.S. and Mahapatra, C. (2004) 'US Strategic Responses to Emerging Problems in Asia', *International Studies* 41(3): 279–298.
Rajagopalan, R. (2005) 'Structural Imperatives of Asian Security' in Sharma, R.R. (ed) *India and Emerging Asia* (New Delhi: Sage): 295–310.
Rajagopalan, R. and Sahni, V. (2008) 'India and the Great Powers: Strategic Imperatives, Normative Necessities', *South Asian Survey* 15(1): 5–32.
Rajan, M.S. (1998) 'The Goal's of India's Foreign Policy', *International Studies* 35(1): 73–105.
Rajghatta, C. (2005) 'Six Asian "Stans" to be United with the States', *The Times of India*, 22 September.
Rajshekar, V.T. (2005) 'Aryan Aggression on Indian Culture' in Khalid, U. (ed), *Authentic Voices of South Asia* (London: Institute of South Asia): 45–83.
Ramakant (ed) (1988) *China and South Asia* (New Delhi: South Asian Publishers).

Ramet, S. (2005) *Thinking about Yugoslavia: Scholarly Debates about the Yugoslav Breakup and the Wars in Bosnia and Kosovo* (Cambridge: Cambridge University Press).
Rana, K.S. (2007) *Asian Diplomacy: The Foreign Ministries of China, India, Japan, Singapore, and Thailand* (New Delhi: Oxford University Press).
Rane, P.P. (2007) 'NATO's Counter-Terrorism Strategies in Afghanistan', *Strategic Analysis* 31(1): 73–91.
Ranganathan, C.V. (1997) 'India-China Relations: An Assessment' in Rasgotra, M. and Chopra, V.D. (eds) *India's Relations with Russia and China: A New Phase* (New Delhi: Gyan Publishing): 145–150.
———. (2002) 'The China Threat: A View from India' in Yee, H. and Storey, Y. (eds) *The China Threat: Perceptions, Myths, and Reality* (London: Routledge Curzon): 281–296.
Rao, V.N. and Alam, M.M. (eds) (2005) *Central Asia: Present Challenges and Future Prospects* (New Delhi: Knowledge World).
Rasgotra, M. and Chopra, V.D. (eds) (1997) *India's Relations with Russia and China: A New Phase* (New Delhi: Gyan Publishing House).
Ray, B.N. (1999) *Tradition and Innovation in Indian Political Thought* (New Delhi: Ajanta Books).
Reddy, K.R. (ed) (2005) *India and ASEAN: Foreign Policy Dimensions for the 21st Century* (New Delhi: New Century Publications).
———. (2007) 'India and China Rapprochement: Cautious Moves' in Reddy, Y.Y. (ed) *Emerging India in Asia-Pacific* (New Delhi: New Century Publications): 207–212.
Rosenau, J. (2003) *Distant Proximities: Dynamics Beyond Globalization* (Princeton, NJ: Princeton University Press).
Roy, M.S. (2001) 'India's Interests in Central Asia', *Strategic Analysis* 24(1): 2273–2298.
Roy-Chaudhury, R. (2008) *India as a Rising Great Power: Challenges and Opportunities* (London: Routledge).
Rummel, R. (1976) *Understanding Conflict and War: The Conflict Helix* (Beverly Hills, CA: Sage).
Sachdeva, G. (2003) 'Understanding Central Asian Economic Models' in Joshi, N. (ed) *Central Asia—The Great Game Replayed: An Indian Perspective* (New Delhi: New Century Publications): 198–256.
———. (2005) 'Economic Developments and Regional Economic Trends in Central Asia: Emerging Asian Linkages' in Sharma, R.R. (ed) *India and Emerging Asia* (New Delhi: Sage): 268–294.
———. (2007) 'Economic Changes in Central Asia and Indian Responses' in Roy, J.N. and Kumar, B.B. (eds) *India and Central Asia: Classical to Contemporary Periods* (New Delhi: Concept Publishing): 251–272.
Sahni, V. (2004) 'From Security in Asia to Asian Security', *International Studies* 41(3): 245–261.
———. (2005) 'A Continent Becomes a Region: Future Asian Security Architectures' in Sharma, R.R. (ed) *India and Emerging Asia* (New Delhi: Sage): 80–101.
Sali, M.L. (1998) *India-China Border Dispute: A Case Study of the Eastern Sector* (Pune: A.P.H. Publishing Corporation).

Sandhu, B. (1988) *Unresolved Conflict: China and India* (New Delhi: Radiant Publishers).
Sareen, A. (1981) *India and Afghanistan* (New Delhi: Seema Publications).
Sarkar, S. (2002) *Beyond Nationalist Frames: Relocating Postmodernism, Hindutva, and History* (New Delhi: Permanent Black).
Sen, K. (2000) 'India, China, and the United States' in Bajpai, K. and Mattoo, A. (eds) *The Peacock and the Dragon: India-China relations in the Twenty-First Century* (New Delhi: Har-Anand Publications): 251– 274.
Sengupta, A. (1997) 'Minorities and Nationalizing States', *International Studies* 34(3): 269–300.
———. (2002) *Frontiers into Borders: The Transformation of Identities in Central Asia* (New Delhi: Hope India Publications).
Seth, S. (1993) '"Nehruvian Socialism": Nationalism, Marxism, and the Pursuit of Modernity', *Alternatives* 18(4): 453–473.
Shah, R. (1993) 'Russia Divided over Ties with India', *Patriot*, 22 January.
Shambaugh, D. (ed) (2005) *Power Shift* (Berkeley, CA: University of California Press).
Shams-ud-Din (1991) 'Disintegration of the Soviet Union and Prospects for Islamic Revivalism in Central Asia', *Journal of West Asian Studies* 7(1): 23–38.
———. (1997) 'The New Great Game in Central Asia', *International Studies* 34(3): 329–341.
———. (ed) (1999) *Nationalism in Russia and Central Asia* (New Delhi: Lancer Books).
Shamsi, N. (2004) *India: A Global Power* (New Delhi: Anmol Publications).
Shani, G. (2007) 'Globalization, the "War on Terror" and Human In/Security in South Asia' in Shani, G., Sato, M. and Pasha, M. (eds) *Human Security in a Post-9/11 World* (Basingstoke: Palgrave Macmillan): 115–130.
Sharan, S. (ed) (1996) *India, Tibet, and China* (New Delhi: ITFS).
Sharma, D. (1987) 'India's Nuclear Policy and the Arms Race in the Southeast Asian Region' in Worsley, P. and Hadjor, K. (eds) *On the Brink: Nuclear Proliferation in the Third World* (London: Third World Books): 223–228.
Sharma, J. (2002) 'Moscow and India', *International Studies* 39(1): 96–98.
Sharma, J.P. (2003) *Foreign Policy Challenges: India and the Afro-Arab World* (New Delhi: Anamika Publishers).
Sharma, L.K. (1998) 'India's Tests Put Nuclear Haves in the Dock', *The Times of India*, 13 May.
Sharma, R.R. (1997) 'Indo-Russian Relations in the Emerging Context' in Rasgotra, M. and Chopra, V.D. (eds) *India's Relations with Russia and China: A New Phase* (New Delhi: Gyan Publishing): 65–74.
———. (2003) 'State-Building in Tajikistan: Problems and Prospect' in Singh, M. (ed) *India and Tajikistan: Revitalizing a Traditional Relationship* (New Delhi: Anamika Publishers): 67–100.
———. (2004a) 'Challenges to Stability in Asia', *International Studies* 41(3): 263–277.
———. (2004b) 'Issues Confronting Central Asia', *International Studies* 41(4): 427–429.

———. (2005) 'Asia's Quest for Identity and Security' in Sharma, R.R. (ed) *India and Emerging Asia* (New Delhi: Sage): 29–51.
———. (2007) 'Political System and Democratic Discourse in Central Asia: A View from Outside' in Roy, J.N. and Kumar, B.B. (eds) *India and Central Asia: Classical to Contemporary Periods* (New Delhi: Concept Publishing): 123–133.
Sharma, S.K. (2005) 'Indian Idea of Good Governance: Revisiting Kautilya's Arthsastra', *Dynamics of Administration* 17(1/2): 8–19.
Sharma, S.L. (1988) *Tibet: Self-Determination among Nations* (New Delhi: Criterion Press).
Sharma, S.R. (2002) *Foundations of Indian Foreign Policy* (New Delhi: Omsons Publications).
Shih, C. (1990) *The Spirit of Foreign Policy* (New York: St. Martin's Press).
Shukla, V. (2005) India's *Foreign Policy in the New Millennium: The Role of Power* (New Delhi: Atlantic Publishers).
Sidhu, W.R.S. (2003) 'Terrible Tuesday and Terrorism in South Asia', *South Asian Survey* 10(2): 215–230.
Singh, J. (1998) 'Against Nuclear Apartheid', *Foreign Affairs* 77(5): 41–52.
———. (1999) *Defending India* (New York: St. Martin's Press).
Singh J.J. (ed) (1998a) *Cooperative Peace in Asia* (New Delhi: IDSA).
———. (ed) (1998b) *Nuclear India* (New Delhi: Knowledge World).
———. (ed) (2000) *Peace and Security in Central Asia* (New Delhi: IDSA).
Singh, K. (2005) *South-Central Asia* (Amritsar: Guru Nana Dev University Press).
Singh, K.G. (2004) 'India and the European Union', *South Asia Analysis Group Paper* 1163, 10 November.
Singh, M. (2003) 'India and Tajikistan: A Perspective for the 21st Century' in Singh, M. (ed) *India and Tajikistan: Revitalizing a Traditional Relationship* (New Delhi: Anamika Publishers): 197–204.
Singh, M. and Krassiltchikov, V. (eds) (2003) *Eurasian Vision: Felicitation Volume on the 70th Birthday of Prof. Davendra Kaushik* (New Delhi: Anamika Publishers).
Singh, M.N. (2001) 'India's Interests in Central Asia', *Strategic Analysis* 24 (12): 2273–2289.
Singh, N. (2006) *India: A Rising Power* (New Delhi: Authors Press).
Singh, S. (2000) 'China's Nuclear Deterrent' in Bajpai, K. and Mattoo, A. (eds) *The Peacock and the Dragon: India-China Relations in the Twenty-First Century* (New Delhi: Har-Anand Publications): 50–76.
———. (2003) *China-South Asia: Issues, Equations, Policies* (New Delhi: Lancer's Books).
Singer, J.D. (1989) 'System Structure, Decision Processes, and Innocence of International War' in Midlarsky, M. (ed) *Handbook of War Studies* (Boston, MA: Unwin Hyman): 1–12.
Sinha, Y. (2004) 'India and Central Asia in the Emerging Security Environment' in Santhanam, K. and Dwivedi, R. (eds) *India and Central Asia: Advancing the Common Interest* (New Delhi: Anamaya Publishers): 5–10.
Snyder, J. (1991), *Myths of Empire: Domestic Politics and International Ambition* (Ithaca, NY: Cornell University Press).

Solingen, E. (1998) *Regional Orders at Century's Dawn* (Princeton, NJ: Princeton University Press).
Soni, S.K. (2002) *Mongolia-Russia Relations: Kiakhta to Vladivostok* (New Delhi: Shipra Publications).
Spear, P. (1970) *A History of India* (New York: Penguin Books).
Spengler, J.J. (1969) 'Kautilya, Plato, and Lord Shang: Comparative Political Economy', *Proceedings of the American Philosophical Society* 113(6): 450–457.
Srinivasan, T.N. (2004) 'China and India: An Update', *Journal of Asian Economics* 15(4): 613–636.
Srivastava, A. (2000) 'Recalibrating India's Relations with China' in Bajpai, K. and Mattoo, A. (eds) *The Peacock and the Dragon: India-China relations in the Twenty-First Century* (New Delhi: Har-Anand Publications): 229–250.
Stobdan, P. (1993) 'China's Forays into Burma: Implications for India', *Strategic Analysis* 16(1): 21–38.
———. (1998) 'Regional Issues in Central Asia: Implications for South Asia', *South Asian Survey* 5(3): 245–263.
———. (2004) 'Central Asia and India's Security', *Strategic Analysis* 28(1): 54–82.
———. (2007) 'India's Tibet Policy', *World Focus* 28(335/336): 417–424.
———. (2009) 'India and Kazakhstan Should Share Complementary Objectives', *Strategic Analysis* 33(1): 1–7.
Stuligross, D. (2006) 'India's Vision—and the BJP's' in Ganguly, S. (ed) *South Asia* (New York: New York University Press): 177–187.
Subramanian, V.K. (1980) *Maxims of Chanakya* (New Delhi: Abhinav Publications).
Subrahmanyam, K. (1998) 'The Nuclear Bomb: Myths and Reality', *The Times of India*, 22 June.
———. (2000) 'From Indira to Gowda: It Was Bomb All the Wat', *The Times of India*, 17 April.
———. (2008[1972]) 'Nehru's Concept of Indian Defence', *Strategic Analysis* 32(6): 1179–1190.
Suganami, H. (2008) 'Narrative Explanation and International Relations: Back to Basics', *Millennium* 37(2): 327–256.
Surayanarayan, S.P. (1993) 'Central Asia: Need for a Bold Policy', *The Hindu*, 11 July.
Syed, A.H. (1974) *China and Pakistan: Diplomacy of an Entente Cordiale* (Oxford: Oxford University Press).
Synnott, H. (1999) *The Causes and Consequences of South Asia's Nuclear Tests* (Oxford: Oxford University Press).
Tavares, S.C. (2007) 'Logrolling and National Government Interests', *Economics and Politics* 19(3): 345–368.
Tellis, A.J. (2004) 'China and India in Asia' in Frankel, F.R. and Harding, H. (eds) *The India-China Relationship: What the United States Needs to Know* (New York: Columbia University Press): 134–177.
Thakur, R. (193) 'Ayodhya and the Politics of India's Secularism: A Double-Standard Discourse', *Asian Survey* 33(7): 645–664.

Thakurta, P.G. and Raghuraman, S. (2004) *A Time of Contradictions: Divided We Stand* (New Delhi: Sage).
The Economic Times (1998) 'The Nuclear Bomb: Myths and Reality', 22 June.
———. (1998) 'After the Bomb, What?', 23 June.
The Hindu (1998) 'How We Learned to Love the Bomb', 7 June.
———. (2003) 'India's Stand on Iraq', 7 April.
———. (2008) 'Central Asia Won't Blow Apart', 18 April.
The Times of India (1998) 'India's Tests Put Nuclear Haves in the Dock', 13 May.
———. (1998) 'We Should Feel Proud', 16 May.
———. (1998) 'Explosion of Nuclear Myths', 17 May.
———. (2006) 'New Effort: India-Myanmar to Begin Talks', 2 September.
———. (2008) 'India Wants Road-Link to Central Asia', 16 March.
The Statesman (1998) 'Tests in Supreme National Interest', 15 May.
Trenin, D. (2003) 'Southern Watch: Russia's Policy in Central Asia', *Journal of International Affairs* 56(2): 119–131.
Udgaonkar, B.M. (1999) 'India's Nuclear Capability, Her Security Concerns, and the Recent Tests', *Current Science* 76(2): 154–166.
———. (2001) 'The International Dimension of National Security: Some Observations', *Strategic Analysis* 24(10): 1773–1794.
Upadhyaya, P. (2009) 'Peace and Conflict: Reflections on Indian Thinking', *Strategic Analysis* 33(1): 71–83.
Varma, S.N. (1999) *Foreign Policy Dynamics: Moscow and India* (New Delhi: Deep and Deep Publications).
Vanaik, A. (2007) 'Making India Strong: The BJP-Led Government's Foreign Policy Perspectives' in McGuire, J. and Copland, I. (eds) *Hindu Nationalism and Governance* (New Delhi: Oxford University Press): 380–404.
Vanaik, S. (1987) 'Nuclear Fallacies in India and Pakistan' in Worsley. P. and Hadjor, K. (eds) *On the Brink: Nuclear Proliferation in the Third World* (London: Third World Books): 62–75.
Varadarajan, S. (2005a) 'India Set to Take Big Leap in Central Asian Backyard', *The Hindu*, 5 July.
———. (2005b) 'Central Asia: China and Russia Up the Ante', *The Hindu*, 8 July.
Varma, P.K. (2004) *Being Indian* (New Delhi: Penguin Books).
Vaughn, B. (2004) 'Indian Geopolitics, the United States and Evolving Correlates of Power in Asia', *Geopolitics* 9(2): 440–459.
Verghese, B.G. (2001) *Reorienting India: The New Geopolitics of Asia* (New Delhi: Konark Publishers).
Verma, S.N. (1995) 'Russia and India: From Hiatus to Resurrection', *Strategic Analysis* 28(4): 569–577.
Vohra, N.N. (ed) (1999) *Culture, Society, and Politics in Central Asia and India* (New Delhi: Shipra Publications).
Vohra, N.N. and Dixit, J. (eds) (1999) *Religion, Politics, and Society in South and Southeast Asia* (New Delhi: Shipra Publication).
Wagner, C. (2006) 'India Moves into the Spotlight', *Deutschland Online*, 27 November.

Walker, M. (2006) 'India's Path to Greatness', *Wilson Quarterly* 30 (3): 22–30.
Waltz, K. (1959) *Man, the State, and War* (New York: Columbia University Press).
Warikoo, K. (ed) (1995) *Central Asia: Emerging New Order* (New Delhi: Har-Anand Publications).
———. (2003) 'The Afghanistan Crisis and Tajikistan' in Singh, M. (ed) *India and Tajikistan: Revitalizing a Traditional Relationship* (New Delhi: Anamika Publishers): 145–154.
Wæver, O. (1998a) 'Explaining Europe by Decoding Discourses' in Wivel, A. (ed) *Explaining European Integration* (Copenhagen: Copenhagen University Press): 100–146.
———. (1998b) 'Insecurity, Security and Asecurity in the West-European Non-War Community' in Adler, E. and Barnett, M. (eds) *Security Communities* (Cambridge: Cambridge University Press): 69–118
White, D. (1971) 'Power and Intention', *International Organization* 65(3): 749–759.
Williams, M.C. (2005) *The Realist Tradition and the Limits of International Relations* (Cambridge: Cambridge University Press).
Wirsing, R. (2005) 'Great-Power Foreign Policies in South Asia' in Hagerty, D.T. (ed) *South Asia in World Politics* (Lanham, MD: Rowman & Littlefield): 135–160.
Woodward, S. (2000) 'Violence-Prone Area or International Transition?' in Das, V., Kleinman, A., Ramphele, M. and Reynolds, P. (eds) *Violence and Subjectivity* (Berkeley, CA: University of California Press): 19–45.
Yasmeen, S. (2008) 'India and Pakistan: From Zero-Sum to Shared Security' in Coicaud, J. and Wheeler, N.J. (eds) *National Interest and International Solidarity* (Tokyo: United Nations University Press): 27–55.
Zolkos, M. (2005) *Conceptual Analysis of the Human Rights and Democracy Nexus* (Copenhagen: Copenhagen University Press).

INDEX

Afghanistan 5–6, 18, 86, 103–105, 126, 183, 186–189, 192–193, 218, 224; *see* 'Northern Alliance', Taliban
Africa 32
Aksai Chin 137, 145
anti-colonialism *see* colonialism
Arthashastra *see* Kautilya
Arunchal Pradesh 137, 152
Ashokan (foreign policy) tradition 13, 35, 213

balance of power 40–43, 54, 120, 158; *see* realpolitik
Bangladesh 54
'bhai-bhai' sentiments *see* China
BJP 58, 61–62, 70, 72–74, 217; *see* Vajpayee
Bulganin, Nikolai 112

Caspian Sea 6
Caucasus 6, 153, 169,
Central Asia 2–7, 15, 21–39, 43–50, 53, 57, 61–70, 74, 77, 81, 83–95, 101, 106, 109, 112, 126, 131, 137–144, 154–157, 160, 167, 172, 176, 179, 181, 183, 187, 190, 193, 195, 197, 204, 210, 218, 220; affairs 5, 19, 64, 85, 89, 92, 97, 104, 107, 123, 129, 155, 158, 167, 204, 220; clan mentality 92, 103; definition of 4–7, 122–123; peoples 4–7, 92, 103, 108, 106, 123–124, 154, 188; states 7, 15, 81, 83–95, 101, 106, 109, 112, 126, 131, 154–157, 160, 167, 181, 183, 187, 190, 204, 210, 218
Chechnya 153
China 7, 16–18, 33, 70, 97, 102, 106, 110, 127, 130, 132, 133–165, 173, 183, 203, 210; 1962 war with India 16, 72, 112–113, 137–138, 141, 143–146, 150, 186, 214, 217; 'bhai-bhai' sentiments 144, 148; relations with Pakistan 16, 39, 106, 112, 127, 133–165, 192; relations with Russia 108, 110, 129–131, 133–165, 170, 178, 183, 190, 197, 199; *see* Mao
'chosen glory' 75–77; *see* mythmaking
clan mentality *see* Central Asia
colonialism 32–33, 42, 137–138, 144, 151, 165, 190, 215; anti-colonialism 145, 190; neo-colonialism 214, 216
complex interdependence *see* interdependence
complexity 6, 11, 18, 23, 25, 28, 65–66, 92, 106, 122, 129, 132, 135,

145, 156, 161, 170, 178, 180, 192, 197, 200, 223; *see* fragmegration
Congress Party (INC) 34, 70, 112; *see* Gandhi, Nehru
cooperative security *see* security
counter-terrorism 18, 119, 187, 193, 201; *see* terrorism

Dalai Lama 141; *see* Tibet
democracy 12, 15, 24–25, 35, 49, 65, 80, 83, 86, 89–95, 98, 101, 111, 123, 128, 158, 175–178, 181, 184, 186, 190, 201, 209, 215, 219
discourse 2, 8, 14, 16, 18, 23, 28, 36, 39, 43, 45, 49, 53, 60, 63, 66, 68, 73, 75, 80, 96, 98, 104, 106, 156, 164, 167, 170, 176, 180, 183, 187, 196, 200, 213; foreign policy 10, 18, 43, 48, 50, 54, 59, 88, 100; *see* discourse analysis
discourse analysis 3–4, 8, 10, 12–18, 28, 38, 43, 45, 48–51, 80, 83, 85, 95, 100, 104, 107, 109, 136, 138, 161, 167, 172, 182, 187, 195, 200, 206; *see* narrative imbrication
discursive articulation 1, 4, 16, 45, 100, 125, 182, 196; assertiveness 200; construction 14–15, 17–18, 47, 60, 84, 132, 161, 167, 169, 183, 206; engagement 3, 80, 82; experience 85; framing 137; formulation 8, 12, 16, 21, 77, 161, 187, 194; intangibles 42; interpretation 172; modality 7, 95–96, 134; multiplicity 132; platform 47, 61, 107; process 8, 48; recognition 189; *see* discourse analysis
disorder 65, 93; *see* order

economic order *see* order
economic security *see* security
energy security *see* security

EU 17, 106, 110, 154, 167, 169, 171–182, 186, 188, 194, 202, 211, 218; enlargement 155, 186, 203
Eurasian 6, 118, 125, 128; *see* Central Asia

foreign policy 2, 6, 8, 11–14, 17, 19, 21–23, 25, 28, 34, 37, 39, 41, 44, 47–78, 81, 84, 90, 93, 101, 104, 107, 109, 113, 118, 122, 134, 138, 162, 168, 171, 173, 175, 177, 179, 181, 183–187, 189, 191, 194, 197, 199, 201, 204, 207–210, 213, 215, 217, 219, 222; articulation 10, 18, 43, 48, 50, 54, 59, 88, 100; democratic 12, 15, 24–25, 35, 49, 65, 80, 83, 86, 89–95, 98, 101, 111, 123, 128, 158, 175–178, 181, 184, 186, 190, 201, 209, 215, 219; 'Gandhian' 44, 69, 215; 'Kautilyan' 13, 35, 40, 48, 213; 'Nehruvian' 31–33, 43–44, 47, 59, 69, 85, 137, 143–145, 148, 199, 208, 217; post-Cold War 1–20, 15, 29–30, 45–58, 84–85;
foreign policy making 2, 6, 8, 11–14, 17, 21–23, 25, 28, 34, 37, 39, 44, 47–78, 84, 90, 93, 101, 104, 109, 113, 118, 122, 134, 138, 162, 168, 183–187, 189, 194, 197, 207–210, 213, 215, 217, 222; *see* foreign policy
foreign policy mythmaking 42, 60, 76, 80, 97, 135, 150, 189, 198, 201; *see* mythmaking
fragmegration 65–67, 69; *see* complexity
fundamentalism 103–104, 117, 125, 220; Islamic 104, 125, 126, 187, 220

Gandhi, Indira 22, 70, 73
Gandhi, Mohandas Karamchand

44, 69, 215
Gandhi, Rajiv 82, 149
geopolitics 18, 35, 37, 51, 79, 82, 99, 105, 108, 114, 120, 123, 182, 205, 213; see realpolitik
geostrategy 27; *see* strategy
global affairs *see* world affairs
global order *see* order
globalization 11, 62, 64–69, 72, 79, 153, 169, 198, 202, 214, 216; *see* interdependence
Gorbachev, Mikhail 113–115,
governance 5, 15, 49, 59, 62, 90, 95, 164, 176, 179, 185, 203, 216; global 175, 179; good 179, 209; poor 5, 95, 176; security 128, 179, 189, 216; *see* order
'great game' 2, 4, 42, 100, 105, 192; new 2, 6, 15–18, 78, 80, 105–109, 131–133, 163, 167, 170, 183, 192–206, 220; old 2, 17, 42, 100, 106, 193; *see* balance of power
'great powers' 3, 43; 48, 77, 94, 100, 105, 107, 124, 135, 156, 160, 207, 215; military 58, 77, 101, 106, 124, 160, 191; regional 77, 101, 106, 108, 128, 156, 207; *see* power

Hindu nationalism see nationalism
Hinduism 22, 61–62, 69–70, 216
Hindutva 60–62, 66–67, 71, 75, 85; *see* Sarvakar

ideology 14, 47, 59, 61, 70, 72, 91, 98, 123, 187, 221,
India 1, 5, 10, 21, 37, 44, 53, 66, 74, 81, 94, 108, 111, 121, 135, 141, 159, 167, 172, 184, 195, 206, 213, 220; Central Asian strategy 3–4, 7, 9, 12, 15–19, 21, 28, 78, 79–110, 112, 118, 126–134, 153, 155–171, 178, 180–193, 195–211, 218, 223; democratic foreign policy 12, 15, 24–25, 35, 49, 65, 80, 83, 86, 89–95, 98, 101, 111, 123, 128, 158, 175–178, 181, 184, 186, 190, 201, 209, 215, 219; 'Gandhian foreign policy' 44, 69, 215; 'Kautilyan foreign policy' 13, 35, 40, 48, 213; national identity 8, 11, 13–15, 23–24, 26–28, 36–37, 42, 57–58, 62, 66, 68, 76, 80, 91–93, 98, 123, 125, 155, 196, 207, 216, 218; national interest 14, 23, 33, 36, 38, 43, 71, 88, 116, 123, 161, 179, 196; national security 25, 28, 41, 44, 74, 88, 158, 213, 217; 'Nehruvian foreign policy' 31–33, 43–44, 59, 69, 85, 137, 143–145, 148, 199, 208, 217; 'post-Cold War Blues' 29–30, 84–85; relations with Afghanistan 5–6, 18, 86, 103–105, 126, 183, 186–189, 192–193, 218, 224; relations with China 7, 16–18, 33, 70, 97, 102, 106, 110, 127, 130, 133–165, 186, 192, 197, 199, 214, 217; relations with the EU 17, 106, 110, 154, 167, 169, 171–182, 186, 188, 194, 202, 211, 218; relations with Kazakhstan 4, 102, 154–155; relations with Kyrgyzstan 4, 154–155; relations with Russia 5, 13, 28, 82, 85, 89, 111–133, 138, 147, 149, 154, 169, 187, 214, 218; relations with Southeast Asia 3, 142; relations with Tajikistan 101–105, 109, 189; relations with Tibet 6, 16, 134, 136, 140–141, 143, 149; relations with Turkmenistan 4, 80; relations with the USA 17, 29–30, 106, 121, 134, 147, 154, 167–171, 182,

185, 194, 201, 204, 207, 211, 218, 220, 224; relations with Uzbekistan 4, 102, 155; self-aggrandizement 14, 59, 75–77, 98, 107, 135, 162, 184, 196, 206, 208
Indian Ocean 142; *see* Myanmar
influence 2, 7, 16, 18, 23, 34, 37, 39, 41, 48, 57, 61, 77, 83, 93, 106–109, 113, 123, 127, 157, 161, 169, 178, 180, 188, 193, 214, 220; no 19, 28, 97, 170, 195–211, 214, 220; *see* power
insecurity 17, 55, 66, 217; ontological 198; *see* security, uncertainty
interdependence 64, 65, 169, 199, 202; complex 134, 137, 202; *see* globalization
internalize 74; *see* socialization
international order *see* order
international security *see* security
Iran 106, 121, 154, 186
Iraq 55, 121
Islamic fundamentalism *see* fundamentalism

Japan 173

Kashmir 6, 87, 96, 103, 138–139, 150, 188, 223; *see* Pakistan
Kazakhstan 4, 102, 154–155
Kautilya 35, 40–41, 44, 48, 204
Kautilyan (foreign policy) tradition 13, 35, 40, 48, 213; paradigm 41, 44, 213; *see* geopolitics, realpolitik
Khrushchev, Nikita 112
Kyrgyzstan 4, 154–155

Latin America 178
logic of mythmaking 51–57; and Indian foreign policy 57–77; *see* mythmaking
'Look East' policy 3, 142; *see* Southeast Asia
'Look North' policy 3–4, 7, 9, 12, 15–19, 21, 28, 78, 79–110, 112, 118, 126–134, 153, 155–171, 178, 180–193, 195–211, 218, 223

Mao Zedong 137–138, 147, 150; *see* China
militarism *see* Kautilyan tradition
military great power *see* great powers
Mongolia 5
moralism *see* Ashokan tradition
Myanmar 141–143, 224
Mujahideen 103, 218; *see* Afghanistan
multilateral strategic partnership *see* strategic partnership
multilateralism 49, 88, 97, 130, 160, 175, 179,
mythmaking 1–5, 7, 9, 15, 21–39, 43–50, 53, 57, 61–70, 74, 77, 81, 83–95, 101, 106, 109, 112, 126, 131, 137–144, 154–157, 160, 167, 172, 176, 179, 181, 183, 187, 190, 193, 195, 197, 204, 210, 218, 220; discursive 2, 58; foreign policy 42, 60, 80, 98, 135, 150, 189, 198; powerful 66, 196; *see* logic of mythmaking, narrative

narrative 3–4, 8, 10, 14–19, 43, 47, 50, 67, 74, 79, 95, 109, 170, 182; complex 99, 167; cultural 74; foreign policy 3, 53, 58, 71, 208; historical 47, 62, 85; mythical/mythmaking 52, 56, 60, 63, 66, 76, 84–85, 101, 172, 195–196, 201, 210; resilient 98; *see* narrative imbrication
narrative account 8, 12, 196; articulation 12, 69; assessment 7; attempt 104; cloak 95; construc-

tion 18–20, 27, 50, 58–59, 73, 77, 89, 133, 202, 206; emplotment 2; explanation 11, 42, 184; framework 223; justification 53, 98, 167; malleability 67; modality 15, 21, 39, 94, 109; outline 76, 80, 82; pattern 170; platform 196; process-tracing 2, 171–172, 197; tendency 4, 189; representation 48; uncertainty 45; *see* narrative imbrication

narrative imbrication 2, 7–12, 14, 171, 197–198; see discourse analysis

national interest 14, 23, 25–26, 33, 36, 38, 43, 71, 74, 88, 111, 116, 123, 125, 161, 179, 196, 198

national security *see* security

nationalism 32, 51, 60–62, 66, 69–72, 75, 196, 216, 220; Hindu 58, 60–62, 67, 69–70, 72, 75, 196

NATO 17, 167–171, 182–183, 191, 194, 218

Nehru, Jawaharlal 31–33, 43–44, 59, 69, 85, 137, 143–145, 148, 199, 208, 217; *see* nonalignment

neo-colonialism *see* colonialism

Nepal 54

new great game *see* great game

new regionalism *see* regionalism

no influence *see* influence

nonalignment 13, 31; failure of 33–37, 43, 113, 147, 214; 'tilted nonalignment' 31, 113–114, 138

normative culture 2, 12, 16, 23, 32, 36, 52, 61, 65, 76, 111, 120, 124, 138, 146, 156, 158, 162, 169, 175, 179, 190, 202, 213; foreign policy 42, 60, 76, 80, 97, 135, 150, 189, 198, 201

'Northern Alliance' 103–104, 187; *see* Afghanistan

nuclear ambiguity 214

nuclear apartheid 58, 68, 70–72, 217

nuclear tests 2, 22, 37–41, 54, 57, 60, 62, 70, 208; 1974 nuclear tests 22, 73; 1998 nuclear tests 2, 13, 17, 22, 37, 41, 43, 54, 57, 70, 74, 80, 88, 111, 150, 179, 185, 213; Pakistan's 37, 138–140

old great game see great game
ontological insecurity *see* insecurity
ontological security *see* security
order 1, 12, 19, 26, 28, 40, 53, 56, 65, 67, 70, 128, 189, 196, 206, 211; economic 26, 42, 65, 77, 190, 207, 211; international/global/world 19, 21, 23, 32, 37, 40, 42, 62, 70, 76, 131, 189, 196, 199, 205, 211, 215; multiethnic 83; social 35, 42, 83, 190, 209, 213; *see* disorder, governance

Pakistan 16, 18, 25, 31, 54, 83–86, 95, 104, 106, 112, 116, 127, 179, 192, 216, 218; relations with Afghanistan 25, 87, 95, 103, 116, 126, 139, 187, 193, 218; relations with China 39, 106, 112–113, 127, 133–165, 192; *see* Kashmir

peaceful coexistence 31–33, 94, 143, 213

power 2–5, 11, 16, 18, 23, 34, 37, 39, 41, 48, 57, 61, 77, 83, 93, 106–109, 113, 123, 127, 157, 161, 169, 178, 180, 188, 193, 214, 220; *see* great powers, influence

pragmatic strategic partnership *see* strategic partnership

process 2, 5, 8, 18, 53, 62, 64, 85, 92, 108, 162, 177, 192, 202, 216; cognitive 91; composite 122, 197; democratization 90; incremental 24; integrating 65; inter-

nal 107, 182; psychological 198; social 8, 18, 48, 224; textual 8, 172; see discursive process; narrative process-tracing
process-tracing see narrative process-tracing
Putin, Vladimir 9, 120, 124–126, 129–130, 153; see Russia

realpolitik 18, 43–44, 52–54, 59, 99, 179, 185, 191, 220; see geopolitics
regional great powers see great powers
regionalism 95–96, 220; new 108, 220
Russia 9, 111–133, 163, 169, 221

Sarvakar, Vinayak Damodar 61; see Hindutva
Saudi Arabia 106
secularism 43, 63, 69–70, 80, 86, 89, 94
securitization 52, 79, 198, 210
security 5, 7, 13, 18, 23, 27, 44, 52, 64, 73, 90, 96, 111, 125, 135, 151, 192, 198, 215; cooperative 43, 96, 157, 163, 188; economic 193; energy 89, 155; international 3, 69, 96, 135, 213; national 25, 28, 41, 44, 74, 88, 158, 213, 217; ontological 63; shared 27, 121
security culture 11, 28; see strategic culture
security dilemma 145, 163, 192
security identity 69, 179
security governance see governance
self-aggrandizement see India
Shanghai Cooperation Organization 97, 130, 153, 155–156, 159–163, 186, 191, 221

shared security see security
'Silk Road' 4, 82, 95–97, 108, 191
'Shawl Road' 96–97
socialization 28, 74, 155–156, 176–177, 203–204; see influence, internalize
South Asia 6, 15, 32, 37, 82, 140, 152, 164, 167, 172, 174, 188, 216; paradox 216
Southeast Asia 3; see 'Look East' policy
sovereignty 25, 38, 53, 66, 84, 120, 130, 145, 152, 158, 162, 165, 177, 190, 196, 223
Soviet Union see USSR
Sri Lanka 54
Stalin, Joseph 112
strategic culture 12, 26, 43, 60, 136, 174; see security culture
strategic partnership 31, 93, 112, 116, 120–121, 126, 128, 130, 162, 171, 173–177, 181–182, 186, 190, 199, 221; multilateral 155; pragmatic 159
strategy 9, 13, 16, 19, 22, 25, 32, 45, 48, 62, 66, 71, 73, 81, 85, 87, 89, 93, 101, 103, 123, 127, 145–146, 154, 157, 173, 182, 190, 197, 201, 205, 214; assertive 45, 125, 188; global 97, 105, 188, 227; military 35–37, 101; moralistic 35–37, 146; offensive 33, 35–37, 188; see geostrategy

Tajikistan 4, 15, 80–81, 101–105, 126, 155, 189, 220; civil war 103, 220; Indian relations with 101–105, 109, 189
Taliban 83, 103–104, 187–188, 193; see Afghanistan
terrorism 5, 18, 79, 96, 119, 125, 183, 187, 193, 201; see counter-terrorism

Tibet 6, 16, 134, 136, 140–141, 143, 149; see Dalai Lama
Turkey 106, 154
Turkmenistan 4, 80

UN 104, 158, 179, 195
uncertainty 21, 27, 30, 45, 64, 66, 72, 82, 116, 146, 159, 163, 185, 199, 221; strategic 21, 45, 84, 117, 127, 146, 163, 185, 199; see complexity, fragmegration
uncovery 21, 25, 51, 172, 197,
USA 17, 29–30, 106, 121, 134, 147, 154, 167–171, 182, 185, 194, 201, 204, 207, 211, 218, 220, 224; invasion of Iraq 55, 121
USSR 5, 13, 28, 82, 85, 89, 111–133, 138, 147, 149, 154, 169, 187, 214, 218; see Russia
Uyghur 154
Uzbekistan 4, 102, 155

Vajpayeee 38, 40, 71, 73, 75, 96, 147–148, 150–151, 195–196, 222; see BJP

world affairs 1, 11, 18, 23, 34, 53, 65, 73, 80, 84, 88, 94, 106, 112, 135, 146, 164, 177–179, 190, 199, 202, 214, 218, 220, 223
world order see order

Xinjiang 6, 140, 146, 154–157, 222; see China, Uyghur

Yeltsin, Boris 116–120, 129, 153, 221
Yugoslavia 89–90, 94, 190–191, 219